ASTON VILLA REVIEW 1997

Published by Sports Projects Ltd

ACKNOWLEDGEMENTS

Aston Villa Review 1997
First published in Great Britain in July 1997
by Sports Projects Limited

© 1997 Sports Projects Limited
188 Lightwoods Hill, Smethwick, Warley,
West Midlands B67 5EH.

ISBN 0 946866 39 2

Printed and bound in Great Britain

Editor: Dennis Shaw

Photographs: Bernard Gallagher, Empics,
Allsport, Neville Williams

Design, layout and graphics: Vic Millward,
Bernard Gallagher, Phil Lees and
Nadine Goldingay

Special thanks to: Rod Evans, Mike Beddow,
Pam Bridgewater.

KEY

❏	Player booked
■	Player sent off
32	Figure in goals column indicates time of goal
†56	First substitute and time of substitution
†	First player substituted
‡56	Second substitute and time of substitution
‡	Second player substituted

Notes:

● *Players are listed in squad number order, except for the goalkeeper, who is always at the top of the list.*

● *Substitute goalkeepers are in squad number order, with (Gk) after their name.*

● *In friendly games, where several substitutes may have appeared, additional symbols are used in the following order: #, §, ††, ‡‡, ##, §§, ≠.*

Also available in this series:

Aston Villa Review 1993
ISBN 0 946866 09 0   Price: £7.95

Aston Villa Review 1994
ISBN 0 946866 19 8   Price: £8.95

Aston Villa Review 1995
ISBN 0 946866 23 6   Price: £8.95

Aston Villa Review 1996
ISBN 0 946866 32 5   Price: £8.95

Top-five finish confirms position amongst the Premiership elite

Coverage of the full five-year, opening period of the FA Premier League is completed by Volume Five of the *Aston Villa Review*, which traces every detail of season 1996-97.

Brian Little's second full season proved to be another eventful one, though overshadowed by the daunting task of attempting to match the previous campaign.

Only when the final whistle of the final match, at home to Southampton, sounded could it be confirmed that a place in the UEFA Cup was regained, by virtue of attaining fifth place in the Premiership.

Thus the manager had succeeded in continuing a progressive record of avoiding relegation in his first half-season, winning a trophy and a European place in his first full season, followed by a return to Europe in his second full season.

This consistency led to his signing a new contract in 1997 to keep him at Villa Park beyond the year 2,000.

Although it was a case of 'so-far-so-good' he had much still to prove after slipping sadly out of Europe at the first hurdle, against the little-known Swedish club, Helsingborg.

While the domestic cup competitions were equally unproductive, Villa were never far away from a Championship challenge, despite spells of inconsistency.

Off the field activity was as high-profile as ever with the club being floated on the Stock Exchange in the Spring and, despite fluctuating prices, being valued at around the £120m mark.

Away from playing affairs the major disappointment was the late and unexpected decision by the planners to put the club's application to re-roof and improve the Trinity Road Stand on hold.

As a result the intention of bringing all four sides of the ground into a co-ordinated modern design had to be put back 12 months. One possibility now is that a restructuring of the North Stand will also take place in a project that could increase the stadium's capacity to 50,000.

Meanwhile, the flotation helped to release resources for further transfer activity and within 48 hours of the end of the season Stan Collymore was on his way from Liverpool to Villa Park for a club record fee of £7m.

Other dealings were also scheduled for a summer of further progress. Any not detailed in the following pages will be faithfully recorded in the next volume of the *Aston Villa Review*.

Those who have purchased each copy from its launch in 1993 now have a comprehensive record of Aston Villa's Premiership history, as it has been played out, match-by-match.

Among the events recorded is the milestone of the one hundred years since the move to Villa Park. This latest edition thus starts the second century of football at the famous stadium.

As previously the match reports are written as they happen and include the background to each fixture, linking up with the game before and the one to follow. It can thus be read as an on-going description of the entire season, with full factual and statistical detail, and also retained as a work of reference and quiz-question solver whenever needed.

The *Aston Villa Review 1997* and its predecessors is the only Aston Villa publication of its type ever produced and can sit on the library shelf forever.

Dennis Shaw May 1997.

CONTENTS

Foreword   *Page 3*

FIRST TEAM MATCHES

Aug 17	A	Sheffield Wednesday	1-2	Johnson	6
Aug 21	H	**Blackburn Rovers**	1-0	Southgate	8
Aug 24	H	**Derby County**	2-0	Joachim, Johnson (pen)	10
Sept 4	A	Everton	1-0	Ehiogu	12
Sept 7	H	**Arsenal**	2-2	Milosevic 2	14
Sept 10	H	**Helsingborg** (UEFA 1/1)	1-1	Johnson	16
Sept 15	A	Chelsea	1-1	Townsend	18
Sept 21	H	**Manchester United**	0-0		20
Sept 24	A	Helsingborg (UEFA 1/2)	0-0	*(Helsingborg win on away goals rule)*	22
Sept 30	A	Newcastle United	3-4	Yorke 3	24
Oct 12	A	Tottenham Hotspur	0-1		26
Oct 19	H	**Leeds United**	2-0	Yorke, Johnson	28
Oct 23	A	Leeds United (CCC3)	2-1	Taylor, Yorke (pen)	30
Oct 26	A	Sunderland	0-1		32
Nov 2	H	**Nottingham Forest**	2-0	Tiler, Yorke	34
Nov 16	H	**Leicester City**	1-3	Yorke	36
Nov 23	A	Coventry City	2-1	Joachim, Staunton	38
Nov 26	A	Wimbledon (CCC4)	0-1		40
Nov 30	H	**Middlesbrough**	1-0	Yorke (pen)	42
Dec 4	A	West Ham United	2-0	Ehiogu, Yorke	44
Dec 7	A	Southampton	1-0	Townsend	46
Dec 22	H	**Wimbledon**	5-0	Yorke 2, Milosevic, Taylor, Blackwell og	48
Dec 26	H	**Chelsea**	0-2		50
Dec 28	A	Arsenal	2-2	Milosevic, Yorke	52
Jan 1	A	Manchester United	0-0		54
Jan 11	H	**Newcastle United**	2-2	Yorke, Milosevic	56
Jan 14	A	Notts County (FAC3)	0-0		58
Jan 18	A	Liverpool	0-3		60
Jan 22	H	**Notts County** (FAC3R)	3-0	Yorke 2, Ehiogu	62
Jan 25	A	Derby County (FAC4)	1-3	Curcic	64
Jan 29	H	**Sheffield Wednesday**	0-1		66
Feb 1	H	**Sunderland**	1-0	Milosevic	68
Feb 19	H	**Coventry City**	2-1	Yorke 2	70
Feb 22	A	Nottingham Forest	0-0		72
Mar 2	H	**Liverpool**	1-0	Taylor	74
Mar 5	A	Leicester City	0-1		76
Mar 15	H	**West Ham United**	0-0		78
Mar 22	A	Blackburn Rovers	2-0	Johnson, Yorke	80
Apr 5	H	**Everton**	3-1	Milosevic, Staunton, Yorke	82
Apr 9	A	Wimbledon	2-0	Milosevic, Wright	84

CONTENTS

Apr	12	A	Derby County	1-2	Joachim	86
Apr	19	**H**	**Tottenham Hotspur**	1-1	Yorke	88
Apr	22	A	Leeds United	0-0		90
May	3	A	Middlesbrough	2-3	Ehiogu, Milosevic	92
May	11	**H**	**Southampton**	1-0	Dryden og	94

FRIENDLY MATCHES

First Team

July	29	A	Walsall	2-0	Taylor, Yorke	96
July	31	A	Lincoln City	1-0	Farrelly	98
Aug	3	A	Wrexham	2-2	Johnson, Yorke	100
Aug	6	A	Oldham Athletic	3-0	Yorke 2, Graham og	102
May	13	A	San José Clash	1-1	Ehiogu	104
May	21	A	Los Angeles Galaxy	1-1	Collymore	105

Reserves

July	23	A	Pelsall Villa	1-1	Byfield	106
July	27	A	Gravesend & Northfleet	2-1	Davis (pen), Jaszczun	107
Aug	1	A	Tamworth	3-0	Burchell, Collins, Farrelly	108
Aug	7	A	Hednesford Town	0-0		109
Aug	12	A	Bedworth United	3-1	Hendrie, Carr, Petty	110
Aug	14	A	Leicester Y.M.C.A.	7-1	Blackwood (2), Walker, Byfield, Hines (pen), Collins, Lee	111
Nov	12	A	Stony Stratford Town	6-0	Byfield 2, Hines, Walker, Kirby, Brock	112

APPENDIX

THE MANAGEMENT TEAM	The men behind the teams	113
CENTENARY CELEBRATIONS	100 years at Villa Park	115
EUROPEAN CHAMPIONSHIPS	Football comes home!	116
PHOTOGRAPH	First team squad 1996-97	117
THE PLAYERS	Pen pictures and playing records	118
SHARE FLOTATION	Villa goes public	131
FA CARLING PREMIERSHIP	Final table, scorers, attendances and statistics	132
STATISTICS OF THE SEASON	Villa facts and figures from 1996-97	134
PLAYERS OF THE PAST	Former Players' Association and obituaries	136
RESERVE & YOUTH	Results, appearances and goalscorers	137
GROUND DEVELOPMENTS	What's new at Villa Park	141
PREMIERSHIP RECORD	Full statistics since conception of Premiership	142
ALL-TIME LEAGUE RECORD	Season-by-season	145
ALL-TIME LEAGUE RECORD	Club-by-club	148
ALL-TIME EUROPEAN RECORD	Match-by-match results	150
SUBSCRIBERS	Fans' roll call	154

Saturday 17th August 1996 • Hillsborough • 3.00pm

SHEFFIELD WEDNESDAY 2 ASTON VILLA 1

Half-time 0-0 • Attendance 26,861

Referee Roger DILKES (Mossley)

Referee's Assistants R. BURTON and A.N. BUTLER

Blue and White Shirts, Blue Shorts		Goals	Claret and Blue Shirts, White Shorts		Goals
1	Kevin PRESSMAN		13	Michael OAKES	
2	Peter ATHERTON		3	Steve STAUNTON	
3	Ian NOLAN		4	Gareth SOUTHGATE	
4	Mark PEMBRIDGE †		6	Andy TOWNSEND	
6	Des WALKER		7	Ian TAYLOR	
7	Guy WHITTINGHAM	82	8	Mark DRAPER	
10	Andy BOOTH		10	Dwight YORKE	
11	Regi BLINKER		11	Tommy JOHNSON	88
18	Dejan STEFANOVIC		14	Alan WRIGHT	
20	Wayne COLLINS		16	Ugo EHIOGU	
25	Ritchie HUMPHREYS ‡	55	24	Scott MURRAY †	
	Substitutes			*Substitutes*	
12	Graham HYDE †72		5	Paul McGRATH	
13	Matt CLARKE (Gk)		12	Julian JOACHIM †63	
14	Steve NICOL		19	Gareth FARRELLY	
16	John SHERIDAN		20	Riccardo SCIMECA	
19	Scott OAKES ‡80		30	Adam RACHEL (Gk)	

BEFORE	P	W	D	L	F	A	pts
Villa	0	0	0	0	0	0	0
Wednesday	0	0	0	0	0	0	0

AFTER		P	W	D	L	F	A	pts
6	Wednesday	1	1	0	0	2	1	3
15	Villa	1	0	0	1	1	2	0

FACTFILE

Michael Oakes makes his Premiership debut... Young keeper Adam Rachel introduced on bench... Villa's second successive league defeat at Hillsborough after seven Premiership meetings without a Wednesday win... First opening-day defeat in the five seasons of the Premiership.

High hopes fade in a slow start

Football is basking in the glow of a close season which has seen the game soar to yet new heights of public interest and expectation.

As Villa kick-off with a threatening opening fixture at Hillsborough attendances are booming around the superb stadia of the Premiership.

The success of Euro 96 played in this country, with four fixtures at Villa Park, has been just one major contributory factor to the general mood of euphoria.

An even bigger factor, however, is the ever-increasing influx of top foreign players with a total of £97,675,000 spent on close-season transfers.

Villa have not been left out, Brian Little having signed Portuguese right back Fernando Nelson for £1.75m from Sporting Lisbon and Serbian Sasa Curcic for a record £4m from Bolton.

On opening day, however, this summer outlay counts for nothing as Curcic awaits a work permit and Nelson is out injured – along with Mark Bosnich and Savo Milosevic.

The new ruling allowing three subs from a total of five leads to several young players being in the 16, including Michael Oakes, introduced for his Premiership debut and teenage keeper Adam Rachel on the bench.

High standards were set in 1995-96, standards which have attracted the nation at large to sit in judgement on whether the club can continue to move forward.

The opening half at Hills-

Michael Oakes' Premiership debut

borough is encouraging enough with some tidy passing moves creating openings and providing hints that last season's form is not far away.

Steve Staunton has kept Paul McGrath on the bench and the back-line makes David Pleat's side look ineffectual with only one serious attack in almost an hour.

Something special is required to break Villa down and a promising newcomer, name of Ritchie Humphreys, provides it with a whiplash volley as Mark Pembridge feeds an ideal pass forward.

Villa have been far less decisive with their own finishing and they are punished again near the end as Guy Whittingham sends a looping header wide of Oakes, who is not to blame for either goal.

Frustratingly for Villa Kevin Pressman has made a number of saves including one from Dwight Yorke, anxious to get his account under way, while Ian Taylor has been off-target a couple of times and blocked out when more accurate.

Although reasonably stylish and balanced in approach a cutting edge has been missing and fans are sent home hoping to see something better against Blackburn at Villa Park next Wednesday.

Villa's only goal was a close range Tommy Johnson header from Alan Wright's centre, and arrived far too late to salvage a badly-needed draw.

It has been a challenging opening day for Gareth Southgate, back to business again after his sad penalty miss in the European Championship semi-final shoot-out against Germany, but he has sailed through, as always, with pride and professionalism intact.

Wednesday 21st August 1996 • Villa Park • 7.45pm

ASTON VILLA 1 BLACKBURN ROVERS 0

Half-time 0-0 • *Attendance* 32,457

Referee Alan WILKIE (Chester-le-Street)

Referee's Assistants J.H. HOLBROOK and B. LOWE

Claret and Blue Shirts, White Shorts	Goals		Blue and White Halved Shirts, Blue Shorts	Goals
13 Michael OAKES			1 Tim FLOWERS	
3 Steve STAUNTON			2 Chris COLEMAN	
4 Gareth SOUTHGATE	64		3 Jeff KENNA	
6 Andy TOWNSEND ❏			4 Tim SHERWOOD	
7 Ian TAYLOR			5 Colin HENDRY	
8 Mark DRAPER			8 Kevin GALLACHER †	
10 Dwight YORKE ❏			10 Lars BOHINEN	
11 Tommy JOHNSON †			20 Henning BERG	
12 Julian JOACHIM			21 Georgios DONIS	
14 Alan WRIGHT			23 Garry FLITCROFT ‡	
16 Ugo EHIOGU			24 Paul WARHURST	
Substitutes			*Substitutes*	
5 Paul McGRATH			7 Stuart RIPLEY ‡75	
15 Fernando NELSON			13 Shay GIVEN (Gk)	
19 Gareth FARRELLY			14 Graham FENTON †59	
20 Riccardo SCIMECA †84			25 Ian PEARCE	
30 Adam RACHEL (Gk)			34 Gary CROFT	

BEFORE	P	W	D	L	F	A	pts	AFTER	P	W	D	L	F	A	pts
15 Villa	1	0	0	1	1	2	0	11 Villa	2	1	0	1	2	2	3
16 Blackburn	1	0	0	1	0	2	0	19 Blackburn	2	0	0	2	0	3	0

FACTFILE

Villa's 35th home win over Blackburn in 65 starts... The news arrives that Sasa Curcic has his permit to play on Saturday... Blackburn stage after-match press conference at Villa Park to announce Director of Football Kenny Dalglish's departure 'by mutual agreement'.

The show's back on the road

The first home match of the season and a slight air of anxiety pervades Villa Park as the unspoken thought prevails that failure to win would virtually leave the new season in the starting blocks. Blackburn Rovers are similarly in a mood of uncertainty following the £15m sale of Alan Shearer to Newcastle United.

Brian Little is acutely aware that his squad is being put through an examination of both its strength in depth and its capacity to recapture last season's excellence.

The continuing absence of a key trio in Mark Bosnich, new signing Fernando Nelson (who is a sub) and Savo Milosevic means that Villa are significantly below strength.

One personnel change has been made compared to Hillsborough last Saturday, with Julian Joachim replacing Scott Murray, though lining up alongside Dwight Yorke with Ian Taylor at right back.

In a below-average first half Tim Flowers touches a Taylor header over the bar and Michael Oakes treats a Tim Sherwood drive from 20 yards in like fashion.

More close calls follow but just before the break Villa are rightly aggrieved to be denied a perfectly good goal. Another Taylor header, as Andy Townsend's corner swings in, clearly crosses the goalline, as proven by the slo-mo TV clips afterwards.

Defender Jeff Kenna makes a late, despairing effort to hook the ball away, knocking it onto the cross bar and back into play.

The mere fact that the rebound off the bar takes the ball sharply back into play is proof enough that it has been struck at an angle from the other side. However, neither the referee nor the referee's assistant see it that way and Villa go in still all-square.

The second half sees Villa a touch sharper and a whole lot more accurate with their passing, but the game still needs a change of script to capture interest.

Appropriately, just such a contribution arrives in the 64th minute from spare-time sports columnist Gareth Southgate who writes the lead story to his own fantasy football page.

On the eve of the season Southgate had called his own press conference to deal with the masses of media inquiries about his recovery or otherwise from his penalty miss against Germany in the Euro 96 semi-final.

The best therapy to purge the pain, though, would be a goal, if not a penalty then a headline-catching show-stopper...just like the little beauty he blasts into the net from 20 yards as Kenna mis-heads another Townsend corner. Rovers, energetically working the Shearer loss out of their system, are organised and industrious but lightweight in front of goal and are never going to pull it back.

In contrast Villa have the chance to make it 2-0 when Joachim is released on a clear run but his first touch lets him down and the ball frustratingly runs away from him.

"I'm feeling relieved more than anything," admits Brian Little "And other results up and down the country went our way to keep us in touch."

With Sheffield Wednesday having won at Leeds last night a new perspective has been put on the Villa's defeat at Hillsborough as the Owls become the only team to win their first two matches.

Gareth Southgate

Saturday 24th August 1996 • Villa Park • 3.00pm

ASTON VILLA 2 DERBY COUNTY 0

Half-time 1-0 • *Attendance 34,646*

Referee Paul ALCOCK (Redhill)

Referee's Assistants P.V. NORMAN and M.A. WILLIAMS

Claret and Blue Shirts, White Shorts		Goals	White Shirts, Black Shorts		Goals
13	Michael OAKES		1	Russell HOULT	
3	Steve STAUNTON		2	Gary ROWETT †	
4	Gareth SOUTHGATE		3	Chris POWELL	
6	Andy TOWNSEND		4	Darryl POWELL ❑	
7	Ian TAYLOR		6	Igor STIMAC ❑	
8	Mark DRAPER		10	Aljosa ASANOVIC	
10	Dwight YORKE †		11	Ron WILLEMS #	
11	Tommy JOHNSON	47pen	16	Jacob LAURSEN	
14	Alan WRIGHT		19	Sean FLYNN	
16	Ugo EHIOGU		22	Christian DAILLY	
26	Sasa CURCIC ‡		23	Paul PARKER ❑	

	Substitutes			*Substitutes*	
5	Paul McGRATH		7	Robin VAN DER LAAN †15 ‡	
12	Julian JOACHIM †15	19	9	Marco GABBIADINI ‡57	
15	Fernando NELSON ‡79		13	Martin TAYLOR (Gk)	
20	Riccardo SCIMECA		14	Paul SIMPSON #74	
30	Adam RACHEL (Gk)		18	Lee CARSLEY	

BEFORE	P	W	D	L	F	A	pts	AFTER	P	W	D	L	F	A	pts
11 Villa	2	1	0	1	2	2	3	4 Villa	3	2	0	1	4	2	6
13 Derby	2	0	2	0	4	4	2	15 Derby	3	0	2	1	4	6	2

FACTFILE

Second win brings joint-third place... Debut for Sasa Curcic and also for Fernando Nelson as a second half substitute... Challenge for places mounts as Steve Staunton shines... "It's a tough season ahead, in four competitions" says Brian Little. "There will be plenty of opportunities for everyone."

Sasa Curcic debut in second victory

An interesting theory has grown on the Villa Park scene, saying: "We're missing Savo Milosevic," which just shows that some players are appreciated more when they're not there.

As the big, under-rated Serbian continues his recovery from an Achilles tendon problem his friend and compatriot Sasa Curcic is free to make his debut in midfield.

During Savo's three-match absence an awareness has dawned that his capacity to 'hold the ball up', and the magic of his left-foot, were a major feature of last term's attacking formula.

However the Yugoslavian international's misfortune has a spin-off for both Tommy Johnson and Julian Joachim in there being a spare shirt temporarily up for grabs.

At kick-off the ex-Leicester City forward is one of the five substitutes after making way for Curcic, but his chance to form a J-J attack arrives after only 15 minutes when Dwight Yorke limps out of the action.

Joachim has barely had time to settle to the pace of the proceedings, in which Curcic has been prominent, when an opportunity to take centre stage is delivered by the simplest of routes in the 19th minute.

Michael Oakes, enjoying his spell as cover for injured Mark Bosnich, sends a huge goal clearance upfield, well into the County half.

Johnson has merely to apply a stragetic forward deflection to send Joachim on a piercing run for goal which he completes with a neat and precise finish.

Derby enjoys spells on the attack, without looking truly dangerous, but it is Villa's forward play which spasmodically takes the eye.

Joachim almost scores a second in a link-up with Ian Taylor, while Johnson smacks one chance against the crossbar.

Villa are looking worthy of a second goal and two minutes into the second half the opportunity arises when Joachim is clearly pushed over by County's summer signing Jacob Laursen.

With a well-meaning, if slightly-indiscreet, thirst for a moment of theatre the crowd call for Gareth Southgate to take the kick.

In the event there was no way the England defender could have got to the ball before Johnson, who quickly realised that with Yorke's departure the spot-kick was on general offer.

"I want to score against my former club," says Johnson, or words to that effect, as with a gesture of admirable confidence and control he beats the keeper, no problem.

As Villa carefully wrap up their second successive home victory in four days Southgate does get a chance to connect with a 25-yard shot to test Hoult as Curcic continues with a satisfying debut.

Oakes proves his Premiership class again with a save from Asanovic, while Steve Staunton is outstanding in confining Paul McGrath to the bench.

The only blot on an improving performance is that both Joachim and Johnson pass up opportunities to stretch the scoreline.

By now, however, Villa are assured of a similar three-match points haul to a year earlier so no-one, least of all Brian Little, is complaining.

Julian Joachim flies into action

Wednesday 4th September 1996 • Goodison Park • 7.45pm

EVERTON 0 ASTON VILLA 1

Half-time 0-0 • *Attendance* 39,115

Referee Martin BODENHAM (Looe)

Referee's Assistants N.E. GREEN and P. WALTON

Blue Shirts, White Shorts	Goals	White Shirts, Claret Shorts	Goals
1 Neville SOUTHALL		13 Michael OAKES	
2 Earl BARRETT		3 Steve STAUNTON ❏	
3 Andy HINCHCLIFFE		4 Gareth SOUTHGATE	
4 David UNSWORTH		6 Andy TOWNSEND ❏	
7 Graham STUART †		8 Mark DRAPER	
9 Duncan FERGUSON		9 Savo MILOSEVIC ‡	
10 Gary SPEED		10 Dwight YORKE	
17 Andrei KANCHELSKIS		14 Alan WRIGHT	
18 Joe PARKINSON		15 Fernando NELSON #	
20 Tony GRANT ❏		16 Ugo EHIOGU	62
21 Craig SHORT		26 Sasa CURCIC †	
Substitutes		*Substitutes*	
8 Paul RIDEOUT †66		1 Mark BOSNICH (Gk)	
11 Anders LIMPAR		5 Paul McGRATH	
14 John EBBRELL		7 Ian TAYLOR †75	
19 Marc HOTTIGER		11 Tommy JOHNSON ‡86	
31 Paul GERRARD (Gk)		20 Riccardo SCIMECA #90	

BEFORE	P	W	D	L	F	A	pts	AFTER	P	W	D	L	F	A	pts
4 Villa	3	2	0	1	4	2	6	2 Villa	4	3	0	1	5	2	9
8 Everton	3	1	2	0	4	2	5	11 Everton	4	1	2	1	4	3	5

FACTFILE

Mark Draper has been chosen, last weekend, as sub for England in Moldova... Nelson makes his full debut... Savo kicks off his season... Ugo Ehiogu's first Premiership goal since Spurs away, August 1995... Away victory takes Villa to clear second in table behind Sheffield Wednesday.

Ugo strikes in Goodison win

The scene is set for what proves to be a sabre-rattling third victory of the season when Brian Little writes down his 16 names an hour before the kick-off.

Savo Milosevic is in for his first appearance of the season, having finally recovered from his Achilles tendon problem, while Fernando Nelson is named for his first start and Dwight Yorke is back after injury.

Also in the squad, but on the bench still a fraction below total fitness, is Mark Bosnich. "Not a bad group of players, there..." says the manager with his flair for the under-statement.

Goodison Park, with Joe Royle getting a considerable act together, is not a venue to offer easy points and, pre-kick-off, supporters would settle for a draw without complaints.

Early in the game the sentiment seems to be confirmed as Everton fashion some impressive football and Villa have to settle in quickly to avoid falling behind.

A major scare is survived in the 12th minute. Andrei Kanchelskis, a quick and skilful menace down the flanks sends in a cunningly-flighted corner which Gary Speed meets with what threatens to be a scoring header. Michael Oakes is unable to get to it, but Alan Wright is doing his job to perfection, covering back to block the ball on the line.

There are further Kanchelskis-inspired close shaves, notably in first-half stoppage time when the Ukrainian flier is released for a piercing run and shot which Bosnich's deputy stops with his knees. The rebound finds the tall and menacing Duncan Ferguson but, to Everton's chagrin, his header rebounds off a post for another Villa escape.

Villa have not been totally pre-occupied with defence, however, as Nelson and Sasa Curcic slot themselves into the scheme of things and Savo settles down to work off the rustiness of previous inactivity.

Nelson has almost caught Neville Southall unprepared with a sudden 30-yard shot, while Mark Draper, a substitute for England in the Moldova World Cup qualifier last weekend, also produces a save from the Welsh international.

Both keepers are kept busy, Oakes denying the lively Kanchelskis again and Southall diving anxiously to keep out Milosevic. In a contest of tit-for-tat attacking Dwight Yorke attempts to sign in with his first goal of the season – but a blistering drive which beats Southall rebounds off the crossbar.

With an hour gone the result could go either way but the break arrives in the shape of Ugo Ehiogu's first league goal for more than a year.

Starting the move himself he is ideally placed to finish it off from six yards when his pass to Nelson leads to Yorke nodding down the Portuguese international's centre.

After that there is no way Villa intend to let go and by the final whistle the verdict is that last season's form and resilience is back in place and with plenty of room for improvement.

In the post-match press conference, the manager shields off probing questions about Villa's championship prospects by observing: "If we could pick these players for every game, and prepare them properly, we would have a chance." An excellent chance, some might feel.

Ugo Ehiogu

Saturday 7th September 1996 • Villa Park • 3.00pm

ASTON VILLA 2 ARSENAL 2

Half-time 1-0 • *Attendance* 37,944

Referee Mike RILEY (Leeds)

Referee's Assistants D.R. CRICK and G.K. HEGLEY

Claret and Blue Shirts, White Shorts	Goals	Red and White Shirts, White Shorts	Goals
13 Michael OAKES		24 John LUKIC	
3 Steve STAUNTON ❑		2 Lee DIXON	
4 Gareth SOUTHGATE		3 Nigel WINTERBURN	
6 Andy TOWNSEND		7 David PLATT ❑	
8 Mark DRAPER		8 Ian WRIGHT ❑	
9 Savo MILOSEVIC ‡	39,63	9 Paul MERSON	70
10 Dwight YORKE		10 Dennis BERGKAMP ‡	
14 Alan WRIGHT		12 Andy LINIGHAN	90
15 Fernando NELSON †		14 Martin KEOWN	
16 Ugo EHIOGU		15 Ray PARLOUR	
26 Sasa CURCIC ❑		18 Steve MORROW ❑ †	
Substitutes		*Substitutes*	
5 Paul McGRATH		11 Glenn HELDER ‡80	
7 Ian TAYLOR †60		16 John HARTSON †68 ❑	
11 Tommy JOHNSON ‡84		26 Lee HARPER (Gk)	
20 Riccardo SCIMECA		27 Paul SHAW	
30 Adam RACHEL (Gk)		31 Matthew ROSE	

BEFORE		P	W	D	L	F	A	pts	AFTER		P	W	D	L	F	A	pts
2	Villa	4	3	0	1	5	2	9	4	Villa	5	3	1	1	7	4	10
5	Arsenal	4	2	1	1	7	5	7	8	Arsenal	5	2	2	1	9	7	8

FACTFILE

Eighth successive meeting with Arsenal without a win... No injury worries from the win at Goodison, so Villa are unchanged, but Mark Bosnich still not 100% fit ... Savo Milosevic opens his scoring account for the season... Seaman and Bould missing for Gunners, but Wright and Platt return to the side.

Gunners stage two-goal revival

Since the mid-week victory at Goodison Park the word has spread among supporters and pundits that Villa are shaping up as Championship material.

Brian Little wisely side-steps the issue, pointing to the large number of teams who will compete this season in what looks to be the Premiership's most wide-open marathon.

In the event Villa illustrate, during the last 20 minutes of normal time plus more than three minutes of stoppage time, how NOT to become champions.

From a comfortable-looking 2-0 lead set up by Savo Milosevic by the 63rd minute, Villa allow themselves to be dragged back to a frustrating home draw with late goals by Paul Merson and Andy Linighan.

The equaliser arrives after the crowd have been 'blowing the whistle' on Referee Michael Riley's behalf for several minutes. An ultimately disappointing affair thus ends in an atmosphere of anger and controversy with Sasa Curcic and Ian Taylor booked for comments about the official's watch.

How the mood can change in 90 minutes. Before kick-off Villa have been relishing the prospect of the Serbian pair Milosevic and Curcic playing together at Villa Park for the first time, in a team which includes a fit-again Dwight Yorke and with Fernando Nelson making his full debut.

Optimism seems justified although, as Brian Little points out, Villa played Gunners four times in 1995-96 without actually beating them over 90 minutes. The quality of the football is as high as anticipated between two deeply-experienced teams collectively boasting a whole parade of internationals.

The first hint of controversy arrives in the 16th minute when Merson's shot cannons off the underside of the bar and Arsenal claim it has crossed the goalline.

More dispute surrounds Villa's 39th minute opening goal. As Mark Draper threads his pass through there are the usual Arsenal claims that Milosevic is off-side, but the Yugoslavian international trundles his way around John Lukic for his first goal of the season.

First-year official Riley is proving to be liberal with the use of the yellow card, just as he has been previously this season, but the stoppages do not prevent Villa running into a golden spell of form, inspired largely by the work of the quick-footed Curcic.

The second goal falls comfortably for Milosevic as Lukic fumbles Dwight Yorke's drive and, although Villa are not aware of it, a share of the Premiership lead is beckoning.

A headed goal by Merson from Dennis Bergkamp's 70th minute centre does not appear to be a disaster as the 90th minute arrives, but a price has to be paid for the stoppages.

Arsenal's famed resilience has not deserted them, but Villa's concentration has. A corner deep into injury-time presents Gunners with a chance to effect one of their well-known dead-ball formats as Merson's kick is flicked on from the near post by Martin Keown to the waiting Linighan.

"Everyone knows Arsenal are dangerous from set-pieces, but we didn't seem to," said the Villa manager.

Two-goal Savo Milosevic

Tuesday 10th September 1996 • Villa Park • 7.45pm

ASTON VILLA 1 HELSINGBORGS IF 1

Half-time 1-0 • Attendance 25,818

Referee Loizos LOIZOU (Cyprus)
Referee's Assistants A. MICHAEL and G. PEKRIS

Claret and Blue Shirts, White Shorts		Goals	White Shirts, Blue Shorts		Goals
13	Michael OAKES		1	Sven ANDERSSON	
3	Steve STAUNTON		3	Ola NILSSON	
4	Gareth SOUTHGATE		4	Roland NILSSON	
6	Andy TOWNSEND		5	Andreas JAKOBSSON	
8	Mark DRAPER		6	Christer FURSTH ❑	
9	Savo MILOSEVIC		8	Peter WIBRÅN	80
10	Dwight YORKE		9	Magnus POWELL †	
11	Tommy JOHNSON	14	11	Mattias JONSSON	
14	Alan WRIGHT		12	Jan ERIKSSON ❑	
15	Fernando NELSON		14	Ulrik JANSSON	
16	Ugo EHIOGU		16	Jesper LJUNG	

Substitutes			*Substitutes*		
5	Paul McGRATH		2	Anders JÖNSSON	
7	Ian TAYLOR		7	Patrik SUNDSTRÖM	
12	Julian JOACHIM		10	Martin PRINGLE †54	
20	Riccardo SCIMECA		15	Marcus LANTZ	
28	Adam RACHEL (Gk)		21	Roger PERSSON (Gk)	

Michael Oakes' European baptism... Dwight Yorke still without a goal this season... A 0-0 draw will put Villa out in Sweden... "No ifs or buts. We have to go and win," said the manager. Ex-Owl Roland Nilsson turns out for Helsingborg.

Tommy Johnson opens the scoring

Low-key start to Euro-campaign

The return to Europe, awaited with such a sense of anticipation, proves to be a bitterly disappointing and low-key affair as a major test is set for the second leg.

Supporters arrive at the ground expecting to see Villa set-up a winning lead in this first leg against little-known Swedish opponents who are playing in European competition for the first time. Brian Little has stressed that, while this is his own first experience as a manager in European competition, he sees no reason to change Villa's playing style.

A team-change is enforced by Sasa Curcic being ineligible until the third round, enabling Tommy Johnson to return. Otherwise Villa start as they did against Arsenal with Mark Bosnich still not quite fit.

With only a very small following of fans from Helsinborg in the North Stand enclosure, and the home following down a little, the atmosphere in the ground lacks its usual intensity.

Villa slot instantly into their 3-5-2 formation with Fernando Nelson wide on the right of midfield and Savo Milosevic and Dwight Yorke hoping for the ammunition to run up a first-leg advantage.

Helsinborg predictably make their intentions clear, namely to mass numbers behind the ball in a damage-limitation exercise.

However, whilst their concentration is emphatically on organised defence, they also show the capacity to move forward in strength, linking up with good passing moves.

There is the danger, as early as the fifth minute, that Villa will go a goal down. As goalkeeper Michael Oakes moves smartly forward to kick away a pass-back the ball rebounds off the advancing Magnus Powell to loop back embarrassingly near to the goal.

Then Ulrik Jansson fires a long drive a shade too high as a dire warning to Villa that the hard-working Swedes acknowledge the value of an away goal.

In response Mark Draper bounces a 12th minute long shot off the cross-bar as Villa begin to dominate the forward play and in the 14th minute the lead arrives.

Mark Draper played a fine cross-field pass out to Alan Wright on the left touch-line, moved up and received a return pass and floated the ball into the crowded goalmouth where Johnson was waiting on the edge of the box as Andy Townsend nodded it back and a blistering drive found its target, bouncing viciously in front of the keeper before hitting the back of the net.

At this point the hope was that Helsingborg would commit a few more players forward in seach of the equaliser and thus open the game up for some more attractive football.

In fact the same predictable pattern continues and intensifies. Villa play the ball across the back looking for a forward pass to be on, but the opposition refuse to be drawn.

The Villa midfielders, always well marked and covered, slow things down in search of space but their passes are generally intercepted and cleared.

Thus, with very few crosses going in, Villa's strikers are never able to find freedom for themselves and this reduces Milosevic to one of his more sombre moods. Yorke, disappointingly, is rarely seen to trouble the Swedes' defence.

A one-goal lead to take to Sweden is looking a poor return in a quiet stadium, but worse is to come as Villa fail to raise their game or vary their approach.

A quick Helsingborg thrust in the 80th minute sees Ola Nilsson square the ball from the left for an unmarked Peter Wibrån to drive it wide of Oakes.

"It's a long time since I saw us play in such straight lines," says Brian Little. It was very frustrating for everyone." Very...

Sunday 15th September 1996 • Stamford Bridge • 4.00pm

CHELSEA 1 ASTON VILLA 1

Half-time 1-1 • *Attendance* 27,729

Referee Jeff WINTER (Middlesbrough)

Referee's Assistants M. TINGEY and S.G. TOMLIN

Blue Shirts, Blue Shorts		Goals	White Shirts, Claret Shorts		Goals
13	Kevin HITCHCOCK		13	Michael OAKES	
2	Dan PETRESCU		3	Steve STAUNTON	
5	Frank LEBOEUF	45	4	Gareth SOUTHGATE	
6	Steve CLARKE		6	Andy TOWNSEND ❑	18
8	Andy MYERS		8	Mark DRAPER	
9	Gianluca VIALLI		9	Savo MILOSEVIC ❑ †	
10	Mark HUGHES		10	Dwight YORKE	
11	Dennis WISE		14	Alan WRIGHT	
14	Craig BURLEY ‡		15	Fernando NELSON ❑	
16	Roberto DI MATTEO ❑		16	Ugo EHIOGU ❑	
18	Erland JOHNSEN †		26	Sasa CURCIC ‡	
	Substitutes			*Substitutes*	
7	John SPENCER ‡86		5	Paul McGRATH	
12	Michael DUBERRY		7	Ian TAYLOR ‡75	
21	Jody MORRIS †45		11	Tommy JOHNSON †65 ❑	
22	Mark NICHOLLS		12	Julian JOACHIM	
23	Nick COLGAN (Gk)		30	Adam RACHEL (Gk)	

BEFORE		P	W	D	L	F	A	pts	AFTER		P	W	D	L	F	A	pts
2	Chelsea	5	3	2	0	8	3	11	3	Chelsea	6	3	3	0	9	4	12
4	Villa	5	3	1	1	7	4	10	7	Villa	6	3	2	1	8	5	11

FACTFILE

Mark Bosnich is told to rest his damaged knee ligaments for a week... Coventry fail in attempt to sign Paul McGrath... Dwight Yorke still in search of his first goal... ineffective Savo Milosevic is replaced by Tommy Johnson after 65 minutes... Liverpool win at Leicester and take Premiership lead.

Dream free-kick earns a point

In his live-on-Sky TV pre-match interview Brian Little hints that to leave Stamford Bridge unbeaten would be a satisfactory outcome of this meeting of early Championship contenders.

The Villa manager is not being negative, but merely underlining the growing respect for Chelsea under Ruud Gullit's leadership.

Strengthened by the foreign signings of Franck Leboeuf, Roberto Di Matteo and Gianluca Vialli Chelsea are being tipped as likely to be challenging for honours.

Yesterday's results have brought a more familiar look to the Premiership with Manchester United top and Newcastle United back in there among the front-runners.

Nonetheless, victory could possibly move either Villa or Chelsea into top spot, a situation which guarantees a tight, competitive game at Stamford Bridge.

Following the disappointing UEFA Cup display against Helsingborgs IF in mid-week Sasa Curcic is recalled in place of Tommy Johnson who reverts to the bench.

Early indications are that Villa's game is back on track with a good deal of mobile attacking play interspersed with solid defending as Chelsea are not allowed to settle.

The promising start prompts the lead being grasped in dynamic and stylish fashion after 18 minutes.

A free-kick in a dangerous position just outside the Chelsea penalty area sees a group of Villa players in a huddle around the ball with no clear indication of who is going to take the kick.

Suddenly they disperse and Dwight Yorke, back to goal, pushes the ball to his right. Andy Townsend is moving in and as the ball arrives perfectly for him he drives it into the net with a magnificent, curling cross-shot.

"We practice it a lot in training, but that's the first time it's ended in the net. The others are in a field next to the training ground," Townsend is to admit afterwards.

In a match packed with talented imports it is a pleasure to see a player brought up and nurtured in the Football League deliver such a stunner, though Townsend's former club must have mixed feelings on the subject.

Townsend almost took the lead earlier with a diving header, while Curcic had made a good chance for himself without finishing it off.

However, with the lead tucked away Villa impress with their football for much of the half but, in stoppage time, Chelsea's equaliser changes the mood of the game.

Chelsea, for all their star names, have achieved little against Villa's confident rearguard, with Steve Staunton in fine form, until Dan Petrescu's angled centre from the right deceives everyone. Everyone, that is, except Leboeuf. As the ball heads towards the far post, at the narrowest of angles, the talented Frenchman moves in to judge his connection to perfection and steer the ball between Michael Oakes' outflung left hand and the upright.

The second-half proves to be a more-or-less uneventful slog with neither side wishing to lose their point. All-in-all an encouraging draw from a difficult game and confirmation of Villa's growing resilience – little sparkle in attack, though.

Andy Townsend

Saturday 21st September 1996 • Villa Park • 3.00pm

ASTON VILLA 0   MANCHESTER UNITED 0

Half-time 0-0 • Attendance 39,339

Referee Stephen LODGE (Barnsley)
Referee's Assistants W.M. JORDAN and P.A. VOSPER

Claret and Blue Shirts, White Shorts		Goals	White Shirts, Black Shorts		Goals
13	Michael OAKES		17	Raimond VAN DER GOUW	
3	Steve STAUNTON		2	Gary NEVILLE	
4	Gareth SOUTHGATE		3	Denis IRWIN	
6	Andy TOWNSEND		6	Gary PALLISTER	
8	Mark DRAPER		7	Eric CANTONA	
9	Savo MILOSEVIC ❏		10	David BECKHAM ❏	
10	Dwight YORKE		11	Ryan GIGGS	
14	Alan WRIGHT		14	Jordi CRUYFF ‡	
15	Fernando NELSON		16	Roy KEANE ❏	
16	Ugo EHIOGU		19	Ronny JOHNSEN	
26	Sasa CURCIC ❏ †		20	Ole Gunnar SOLSKJAER †	

	Substitutes			*Substitutes*	
5	Paul McGRATH		9	Andy COLE †45	
7	Ian TAYLOR †84		13	Brian McCLAIR	
11	Tommy JOHNSON		15	Karel POBORSKY ‡78	
12	Julian JOACHIM		18	Paul SCHOLES	
30	Adam RACHEL (Gk)		29	Michael APPLETON	

BEFORE	P	W	D	L	F	A	pts		AFTER	P	W	D	L	F	A	pts
2 Man Utd	6	3	3	0	16	6	12		4 Man Utd	7	3	4	0	16	6	13
7 Villa	6	3	2	1	8	5	11		6 Villa	7	3	3	1	8	5	12

FACTFILE

A fourth Villa draw on the trot... Dwight Yorke's eighth game without a goal this season... Villa's 16th home league draw against United in 64 starts which include 32 Villa victories... Villa unchanged for the fourth consecutive time in Premiership matches.

Goals still in short supply

The visit of reigning champions Manchester United inevitably rekindles memories of last season – when Alex Ferguson's otherwise triumphant side lost at Villa Park and were held at Old Trafford.

Brian Little is reminded of Ferguson's post-match comments, after the second of those games, that Villa had been 'dour' and 'unentertaining' but shrugs them off as unimportant.

The view is that the United boss was reacting in a sense of frustration that Villa had slowed down their charge to catch leaders Newcastle and 'we took his words as a compliment'.

A full-house of nearly 40,000 was assured well in advance of the day, though the fixture arrives in an awkward period for both teams.

Next week Villa play the away leg of the UEFA Cup-tie in Sweden, while Rapid Vienna are to visit Old Trafford in the European Champions League as the season truly takes off.

For Villa September is a crucial month as the manager repeatedly emphasises with a trip to Newcastle due a week on Monday and a great deal is at stake.

With Mark Bosnich still unfit, and due to see a specialist about the knee injured in training, the fixture emerges as Michael Oakes' greatest test, one he is to pass with flying colours.

The visitors are also without their first-choice keeper as Raimond Van der Gouw replaces the unavailable Peter Schmeichel.

United are on top in a first-half full of high-speed action but in which defences are mostly dominant. Oakes has to finger-tip away a Jordi Cruyff shot in the early minutes.

Soon after he deals comfortably with a shot from new England squad man David Beckham when fed by Eric Cantona as Villa struggle to get their game together smoothly.

Sasa Curcic attempts a couple of long-range efforts and, with the strikers Savo Milosevic and Dwight Yorke well policed, a moment of aggro arrives when the Serb is struck by Gary Pallister's elbow. Beckham is booked in another little outburst after a clash with Steve Staunton and half-time arrives with the feeling that Villa have weathered a storm.

United take off their new Norwegian Ole Gunnar Solskjaer at half time and bring on the out-of-form Andy Cole, a clear sign that their attack has been frustrated.

Villa have more of a say in the attacking play in the second half, though a Yorke effort is off-target and Van Der Gouw saves from Milosevic. Although there are no goals it is a reasonably entertaining game with Ryan Giggs showing his skill as he breaks through and rebounds a shot off the post.

Curcic is in the thick of some high-tension exchanges and is upended by the goalkeeper on one run on goal. Villa feel it should be a penalty, but the referee sees no offence.

United rattle the woodwork again when Giggs' centre is headed against the crossbar by Cole, while both players are close to scoring late on in the highly-competitive game.

Yorke finds the net when Mark Draper's pass is headed on by Milosevic, but the referee rules the effort out for hand-ball by Yorke and Milosevic is booked for dissent.

A stubborn display by Villa, but two home points have drifted and a five-point gap now separates them from the new leaders, Liverpool.

Dwight Yorke – had a 'goal' disallowed

Tuesday 24th September 1996 • Olympia • 8.00pm

HELSINGBORGS IF 0 ASTON VILLA 0

Aggregate score 1-1 • Helsingborg win 2-1 on away goals rule
Half-time 0-0 • Attendance 10,103
Referee Roger PHILIPPI (Luxembourg)
Referee's Assistants R. WEICKER and C. BIRENBAUM

Red and Blue Shirts, Blue Shorts	Goals	White Shirts, Claret Shorts	Goals
1 Sven ANDERSSON		13 Michael OAKES	
3 Ola NILSSON		3 Steve STAUNTON	
4 Roland NILSSON		4 Gareth SOUTHGATE	
5 Andreas JAKOBSSON		6 Andy TOWNSEND	
6 Christer FURSTH ❏ ‡		7 Ian TAYLOR	
8 Peter WIBRÅN		8 Mark DRAPER	
9 Magnus POWELL †		9 Savo MILOSEVIC ‡	
11 Mattias JONSSON		10 Dwight YORKE	
12 Jan ERIKSSON		14 Alan WRIGHT ❏	
14 Ulrik JANSSON		15 Fernando NELSON †	
15 Marcus LANTZ #		16 Ugo EHIOGU	
Substitutes		*Substitutes*	
2 Anders JÖNSSON #88		5 Paul McGRATH †61	
7 Patrik SUNDSTRÖM		11 Tommy JOHNSON ‡84	
10 Martin PRINGLE †57		12 Julian JOACHIM	
16 Jesper LJUNG #83		20 Riccardo SCIMECA	
21 Roger PERSSON (Gk)		28 Adam RACHEL (Gk)	

FACTFILE

Adam Rachel introduced as keeper substitute... Dwight Yorke's goalless spell drags on... Paul McGrath's first action of the season... Brian Little's European baptism as a manager ends in acute disappointment.

The Captains exchange pennants prior to the kick-off

Sterile Swedes retreat to victory

The club's first trip into Europe under Brian Little's managership is to prove their last, for this season at least, as the necessary breakthrough fails to arrive.

With the advantage of their away goal on which to build their tactics the Scandinavians are obviously in the driving seat and, to their credit, they steer their way safely through into the next round.

As a result of a low-key night of deep frustration the following of some 300 followers are left with nothing to enthuse over on a sad return flight straight after the goalless draw.

Apart from the opportunity to visit the shipshape and hospitable Scandinavian port in clear, pleasant weather conditions, the UEFA Cup journey comes to an end in very negative fashion for the English contingent.

Sasa Curcic's place goes to Ian Taylor but, this change apart, the now-familiar 3-5-2 formation sets about the task of turning the tie around.

Reine Almqvist, the Helsingborg manager, has insisted beforehand that his game plan will not be to simply go for the 0-0 option. Indeed, the club's publicity literature emphasises just how much they favour an enterprising and entertaining style of play.

Fine words, but the first whistle casts doubts on them as the Swedes retreat instantly behind the ball in large numbers and invite Villa to search out a way through.

Alan Wright

A crowd of just over 10,000 packed into the small Olympia stadium are largely silent as the predictable pattern unfolds. There is, indeed, nothing to lift the mood. Even a half-hearted attempt at a Mexican Wave dies out into a desultory ripple.

But for the change in the surrounds and absence of the two goals scored at Villa Park it could all be a slightly depressing action-replay of the first leg.

Helsingborg make the occasional break, showing neat control and movement off the ball, but it is basically a case of Villa's predictable attacks against the opposition's massed reguard. Andy Townsend gets in a long-range drive and a free kick ploy supplies Dwight Yorke with a shooting chance, but goalkeeper Andersson saves comfortably.

Just before the break Michael Oakes, on his European baptism, thinks quickly in dashing beyond his 18-yard line to head the ball away from Mattias Jonsson as the Swede chases onto a forward lob.

Mid-way through the second-half Villa feel they should be awarded a penalty when there is a clear hand-ball, but the referee blows for an offence against Villa instead.

So the game pursues its sterile pattern with Villa unable to conjure the one goal needed to go through. Paul McGrath is introduced as substitute in place of Fernando Nelson, enabling Ugo Ehiogu to push forward, but without any new impact being made.

Moments before the final whistle a 25-yard blast by Alan Wright looks promising, but Andersson flings himself to his left to finger-tip the powerful drive onto the woodwork.

"I think English teams should play as they do in the Premiership and not attempt to play the European style," says Almqvist who insists that the decision to go for a 0-0 draw was not made until half-time.

That highly-suspect explanation falls flat on English ears.

Monday 30th September 1996 • St. James' Park • 8.00pm

NEWCASTLE UNITED 4 ASTON VILLA 3

Half-time 3-1 • *Attendance 36,159*

Referee David ELLERAY (Harrow-on-the-Hill)
Referee's Assistants A.S. HOGG and M.D. MESSIAS

Black and White Striped Shirts, Black Shorts	Goals	Claret and Blue Shirts, White Shorts	Goals
1 Pavel SRNICEK		13 Michael OAKES	
3 John BERESFORD		3 Steve STAUNTON	
4 David BATTY		4 Gareth SOUTHGATE	
5 Darren PEACOCK		7 Ian TAYLOR	
6 Steve HOWEY	67	8 Mark DRAPER ❏ ■42	
7 Robert LEE		9 Savo MILOSEVIC	
9 Alan SHEARER	38	10 Dwight YORKE	4,59,69
10 Les FERDINAND	5,22	14 Alan WRIGHT	
14 David GINOLA †		15 Fernando NELSON	
18 Keith GILLESPIE		16 Ugo EHIOGU	
19 Steve WATSON		26 Sasa CURCIC	
Substitutes		*Substitutes*	
11 Faustino ASPRILLA †65		11 Tommy JOHNSON	
15 Shaka HISLOP (Gk)		12 Julian JOACHIM	
26 Robbie ELLIOTT		17 Lee HENDRIE	
27 Philippe ALBERT		20 Riccardo SCIMECA	
28 Paul KITSON		30 Adam RACHEL (Gk)	

BEFORE		P	W	D	L	F	A	pts
5	Newcastle	7	5	0	2	10	7	15
7	Villa	7	3	3	1	8	5	12

AFTER		P	W	D	L	F	A	pts
2	Newcastle	8	6	0	2	14	10	18
8	Villa	8	3	3	2	11	9	12

FACTFILE

Andy Townsend suffers a muscle-spasm in his back, and makes a late withdrawal from the squad... Man-of-the-match Dwight Yorke's first goals of the season... Sasa Curcic shows his class... Another fine game for young Michael Oakes... Villa without a Premiership win over Newcastle in seven attempts.

Draper off in 7-goal stunner

The visit to St James' Park, with Newcastle on a roll, coincides with Villa being criticised for their Euro-exit and Paul McGrath pushing for a move.

The Irish international has been left out of the travelling party after making critical comments about Villa's reluctance to give him a free transfer in a local paper and Brian Little's squad is under pressure to deliver a notable display.

A late fitness problem results in Andy Townsend being unable to play and Ian Taylor is called up to deputise. In front of the usual full house of vociferous Geordies Villa claim the early initiative by retaining possession with a whole series of sweet-passing moves.

The positive opening earns a right wing corner which is curled in by Mark Draper and though Pavel Srnicek and centre-back Darren Peacock appear to have it covered Dwight Yorke gets his head in first for the tonic of a 1-0 lead. The West Indian's slightly-disturbing goal drought had stretched back to last Easter Monday and the relief of ending it proves to be the launching pad for a brilliant hat-trick.

Yet even this virtuoso performance is not enough to halt Newcastle's march. Within a minute the equaliser arrives. A David Ginola free-kick is shielded brilliantly by Alan Shearer, with his back to goal, and as he directs a low instinctive pass towards Michael Oakes' left-hand post the predatory Les Ferdinand is there to ram it in.

To Villa's credit they absorb the disappointment and set off on more raids to go within a whisker of the lead as Yorke blasts a shot against the upright.

However by mid-way through the half Kevin Keegan's rampant marauders are in charge as confirmed by Ferdinand's second goal, a powerful header on the run to meet Keith Gillespie's cross from the right.

As Newcastle pile on the pressure Oakes is in superb form, as is Steve Staunton in an over-worked back line. Ominously, as it is to prove, Mark Draper receives a yellow card for a mild 'pushing' offence against Keith Gillespie and Newcastle zoom into a 3-1 lead.

The dual menace of the opposition's £21m strike duo creates havoc again as Ferdinand's drive is blocked on the line by Yorke, but rebounds invitingly for Alan Shearer to pounce in his renowned fashion.

By now Villa are looking ready to be over-run, a feeling which increases when Draper commits an undisciplined foul tackle on John Beresford and is sent off for his second yellow card offence in the 42nd minute.

Reduced to ten-men and facing a rampant, Championship-chasing side savouring the scent of blood, Villa seem destined for a second-half battering. The reverse gloriously proves to be the case in a display which has the Live-on-Sky TV team drooling with admiration.

Yorke's second goal is a masterpiece as he chases a long ball from Staunton, outpaces and outwits defenders, draws Srnicek and blasts an unstoppable shot past him. Wonderful.

Villa's football is accurate, incisive and totally committed, with Sasa Curcic carving swathes through the centre of the Magpies' midfield to off-set Draper's absence. Fittingly it is a lovely forward delivery by the Serb which releases Yorke to complete his hat-trick but, by now, Steve Howey has moved off his marker to head in Gillespie's centre unchallenged.

Only a linesman's flag denies Yorke a fourth goal with nine minutes to go; a decision later proved to be incorrect by television evidence; and what a well deserved equaliser it would have been. The final whistle finally removes the strain from the face of Kevin Keegan who has seen his team score four goals – while being subjected to untold mental anguish.

Saturday 12th October 1996 • White Hart Lane • 3.00pm

TOTTENHAM HOTSPUR 1   ASTON VILLA 0

Half-time 0-0 • Attendance 32,847

Referee Peter JONES (Loughborough)
Referee's Assistants M. TINGEY and S.G. TOMLIN

White Shirts, Dark Blue Shorts		Goals	Claret and Blue Shirts, White Shorts		Goals
1	Ian WALKER		1	Mark BOSNICH ❑	
4	David HOWELLS		3	Steve STAUNTON	
5	Colin CALDERWOOD		6	Andy TOWNSEND #	
7	Ruel FOX		7	Ian TAYLOR ❑	
8	Allan NEILSEN ‡	61	8	Mark DRAPER ‡	
10	Teddy SHERINGHAM ❑		9	Savo MILOSEVIC †	
11	Chris ARMSTRONG		10	Dwight YORKE	
15	Clive WILSON		14	Alan WRIGHT	
23	Sol CAMPBELL		15	Fernando NELSON	
25	Steve CARR		16	Ugo EHIOGU	
27	Andy SINTON †		26	Sasa CURCIC	
	Substitutes			*Substitutes*	
2	Dean AUSTIN		11	Tommy JOHNSON †80	
3	Justin EDINBURGH †38		12	Julian JOACHIM ‡80	
13	Espen BÅRDSEN (Gk)		13	Michael OAKES (Gk)	
14	Stuart NETHERCOTT ‡90		18	Carl TILER #80	
20	Neale FENN		19	Gareth FARRELLY	

BEFORE		P	W	D	L	F	A	pts	AFTER		P	W	D	L	F	A	pts
8	Villa	8	3	3	2	11	9	12	8	Villa	9	3	3	3	11	10	12
14	Spurs	8	2	2	4	6	8	8	11	Spurs	9	3	2	4	7	8	11

FACTFILE

Villa's first defeat by Spurs in 15 Cup and League starts... Seven games without a win... Savo Milosevic, who scored a hat-trick for Yugoslavia against Faroe Islands in mid-week, has found the net in only one of his last 16 games... Paul McGrath, unsettled at being out of the team, has moved to Derby County.

Run without a win drags on

A day that begins with optimistic talk of Villa's 'horses for courses' record against Spurs and the London club's poor home record, ends with a miserable return journey to the Midlands.

It's not only the statistics talk that has done a u-turn, to Villa's acute discomfort. The weekend headlines also put Villa in a bad light for an incident that has little to do with football.

In the centre of it all is Mark Bosnich, recalled for his first game of the season after knee trouble and suddenly embroiled in a so-called racist row.

From the start the White Hart Lane crowd have baited the Villa goalkeeper over the incident two years ago when Jürgen Klinsmann was injured in a collision with Bosnich at Villa Park.

The 24-year-old keeper has given no response throughout an evenly-matched first half which contains some attractive football from Villa, but with no cutting edge.

A third goalless draw in four games looks a distinct possibility until everything turns sour in a dreadful spell for Villa during the second half.

Another rash of Klinsmann chants provokes Bosnich into making the Nazi salute, while holding a finger of his right hand to his lip to denote an Adolf Hitler moustache.

The crowd reacts angrily, the gesture is reported to the referee by a linesman and the Australian is shown the yellow card for 'ungentlemanly conduct'.

Worse is to follow after the game as Bosnich and Brian Little are seen by the referee and by the police. The incident has been photographed by the press and is to be splashed across front and back pages adding to the call for action by the FA, for a possible disrepute charge, and by the police for its racist overtones.

Back on the footballing front, which has been largely over-shadowed, the 61st minute sees a Ruel Fox centre for the Dane Allan Nielsen to score his first goal since his summer move to White Hart Lane.

Villa are playing with a changed back-three. Gareth Southgate, injured playing for England in mid-week, has been replaced by Ian Taylor, whom Brian Little sees as an ideal 'play-anywhere' replacement.

Although Sasa Curcic is outstanding in midfield Villa produce very little by way of goal threat and Savo Milosevic is replaced by Julian Joachim. Before he goes, however, the Serb is involved in Spurs accusations of feigning injury and is reprimanded by manager Brian little for a finger-waving incident with a linesman.

Not a happy afternoon and even the depressed journey home sees the controversy drag on as the Radio 5 Live's phone-in show is deluged with calls about the Nazi salute row.

In the Villa coach Bosnich is so upset by hearing the comments that he rings in to the programme on the mobile telephone to publicly apologise for any distress caused and to express amazement that an action he intended as a 'joke' has been taken as an insult to Spurs' largely Jewish following.

Villa officials are to meet with Bosnich on Monday to discuss all likely ramifications.

Mark Bosnich

Saturday 19th October 1996 • Villa Park • 3.00pm

ASTON VILLA 2 LEEDS UNITED 0

Half-time 0-0 • Attendance 39,051

Referee Graham POLL (Tring)
Referee's Assistants D.S. BRYAN and D.C. RICHARDS

Claret and Blue Shirts, White Shorts	Goals	White Shirts, White Shorts	Goals
1 Mark BOSNICH		1 Nigel MARTYN	
3 Steve STAUNTON †		2 Gary KELLY	
6 Andy TOWNSEND		4 Carlton PALMER ❏ ‡	
7 Ian TAYLOR		5 Lucas RADEBE ❏	
10 Dwight YORKE	57	6 David WETHERALL †	
11 Tommy JOHNSON ‡	64	7 Lee SHARPE	
14 Alan WRIGHT		8 Rod WALLACE	
15 Fernando NELSON		9 Ian RUSH ❏	
16 Ugo EHIOGU ❏		16 Richard JOBSON ❏	
18 Carl TILER		22 Mark FORD ❏	
26 Sasa CURCIC		30 Mark HATELEY	

Substitutes		*Substitutes*	
12 Julian JOACHIM ‡81		15 Mark BEENEY (Gk)	
13 Michael OAKES (Gk)		20 Ian HARTE	
17 Lee HENDRIE		23 Andrew COUZENS ‡87	
19 Gareth FARRELLY		26 Paul BEESLEY †63	
20 Riccardo SCIMECA †41		29 Mark JACKSON	

BEFORE	P	W	D	L	F	A	pts		AFTER	P	W	D	L	F	A	pts
9 Villa	9	3	3	3	11	10	12		7 Villa	10	4	3	3	13	10	15
14 Leeds	9	3	1	5	8	13	10		16 Leeds	10	3	1	6	8	15	10

FACTFILE

Italian and Spanish clubs are said to be interested in the displaced Savo Milosevic... Tommy Johnson's fourth goal in five appearances... Carl Tiler's second start in his 12 months at Villa Park... Mark Draper misses the game with a one-match suspension... Steve Staunton suffers a first-half hamstring injury.

Savo left out as sparkle returns

Throughout the week there has been, alongside the 'Bosnich Salute' controversy, the feeling that Savo Milosevic would be rested after seven games without a win.

Bosnich has patiently answered all media inquiries about the White Hart Lane affair with, seemingly, an apology each day, but still the FA have charged him with 'misconduct'.

In contrast, Brian Little's focus has been firmly on the need to start winning again and the players have been told in no uncertain manner what their priorities must be.

Sweet football and crowd-pleasing displays are all very well, provided they keep the points flowing in at an acceptable rate. In recent weeks they have not and changes are on the cards.

Speculation that the £3.5m Serb, who has scored in only one match this season, will lose his place is confirmed as Tommy Johnson is called in.

Brian Little softens the blow by explaining afterwards that Milosevic, who did not remain at the ground to watch the the game, has 'not been too well' all week.

Out on the pitch, however, things have been much better, albeit against a mediocre Leeds side who so far have not been lifted greatly by George Graham, having replaced Howard Wilkinson as manager.

With Gareth Southgate still injured and Mark Draper suspended, Carl Tiler is in the backline with Ian Taylor in midfield. A further change is to arrive before half-time when the luckless Steve Staunton is injured again and Riccardo Scimeca takes over.

Villa's football is attractive and incisive with Sasa Curcic driving midfield with the kind of aggressive forward play he unfolded in the memorable second-half at Newcastle.

Yorke hit the bar in the 37th minute with a scorching 20-yard drive after a neat build-up.

Half-time arrives with the absence of an end-product still undermining Villa's work, but a seven-minute spell early in the second half blows away such negative thoughts.

The afternoon's largest Premiership crowd is warmed by the 57th minute opener which emerges from Curcic being allowed the 'advantage' after riding a foul tackle by Mark Ford.

Curcic finds Johnson, who transfers the ball to Yorke who beats Martyn from wide of his left hand post with the sort of precisely-placed cross-shot that has become his hallmark and his first Villa Park goal of the season.

Goal No. 2 is another little gem as Yorke unhinges his marker to place an ideal centre for Johnson to tuck away from ten yards out. The goal is a just return for the Geordie's unceasing efforts and makes up for a couple of squandered chances earlier.

Leeds had been a minimal threat before the double-strike. Afterwards it is simply no contest, as Curcic continues to delight the large crowd.

"I have told the players that those who win matches will keep their place," says Brian Little, a strong hint that Milosevic may be facing a spell on the sidelines.

Johnson's inclusion has certainly co-incided with a livelier, more menacing approach.

Pre-match fears that Bosnich would face orchestrated taunts from opposition fans over 'that salute' prove to be virtually groundless.

The travelling hordes from Elland Road clearly have problems enough of their own.

Tommy Johnson

Wednesday 23rd October 1996 • Elland Road • 7.45pm

LEEDS UNITED 1 ASTON VILLA 2

Half-time 0-0 • Attendance 15,803

Referee Jeff WINTER (Stockton-on-Tees)

Referee's Assistants D.J. ADCOCK and S.R. BRAND

White Shirts, White Shorts	Goals	Claret and Blue Shirts, Blue Shorts	Goals
1 Nigel MARTYN		1 Mark BOSNICH	
2 Gary KELLY		6 Andy TOWNSEND	
3 Lee SHARPE	69	7 Ian TAYLOR	70
4 Carlton PALMER		10 Dwight YORKE	77 pen
5 Paul BEESLEY ‡		11 Tommy JOHNSON ❑	
6 Richard JOBSON		14 Alan WRIGHT	
7 Mark FORD		15 Fernando NELSON †	
8 Rod WALLACE		16 Ugo EHIOGU	
9 Ian RUSH		18 Carl TILER	
10 Andrew COUZENS		20 Riccardo SCIMECA	
11 Lucas RADEBE †		26 Sasa CURCIC	
Substitutes		*Substitutes*	
12 David WETHERALL †72		. 8 Mark DRAPER †77	
14 Ian HARTE ‡85		12 Julian JOACHIM	
15 Mark BEENEY (Gk)		13 Michael OAKES (Gk)	

FACTFILE

Fourth round draw means Villa must travel to either Wimbledon or Luton Town... Villa have lost only once in their last 20 Coca-Cola Cup matches, including two Wembley wins... Villa's fourth successive cup and league win over Leeds with a 10-1 aggregate scoreline... Another injury as Nelson comes off at Elland Road with a hamstring strain.

Riccardo Scimeca – making his first start of the season

Taylor and Yorke strike for victory

Since last Saturday's 2-0 Premiership victory over Leeds at Villa Park the club has confirmed that Savo Milosevic could be leaving, either for Italy or for Spain.

Brian Little has voiced his disappointment with the way the Serb has been performing and his absence even from the subs bench suggests a forthcoming parting of the ways.

The tie is live on Sky, who build the game up as a repeat of the 1995 Final, though a comparatively small crowd robs the occasion of anything resembling the Wembley atmosphere.

Steve Staunton has not recovered from the injury suffered on Saturday, which means a chance in defence for Riccardo Scimeca.

Early in the game Villa find themselves under siege for spells as Leeds go all out for the revenge result that they and their supporters would dearly like to savour.

A curling shot by Andy Couzens is clawed away by Mark Bosnich, while Rod Wallace is only narrowly off target after Lee Sharpe's free kick is diverted to him.

Scimeca is proving himself equal to the challenge as the defence absorbs all the home side can offer and gradually it is Villa's turn to dictate the flow.

With Mark Draper unable to reclaim his place in the starting line-up Sasa Curcic takes centre stage once again with his speedy, penetrating runs and capacity to exchange passes at full pace.

Curcic and Andy Townsend are to be re-joined in midfield mid-way through the second half by Draper when Fernando Nelson leaves the field and Ian Taylor goes to right wing back.

After 22 minutes Villa are denied what should have been a penalty when the Serb is clearly hooked down by the fallen Richard Jobson. Brian Little leaps from his seat in an uncharacteristic display of disbelief at the decision and at half-time referee Jeff Winter admits that he didn't see the incident clearly.

Both teams miss good chances, Lee Sharpe in front of an open goal and Dwight Yorke, after a brilliant Villa move, when his lunging header ought to have been directed wide of Nigel Martyn's clutches.

By half-time Villa are undeniably the better side with Curcic increasingly outstanding, but it is Leeds who take the lead 24 minutes into the second half with Lee Sharpe hitting an unstoppable drive into the roof of the net after a swift break down Villa's left flank.

Oddly, that proves to be Leeds' last chance of survival as their lead lasts merely a few seconds. Villa hit back with a snaking ball across goal by Curcic following a fine left wing run, which the falling Jobson can only tee up at the far post for Ian Taylor to knock in the equaliser.

After 77 minutes, with Villa in command, Paul Beesley tackles Dwight Yorke clumsily just inside the box and the West Indian places the ball on the spot. Calm as ever, he waits for Martyn to inch to his left before stroking the ball wide of the keeper on the other side.

"This is a competition we want to win again," says Yorke afterwards. "We take it very seriously." Leeds never had cause to doubt it...

Ian Taylor

Saturday 26th October 1996 • Roker Park • 3.00pm

SUNDERLAND 1 ASTON VILLA 0

Half-time 1-0 • *Attendance* 21,059

Referee Paul ALCOCK (Redhill)

Referee's Assistants D.S. BABSKI and I. BLANCHARD

Red and White Striped Shirts, Black Shorts		Goals	Navy Blue Shirts, Light Blue Shorts		Goals
30	Lionel PEREZ		1	Mark BOSNICH ❏ †	
2	Dariusz KUBICKI		4	Gareth SOUTHGATE	
4	Paul BRACEWELL		6	Andy TOWNSEND	
5	Kevin BALL		7	Ian TAYLOR	
6	Andrew MELVILLE		8	Mark DRAPER #	
7	Michael GRAY ❏		10	Dwight YORKE	
8	Richard ORD		11	Tommy JOHNSON ❏	
10	Paul STEWART	25	14	Alan WRIGHT	
12	Gareth HALL		16	Ugo EHIOGU	
16	David KELLY		18	Carl TILER	
19	Michael BRIDGES †		26	Sasa CURCIC ‡	
	Substitutes			*Substitutes*	
9	Craig RUSSELL †85		12	Julian JOACHIM ‡61	
14	Lee HOWEY		13	Michael OAKES (Gk) †57	
15	Alex RAE		17	Lee HENDRIE #61	
18	Martin SMITH		19	Gareth FARRELLY	
28	Philip NAISBETT (Gk)		20	Riccardo SCIMECA	

BEFORE		P	W	D	L	F	A	pts	AFTER		P	W	D	L	F	A	pts
7	Villa	10	4	3	3	13	10	15	7	Villa	11	4	3	4	13	11	15
15	Sunderland	10	2	4	4	8	11	10	13	Sunderland	11	3	4	4	9	11	13

FACTFILE

Fourth away Premiership defeat of season... Only one win in seven Premiership games... Bosnich will be out for a month following keyhole surgery on his suspect knee... Coach John Gregory has joined Wycombe Wanderers as manager and taken reserve striker Neil Davis on a month's loan.

Rock bottom form at Roker

Brian Little remained behind when the players travelled north on the eve of the game to take part in negotiations for the sale of striker Savo Milosevic to Perugia.

Officials of the Italian Serie A club were in Birmingham to conclude agreement at a fee of £4.5m, a good return on a player who had lost his place after a string of ineffectual displays.

Arriving on Wearside in plenty of time for the game the manager recalls Gareth Southgate in defence with Ian Taylor at right wing-back in place of the injured Fernando Nelson.

Villa badly need to build on the two victories over Leeds United in order to get some consistency into the sequence of results, but in an uninspired 90 minutes they never look like achieving that aim.

From the 25th minute, when Paul Stewart gives Peter Reid's side the lead after a disputed penalty, Villa are disturbingly short of conviction in all departments.

The award is given when Mark Bosnich collides with Stewart, though the goalkeeper is insistant that, despite a booking for the offence, it was a complete accident as he went for the ball in a tight situation.

Lee Hendrie – first appearance of the season

That moment is a rare blot on Bosnich's display which prevents Sunderland gaining a bigger lead, until he has to leave the field in the 57th minute when aggravating his knee injury in a collision with Michael Bridges.

Michael Oakes takes over in goal and Brian Little, frustrated by the manner in which Sunderland's more aggressive tactics have negated Villa's efforts then makes a surprising change in midfield. Both Mark Draper and Sasa Curcic are withdrawn to be replaced by Lee Hendrie and Julian Joachim, though there is little noticeable improvement.

In the entire 90 minutes Villa have but two goal-scoring attempts, neither of them especially dangerous. Substitute Joachim forces a routine save from Perez, while Johnson steers a good opening wide of the target when a long upfield pass by Southgate unhinges the otherwise impregnable Sunderland defence.

Even Villa's defence, normally so secure and assured, is out of sorts with Ugo Ehiogu, Southgate and Carl Tiler, who is desputising for the injured Steve Staunton on the left, unsettled by Sunderland's scrambling persistence.

Villa have simply found themselves dominated by the opposition's industrious determination to control and dictate the pace and are never able to come to terms with it.

In the swirling wind and frenetic atmosphere Villa are swept along to a defeat which has been inevitable from the moment Sunderland took the lead.

Many regard the performance as possibly the poorest under Brian Little's command, one which drives home the message that a reliable replacement for Milosevic must be found as quickly as possible.

"It's been a bad day at the office,"admits the concerned Villa manager who confirms that moves are afoot to improve the strike force. "We've not played worse this season," he adds as a sad epitaph to a display that was well below the high standards which have been set.

Saturday 2nd November 1996 • Villa Park • 3.00pm

ASTON VILLA 2 NOTTINGHAM FOREST 0

Half-time 1-0 • *Attendance* 35,310

Referee Roger DILKES (Mossley)
Referee's Assistants M. RYAN and M.R. SIMS

Claret and Blue Shirts, White Shorts	Goals		Yellow Shirts with Navy Blue Trim, Navy Blue Shorts	Goals
13 Michael OAKES			1 Mark CROSSLEY	
4 Gareth SOUTHGATE			2 Des LYTTLE	
6 Andy TOWNSEND			3 Stuart PEARCE	
7 Ian TAYLOR			4 Colin COOPER	
10 Dwight YORKE	64		5 Steve CHETTLE	
11 Tommy JOHNSON			7 David PHILLIPS †	
14 Alan WRIGHT			8 Scot GEMMILL	
15 Fernando NELSON			9 Dean SAUNDERS	
16 Ugo EHIOGU			12 Jason LEE	
18 Carl TILER	19		14 Ian WOAN ❑	
26 Sasa CURCIC			18 Alf Inge HÅLAND ❑	

Substitutes		*Substitutes*
8 Mark DRAPER		13 Alan FETTIS (Gk)
12 Julian JOACHIM		16 Nikola JERKAN
19 Gareth FARRELLY		17 Chris ALLEN
20 Riccardo SCIMECA		19 Stephen HOWE
30 Adam RACHEL (Gk)		22 Bryan ROY †78

BEFORE	P	W	D	L	F	A	pts	AFTER	P	W	D	L	F	A	pts
7 Villa	11	4	3	4	13	11	15	7 Villa	12	5	3	4	15	11	18
18 Forest	11	1	5	5	10	18	8	18 Forest	12	1	5	6	10	20	8

FACTFILE

Fernando Nelson and Gareth Southgate pass late fitness tests, Steve Staunton fails his... Carl Tiler proves he's back after his lengthy lay-off with a hamstring injury – The ex-Forest defender scores his first goal for Villa and his first in the League for five years... Villa unbeaten by Forest in five cup and league matches.

Tiler signs-in with timely goal

With the impending sale of Savo Milosevic having not yet gone through and Villa's form and results less consistent than last season there is an air of uncertainty at Villa Park.

The arrival of Midland rivals Nottingham Forest lacks the usual atmosphere of expectation with the opposition in serious decline and Villa themselves slightly unsettled.

Brian Little, less certain than in the past of his most effective line up and agreeing that things are not quite right, has demoted Mark Draper to the bench and selected Tommy Johnson ahead of Julian Joachim to join Dwight Yorke in attack.

Happily, Villa's attendance is as strong as ever and the home victory anticipated by the claret and blue faction is duly delivered, if a shade less fluently than the majority would have liked.

Reflecting that mood succinctly in the Birmingham Post on the Monday Rob Bishop writes: "Not all football matches are capable of setting the pulses racing. For some strange reason I can't quite put my finger on, this was one of them."

Part of that reason, perhaps, was that while Villa would like to delight the eye with the quality of their football, the more realistic aim is to achieve a crucial home win after the poor display last week at Roker Park.

If they have to grind out a result, rather than achieve it with flair and panache, then so be it...

One nightmare scenario to be avoided is that of Dean Saunders plundering a goal or goals against his former club and the first half sees the home team concentrating on containment rather than a win-at-all-costs approach.

In typical Forest fashion they play some attractive approach football, finding their men well and forcing Villa to work hard in midfield.

Fernando Nelson has returned to right wing-back enabling Ian Taylor to adopt the midfield role he prefers and overall the team balance looks better for it.

As Saunders beavers away with characteristic enthusiasm, mainly along the flanks, the first goal of the game is provided for Villa, ironically, by a Forest 'old boy'.

The opening emerges in the 19th minute from a free kick which Andy Townsend touches to Dwight Yorke whose shot strikes team mate Taylor, positioned in the Forest wall of defenders. For a moment the visitors seem to have survived but Tiler pounces onto the loose ball to drive it wide of Mark Crossley. It is a sickening moment for Forest who by now have seen their front man, Jason Lee, fail with two or three openings which he ought to have put away.

By half time Villa supporters feel fortunate that their team is ahead but many positive signs are emerging with Sasa Curcic again unveiling his repertoire of ball skills and Taylor providing the hard running.

However, any hope Forest had of ending their slide down the table was now disappearing unchecked as Villa take control. A 64th minute Townsend corner evades the grasp of Crossley, under pressure from Ugo Ehiogu, and Yorke completes the scoring with a spectacular overhead kick.

Carl Tiler and Jason Lee

Saturday 16th November 1996 • Villa Park • 3.00pm

ASTON VILLA 1 LEICESTER CITY 3

Half-time 1-2 • Attendance 36,193

Referee David ELLERAY (Harrow-on-the-Hill)
Referee's Assistants L.E. CABLE and P.R. SHARP

Claret and Blue Shirts, White Shorts		Goals	Blue Shirts, Blue Shorts		Goals
13	Michael OAKES		13	Kasey KELLER	
4	Gareth SOUTHGATE		2	Simon GRAYSON	
6	Andy TOWNSEND ❑		3	Michael WHITLOW	
7	Ian TAYLOR		4	Julian WATTS	
10	Dwight YORKE	16	5	Steve WALSH	
11	Tommy JOHNSON		6	Mustafa IZZET	84
14	Alan WRIGHT		7	Neil LENNON	
15	Fernando NELSON †		9	Steve CLARIDGE	8
16	Ugo EHIOGU		10	Garry PARKER	44pen
18	Carl TILER		11	Emile HESKEY ❑	
26	Sasa CURCIC ‡		17	Spencer PRIOR	
	Substitutes			*Substitutes*	
8	Mark DRAPER †56		1	Kevin POOLE (Gk)	
12	Julian JOACHIM ‡60		14	Colin HILL	
19	Gareth FARRELLY		20	Ian MARSHALL	
20	Riccardo SCIMECA		21	Jamie LAWRENCE	
30	Adam RACHEL (Gk)		24	Stuart SLATER	

BEFORE		P	W	D	L	F	A	pts
7	Villa	12	5	3	4	15	11	18
13	Leicester	12	4	2	6	9	15	14

AFTER		P	W	D	L	F	A	pts
9	Villa	13	5	3	5	16	14	18
10	Leicester	13	5	2	6	12	16	17

FACTFILE

Villa's first home defeat of season... Still-injured Mark Bosnich has been fined £1,000 for his 'Basil Fawlty' salute at White Hart Lane... After the weekend, Savo, tiring of the protracted transfer negotiations, announces his desire to stay at Villa Park, regardless of what the two clubs decide.

Penalty decisions go against Villa

After three months of inconsistency, Villa's season arrives at a crossroads as supporters are sent home disappointed not only by the defeat, but by the poor level of form.

The previous week has been punctuated by press talk of Stan Collymore being purchased from Liverpool with the proceeds of the Savo Milosevic sale, but there is no actual evidence of either transaction reaching fruition.

It emerges, in fact, that Milosevic has been recalled to Villa Park because negotiations with the Italian club Perugia have faltered on the size of the fee. As a result there remains a feeling of uncertainty at the club as, unlike a year earlier, there is no settled line-up and no meaningful title challenge.

Brian Little's former club has settled impressively into the Premiership and has been proving tough opposition for anyone. This they emphatically confirm with a Villa Park display against repeated chants from Leicester fans of "Brian, Brian ... what's the score?".

Kevin MacDonald has been appointed first-team coach in succession to the departed John Gregory and it becomes clear that he has some tactical sorting out to achieve.

Villa seem uncertain and ill-at-ease in all departments as Leicester set about their task in a far more co-ordinated manner.

The game is only seven minutes old when some ineffectual defending allows Steve Claridge to plunder the lead from the simplest of chances in front of goal. For a time, however, a sense of optimism returns when Dwight Yorke chases out to the right of the goal onto a half-save by Kasey Keller from Alan Wright's well-struck shot.

The Villa's striker's cross-shot deflects off the goalkeeper for the equaliser, but by half-time Leicester are, very fortuitously, back in the lead from a highly-debatable penalty.

Gareth Southgate has cleared a dangerous ball away from Emile Heskey. Meanwhile, Michael Oakes is running out intending to gather the ball and his impetous sweeps him into an unnecessary collision with the young Leicester striker.

From 50 yards away, near the centre spot, referee David Elleray awards a penalty for what was clearly an accidental collision; leaving ex-Villa midfielder Garry Parker to neatly tuck away the resulting spot kick.

Villa toil untidily in their attempts to create a second equaliser, but Leicester often have ten men guarding their goal and are rarely troubled.

Brian Little's out-of-touch team needs a spot of luck but, in reality, fortune is smiling in the opposite direction. A 63rd minute centre by Ian Taylor is knocked down clearly by Steve Walsh's outflung arm, but referee Elleray waves play on amid an angry reaction from the Holte End of the ground.

At this stage there is the feeling that Leicester are a touch fortunate to be in the lead, though all this changes with the arrival of their 84th minute third goal.

A neat pass by Claridge sends Mustafa Izzet away and the nippy midfield player beats Villa's defence on his own to draw Oakes and slot the ball past him.

By then Brian Little has changed from 3-5-2 to 4-3-3 by replacing Nelson and Curcic with Mark Draper and Julian Joachim, but without effecting the desired improvement.

Julian Joachim

Saturday 23rd November 1996 • Highfield Road • 3.00pm

COVENTRY CITY 1 ASTON VILLA 2

Half-time 0-1 • Attendance 21,340

Referee Paul DURKIN (Portland)

Referee's Assistants J.W. PETTITT and J.J. ROSS

Sky Blue and Navy Blue Striped Shirts, Navy Blue Shorts	Goals
1 Steve OGRIZOVIC	
2 Richard SHAW ‡	
3 David BURROWS †	
4 Paul WILLIAMS	
5 Liam DAISH ❏	
7 Eoin JESS	
8 Noel WHELAN ❏	
9 Dion DUBLIN	75
10 Gary McALLISTER	
11 John SALAKO	
14 Peter NDLOVU #	
Substitutes	
12 Paul TELFER ‡67	
13 John FILAN (Gk)	
16 Brian BORROWS †24 ❏	
17 Willie BOLAND	
28 Darren HUCKERBY #73	

Claret and Blue Shirts, White Shorts	Goals
13 Michael OAKES	
3 Steve STAUNTON	85
4 Gareth SOUTHGATE	
6 Andy TOWNSEND ❏	
8 Mark DRAPER ❏ #	
11 Tommy JOHNSON ❏	
12 Julian JOACHIM ‡	30
14 Alan WRIGHT	
15 Fernando NELSON	
16 Ugo EHIOGU	
26 Sasa CURCIC †	
Substitutes	
7 Ian TAYLOR †60	
9 Savo MILOSEVIC ‡76	
18 Carl TILER	
20 Riccardo SCIMECA #89	
30 Adam RACHEL (Gk)	

BEFORE		P	W	D	L	F	A	pts
9	Villa	13	5	3	5	16	14	18
18	Coventry	13	1	7	5	7	17	10

AFTER		P	W	D	L	F	A	pts
8	Villa	14	6	3	5	18	15	21
18	Coventry	14	1	7	6	8	19	10

FACTFILE

Villa undefeated by Coventry in last eight Premiership meetings... Villa have won last three against Sky Blues... Savo returns to take his place on the subs bench... Ian Taylor and Carl Tiler step down to make way for Mark Draper and Steve Staunton... Steve Staunton's first Premiership goal since May 1995 at Norwich.

Steve Staunton's late super strike

The news that Savo Milosevic, scorer of five goals against them last season, is back in the Villa squad must seem an ominous warning for already-struggling Coventry City.

In the event, however, the £3.5m Serb spends most of the game on the bench until a very brief appearance late on when the Sky Blues have just equalised at 1-1.

The dominant force in this welcome victory is to be Republic of Ireland international Steve Staunton, who returns after injury to set a magnificent example in both defence and attack.

With Dwight Yorke away on World Cup duty for Trinidad & Tobago, Villa have a slightly lightweight-looking front two in the shape of Tommy Johnson and Julian Joachim.

They are confronted by a Coventry side in the mood to fight for their Premiership lives with Gordon Strachan making his home debut as manager since Ron Atkinson's elevation to technical director.

Coventry have drawn their previous six Premiership games, while Villa players have been called to a special team meeting on the morning of the match to ensure no repetition of last Saturday's poor performance against Leicester City.

The outcome is a fiercely competitive Midland derby, played at pace and packed with physical defiance and incident.

Clearly, scoring chances will not be cheaply earned and Villa hearts sink briefly when Ugo Ehiogu steers wide when well-placed to score from six yards out after 26 minutes.

Yet such is the irony of foot-ball that, four minutes later, when Julian Joachim gets possession from a moment of mishandling by Steve Ogrizovic near the junction of the 18-yard line and the keeper's right-hand goalline the Villa striker curves in a scoring shot which is later described on BBC Match-of-the-Day as a 'conjuring trick'.

Tommy Johnson misses a good chance to make it 2-0 and Joachim flicks a header against the inside of the post and out again on the stroke of half-time.

Coventry could have been down and out, but they come back in admirable pursuit of the equaliser, which is to arrive when Strachan sends on his new £1m signing – Darren Huckerby. The former Newcastle forward's very first involvement for his new club sweeps him around the left of Villa's defence to lay the ball right in the path of Dion Dublin for 1-1.

Brian Little promptly sends on Milosevic as Villa strive to regain the lead with the atmosphere becoming increasingly frenetic. In the thick of it all Staunton storms upfield to unleash a 30-yard drive that takes a deflection on its way to winning the points.

Now passions are boiling over and as Noel Whelan goes in hard on Andy Townsend near the fallen body of Paul Williams, a melee of feuding, jostling players develops around the sorely-pressed referee.

Quickly law and order returns as Whelan is booked for his challenge and Townsend, who has already been booked, is severely lectured by the official for his agitated response.

Villa are glad to hear the final whistle which quickly follows, leaving Coventry with the feeling that maybe they deserved a seventh draw on the trot and Villa contented with a job well done.

Steve Staunton

Wednesday 26th November 1996 • Selhurst Park • 7.45pm

WIMBLEDON 1 ASTON VILLA 0

Half-time 1-0 • *Attendance* 7,573

Referee Peter JONES (Loughborough)

Referee's Assistants P. GRIFFIN and C. FRANCIS

Dark Blue Shirts, Dark Blue Shorts		Goals	White Shirts, Claret Shorts		Goals
1	Neil SULLIVAN		13	Michael OAKES	
2	Kenny CUNNINGHAM		3	Steve STAUNTON	
3	Alan KIMBLE		4	Gareth SOUTHGATE ‡	
4	Vinny JONES ❑		6	Andy TOWNSEND	
5	Dean BLACKWELL		7	Ian TAYLOR	
7	Øyvind LEONHARDSEN		8	Mark DRAPER	
8	Robbie EARLE		10	Dwight YORKE	
9	Efan EKOKU †		12	Julian JOACHIM †	
11	Marcus GAYLE ‡	44	14	Alan WRIGHT	
12	Chris PERRY		15	Fernando NELSON	
18	Neal ARDLEY		16	Ugo EHIOGU	
	Substitutes			*Substitutes*	
20	Mick HARFORD †71		9	Savo MILOSEVIC †67	
22	Andy CLARKE ‡71		18	Carl TILER	
24	Peter FEAR		20	Riccardo SCIMECA ‡82	

FACTFILE

Dwight Yorke returns unscathed from his international duties... First Coca-Cola Cup-tie defeat since Crystal Palace, Selhurst Park November '94... Only the second since Ipswich, December '93... Including 1st leg semi-final defeat by Tranmere Villa have lost only three of last 26 Coca-Cola Cup games dating back to the start of the '92/93 season.

Mark Draper

Sucker punch lands unlucky KO

This was always going to be an uncomfortable and testing obstacle in defence of the trophy so proudly won and so it is to prove on a night of abject disappointment.

The combination of Wimbledon and Selhurst Park brings back unhappy memories of past disasters and few are truly surprised when this simply proves to be another.

Before the kick-off, however, there has been some degree of optimism with the return from World Cup duty of Dwight Yorke, to replace Tommy Johnson, following on to the impressive display at Coventry last Saturday.

The stomach bug which troubled Sasa Curcic at Highfield Road has not cleared up, so Ian Taylor returns to the Villa midfield as they set about the task in hand with plenty of attacking aggression.

Apart from the occasional Wimbledon thrust Villa dictate the play with Mark Draper linking up well with Nelson down the right-hand side. Alan Wright is equally prominent down the left touchline.

Yorke, Taylor and Draper all promise a Villa lead before the Dons sneak ahead, helped by some questionable Villa defending, just a few seconds before half-time.

There seems no real threat as Steve Staunton carefully shields Marcus Gayle from the goal as the Wimbledon forward cuts a path through the inside-left position.

Virtually on the goal-line, however, Staunton appears to relax, as though his job is completed. Simultaneously, Michael Oakes has advanced from his goal towards the two players.

In that unguarded split-second Gayle tries a hopeful shot from seemingly sideways on and the ball threads off the surprised keeper's arm and his right-hand post.

To go in a goal down to such a hit-or-miss affair is a sickener for Villa and the disgust shows on Brian Little's face as he heads for the dressing room.

Oakes quickly sets about making amends for not blocking the shot by tipping away a Neal Ardley free-kick in the 58th minute, but it is mainly a case of the home team closing down and defending their slender lead.

Villa have their chance to draw level when Dwight Yorke is put into possession only six yards out, but the West Indian's full-blooded volley is brilliantly kept out by goalkeeper Neil Sullivan who dives full-stretch to save.

Waves of Villa attacks sweep Dons constantly back into defence as Villa go full-throttle for a replay, but though Savo Milosevic is involved in the penalty area action the break-through never arrives.

To add to the night's frustration Gareth Southgate lands awkwardly after a hard challenge and is taken from the scene with what looks to be a severe aggravation of the ankle injury which has kept him out previously.

As with the departure from the UEFA Cup, an entrance door marked 'Europe' closes firmly in Villa faces.

Fernando Nelson

Saturday 30th November 1996 • Villa Park • 3.00pm

ASTON VILLA 1 MIDDLESBROUGH 0

Half-time 1-0 • *Attendance* 39,053

Referee Gary WILLARD (Worthing)

Referee's Assistants M.D. DEARING and G.M. LEE

Claret and Blue Shirts, White Shorts	Goals	White and Blue Shirts, Blue Shorts	Goals
13 Michael OAKES		13 Gary WALSH ❑	
3 Steve STAUNTON		2 Neil COX	
6 Andy TOWNSEND		3 Derek WHYTE	
7 Ian TAYLOR		8 Robbie MUSTOE ❑	
8 Mark DRAPER		9 Mikkel BECK	
9 Savo MILOSEVIC ❑		10 JUNINHO †	
10 Dwight YORKE	39pen	11 Fabrizio RAVANELLI	
14 Alan WRIGHT ❑		14 Curtis FLEMING ❑	
15 Fernando NELSON		20 Philip STAMP	
16 Ugo EHIOGU		21 Craig HIGNETT	
20 Riccardo SCIMECA		26 Chris MORRIS	
Substitutes		*Substitutes*	
12 Julian JOACHIM		15 Phil WHELAN	
17 Lee HENDRIE		22 Craig LIDDLE	
18 Carl TILER		23 Jan Aage FJORTOFT	
26 Sasa CURCIC		25 Ben ROBERTS (Gk)	
30 Adam RACHEL (Gk)		32 Andrew CAMPBELL †59	

BEFORE		P	W	D	L	F	A	pts	AFTER		P	W	D	L	F	A	pts
8	Villa	14	6	3	5	18	15	21	7	Villa	15	7	3	5	19	15	24
15	Boro	14	3	5	6	20	25	14	16	Boro	15	3	5	7	20	26	14

FACTFILE

Third Premiership win out of four... Gareth Southgate's ankle injury, sustained at Wimbledon, means he will be out for some time, Southgate hoping to be fit for England's game with Italy in early February... Yorke's eighth goal in last nine appearances... Villa's seventh point from nine since Boro's promotion.

Yorke penalty wins points

Exit from the Coca-Cola Cup allied to home defeat by Leicester City has put Villa's season under close scrutiny and Brian Little is well aware that a slip-up against Middlesbrough would go down badly with supporters.

The Villa manager heralds the game in his match-day programme notes as likely to produce a 'smashing game of football' in the light of Bryan Robson's high-profile imports.

Secretly, however, he might well fear that, because of their lowly position in the Premiership, the Teessiders might go for safety-first ahead of entertaining attacking aggression. This is to prove the case...

Certainly there is a workmanlike look about the Villa line-up with Ian Taylor forcing Sasa Curcic onto the bench and Riccardo Scimeca keeping Carl Tiler out of the back three.

Mark Bosnich and Gareth Southgate are still absent, but the strength of Villa's squad is able to overcome their temporary loss through injury.

From the very outset Middlesbrough, by their tactics, illustrate that their intention is to curb, as much as possible, Villa's attacking potential in front of a virtual full-house attendance.

Many of those fans, no doubt, are here hoping to see at first-hand the attacking skills of the Brazilian Juninho and the Italian Ravanelli. In the event Boro's defensive strategy denies these players much opportunity to express themselves and show their undoubted abilities.

The onus is very much on Villa to make a match of it rather than settle for a negative, defensive stalemate and this they attempt to do.

Much of Villa's passing is of the very highest quality, but it is performed in the face of a massed rearguard seeking to deny space at every turn.

It takes 39 minutes for Villa to achieve the breakthrough which their efforts deserve and this arrives in the shape of a penalty that is vehemently disputed by the opposition.

The offence is a tug of Dwight Yorke's shirt in the penalty area, by former Villa defender Neil Cox, though many are unable to see what has taken place. Undeterred by any protestations Yorke tucks the spot-kick away for a slender lead which Middlesbrough rarely threaten to cut back and Villa are unlikely to relinquish.

Such is Villa's supremacy that a far-wider margin of victory would be appropriate, but for the shortage of clinical finishing outside of Yorke's re-emergence among the Premiership's most lethal strikers.

Staunton is supreme at the back, supported confidently by Ugo Ehiogu and Scimeca, while Nelson and Alan Wright provide the required wing-back service.

On his first full appearance since the breakdown of his proposed transfer to Italian club Perugia Savo Milosevic also plays his part. He blends the attack together by 'holding the ball up' well, but is unable to add to the two goals he scored in the 2-2 home draw with Arsenal on September 7.

The frustrating fact is that if the Yugoslavian could score more consistently Aston Villa would once again be mounting a real challenge for the Championship.

Dwight Yorke

Wednesday 4th December 1996 • Upton Park • 7.45pm

WEST HAM UNITED 0 ASTON VILLA 2

Half-time 0-1 • *Attendance* 19,105

Referee Mike KELLY (Leeds)

Referee's Assistants E.W. GREEN and G.K. HEGLEY

Claret and Blue Shirts, White Shorts	Goals	White Shirts, Claret Shorts	Goals
1 Ludek MIKLOSKO		13 Michael OAKES	
2 Tim BREACKER ‡		3 Steve STAUNTON	
3 Julian DICKS		6 Andy TOWNSEND	
7 Ian BISHOP		7 Ian TAYLOR	
8 Marc RIEPER		8 Mark DRAPER	
11 Florin RADUCIOIU		9 Savo MILOSEVIC	
12 Keith ROWLAND †		10 Dwight YORKE	74
14 Iain DOWIE		14 Alan WRIGHT	
16 John MONCUR ❑		15 Fernando NELSON	
24 Michael HUGHES ❑		16 Ugo EHIOGU	38
28 Slaven BILIC		20 Riccardo SCIMECA	
Substitutes		*Substitutes*	
17 Stan LAZARIDIS †45		12 Julian JOACHIM	
18 Ilie DUMITRESCU		17 Lee HENDRIE	
20 Mark BOWEN ‡68		18 Carl TILER	
21 Les SEALEY (Gk)		26 Sasa CURCIC	
26 Frank LAMPARD		31 Stuart BROCK (Gk)	

BEFORE		P	W	D	L	F	A	pts	AFTER		P	W	D	L	F	A	pts
6	Villa	15	7	3	5	19	15	24	5	Villa	16	8	3	5	21	15	27
14	West Ham	15	4	5	6	13	18	17	15	West Ham	16	4	5	7	13	20	17

FACTFILE

Three wins on the trot hoist Villa into fifth Premiership place... Dwight Yorke's ninth goal in ten games... Ehiogu's first goal since his winner at Goodison on September 4... First win of the season against a London club in five attempts... Young keeper, Stuart Brock, makes his debut on the first team subs' bench.

Ugo and Dwight head for victory

An unchanged team, a place on the substitutes bench again for Sasa Curcic and Carl Tiler and another thoroughly professional display by table-climbing Villa.

Both Tiler and Curcic have discussed their position with Brian Little, who can only restate the obvious that, in the necessary squad system, only eleven players can start the match.

When those eleven players are bringing results then they deserve, in most cases, the chance to carry on the good work. And carry on they do for another victory which confirms that the season is well on track.

With West Ham far more inclined to attack than Middlesbrough had been four days earlier, there is a little more freedom for Villa to make their football flow and the odd hiccup apart, they fashion the shape of the game from the start.

Danger lurks, however and twice the lively Hammers could have taken the lead, Iain Dowie shooting against Michael Oakes' legs before Mark Bosnich's deputy then makes a superb save from Tim Breacker as he dives bravely at the opponent's feet when he is in an excellent scoring position after a left wing cross from Keith Rowland falls invitingly at his feet.

The threat lingers briefly as the rebound falls just right for Raducioiu, but the Rumanian is too hurried and lofts his chance over the bar. West Ham are given very good cause to later lament their wastage of rather better openings than Villa have created.

Throughout a competitive, Villa-dominated match Andy Townsend is beavering away industriously in midfield, but Villa's approaches contain far more passes than clear goalscoring opportunities.

Ian Taylor forces the Hammers keeper into a fine save, while Townsend is a touch too high with a drive that keeps the opposition goal under pressure.

After mesmerising Julian Dicks and Slaven Bilic, Savo Milosevic slams in a 35th minute drive which Ludo Miklosko finger-tips over the bar as a prelude to the 38th minute opener.

After a lengthy period of concerted attacking, a corner by Mark Draper falls invitingly into a crowded goalmouth and there waits a determined Ugo, rising high above the West Ham defence to plunder a deserved lead.

Villa had several chances to increase their lead, notably through Fernando Nelson, who exploded into the heart of the Hammers defence, played a smart one-two with Savo, nut-megged Dicks and blasted the ball high and wide with only Miklosko to beat.

Then Yorke forced a full-length save from the beleagued West Ham keeper. But the respite was brief for the home side.

In the 74th minute the decisive second goal is scored by Dwight Yorke, another goalmouth header from a right wing corner, this time supplied by Townsend and there is no way back for well-beaten West Ham as the Tobagan somehow finds space in a crowded six-yard box to plant a far post header past Miklosko, the ball appearing to hit the keeper on the shoulder on its way into the net.

From Villa's viewpoint the horizon is looking far brighter, though Brian Little is at pains to play down the improvement in results, just as he remained calm when minor wobbles took place.

"We won't get carried away," he stresses in typical style. "This was a good result for us, but there were things in the game we would want to improve on. At times our passing wasn't as good as it should have been.

"There are a lot of teams in the top ten who will have a major say (in the Championship race). A few weeks ago we were starting to slip but now we are back in contention."

Saturday 7th December 1996 • The Dell • 3.00pm

SOUTHAMPTON 0 ASTON VILLA 1

Half-time 0-1 • Attendance 15,232

Referee Stephen LODGE (Barnsley)

Referee's Assistants D.R. CRICK and K.D. HILL

Red and White Striped Shirts, Black Shorts	Goals	Navy Blue Shirts, Light Blue Shorts	Goals
1 Dave BEASANT		13 Michael OAKES	
2 Jason DODD		3 Steve STAUNTON ❑	
8 Gordon WATSON #		6 Andy TOWNSEND	34
10 Neil MADDISON ‡		7 Ian TAYLOR ❑	
12 Graham POTTER †		8 Mark DRAPER ❑	
18 Matthew OAKLEY		9 Savo MILOSEVIC ❑	
19 Richard DRYDEN		10 Dwight YORKE †	
22 Claus LUNDEKVAM		14 Alan WRIGHT	
29 Eyal BERKOVIC		15 Fernando NELSON	
30 Egil ØSTENSTAD		16 Ugo EHIOGU	
32 Ulrich VAN GOBBEL ❑		20 Riccardo SCIMECA	
Substitutes		*Substitutes*	
4 Jim MAGILTON ‡58		12 Julian JOACHIM †54	
6 Ken MONKOU #76		17 Lee HENDRIE	
13 Neil MOSS (Gk)		18 Carl TILER	
20 Robbie SLATER †50		26 Sasa CURCIC	
27 Steven BASHAM		31 Stuart BROCK (Gk)	

BEFORE	P	W	D	L	F	A	pts	AFTER	P	W	D	L	F	A	pts
5 Villa	16	8	3	5	21	15	27	4 Villa	17	9	3	5	22	15	30
17 Saints	16	3	4	9	24	31	13	18 Saints	17	3	4	10	24	32	13

FACTFILE

Four successive Premiership wins take Villa to fourth place... Run makes Villa one point better than same stage last season... Third successive Premiership win over Saints... Third clean sheet on the trot for Michael Oakes and Co... Dwight Yorke has to come off as a precaution after receiving a knock.

...Villa march into top four

After three successive victories in the Premiership Aston Villa's resolve and application are put to another searching test at The Dell where Southampton desperately need the points.

The need for continuity and consistency are on top of Brian Little's list of priorities as the important feel of a steady run takes shape.

This is reflected by another unchanged line-up, a situation which has caused Carl Tiler to wonder whether his future lies elsewhere after an 18-month spell of comparatively little competitive football.

For the manager, however, there is one major target, namely to keep the winning habit going while keeping faith with players who are contributing to the season's improving atmosphere.

Graeme Souness's side are charged with the imperative to bring a poor run to an end and with no Matthew Le Tissier available to conjure magical goals, their brief will be to close ranks and smother Villa wherever possible.

Villa have to dig in with a display of industry and determination with the desire to entertain a mere secondary consideration, as several leading clubs become involved in the Championship chase.

Strangely, the required breakthrough arrives at a similar time as in the previous two victories, namely during the spell leading up to half-time after half-an-hour or so of consolidation.

With the goal, a virtual tap-in by Andy Townsend, arrives a storm of protest and controversy, but it seals the result that Villa desire and no-one would logically claim that it was anything but

Andy Townsend

deserved on the balance of play and the merits of the respective sides.

The move leading up to the simple finish leaves Villa's travelling contingent drooling with appreciation. Alan Wright wins a tackle on the half-way line to put Savo Milosevic in possession and the Serb's immaculate crossfield pass sends Wright forging down the left-wing to supply Townsend with a perfectly-weighted low centre.

Although the goal is a classic of simplicity there are emphatic claims for off-side and when the interval arrives Souness appears to exchange words with the officials as they leave the field.

The home fans are equally charged with a sense of injustice, but the Saints are never going to recover from the set-back and indeed, only a brilliant save from Dave Beasant keeps out a scorching drive from Milosevic, who is playing a significant role in Villa's attacking play.

It becomes simply a question of playing out time for Villa to make it 12 points out of 12.

"I have always said that Savo is a talented player who is important to us," observes the Villa Manager. "He has played three full games since he returned from Italy and we have won all three. I have no problem with him."

On the broader landscape he adds: "That's five wins in the last six Premiership games and it has made a big difference to our season.

"We set our stall out to be hard to beat and while that may sound negative we have actually been winning games because of it. Before long someone might be writing that we will have a big say in what happens this season.

"We have a couple of weeks break now and then we play half-a-dozen games against teams who are with us in the leading group. This spell will tell us a lot about ourselves."

Sunday 22nd December 1996 • Villa Park • 4.00pm

ASTON VILLA 5 WIMBLEDON 0

Half-time 2-0 • Attendance 28,875

Referee Steve DUNN (Bristol)
Referee's Assistants D.M. HORLICK and P.J. JOSLIN

Claret and Blue Shirts, White Shorts		Goals	Dark Blue Shirts, Dark Blue Shorts		Goals
1	Mark BOSNICH		1	Neil SULLIVAN	
3	Steve STAUNTON †		2	Kenny CUNNINGHAM †	
6	Andy TOWNSEND		3	Alan KIMBLE ❏	
7	Ian TAYLOR	60	4	Vinny JONES	
8	Mark DRAPER ‡		5	Dean BLACKWELL	74og
9	Savo MILOSEVIC	41	7	Øyvind LEONHARDSEN	
10	Dwight YORKE	38,86	8	Robbie EARLE	
14	Alan WRIGHT		9	Efan EKOKU	
15	Fernando NELSON		11	Marcus GAYLE	
16	Ugo EHIOGU		12	Chris PERRY ‡	
20	Riccardo SCIMECA		18	Neal ARDLEY	
Substitutes			*Substitutes*		
11	Tommy JOHNSON		10	Dean HOLDSWORTH †67	
12	Julian JOACHIM		17	Brian McALLISTER ‡83	
13	Michael OAKES (Gk)		20	Mick HARFORD	
18	Carl TILER †73		24	Peter FEAR	
26	Sasa CURCIC ‡80 ❏		33	Brendan MURPHY (Gk)	

BEFORE		P	W	D	L	F	A	pts	AFTER		P	W	D	L	F	A	pts
3	Wimbledon	17	10	4	3	30	17	34	3	Wimbledon	18	10	4	4	30	22	34
6	Villa	17	9	3	5	22	15	30	4	Villa	18	10	3	5	27	15	33

FACTFILE

*Nelson recovers from flu to keep his place... Villa's fifth successive victory...
The best run of success for five years... The best-ever run in the Premiership...
Title odds are slashed by half from 16-1 to 8-1... Mark Bosnich returns after
injury, Michael Oakes stands down after keeping three consecutive clean sheets.*

Festive romp sets up title bid

All the pre-match talk is of Wimbledon's unbeaten sequence of nineteen games, Villa's four successive wins and of a forthcoming close encounter of the low-scoring kind.

Even in the build-up to the live transmission on Sky, studio analyst John Gregory, the ex-Villa coach, reflects a popular line of thought by predicting a goalless draw.

With neither side willing to concede valuable points in the 'top-five' confrontation, no-one expects the pre-Christmas goal-rush that is to unfold appetisingly for the claret and blue masses.

Proximity to Christmas, live screening in homes, pubs and clubs on Sky, plus possibly, Wimbledon's shortage of 'glamour' names restricts the attendance to below 30,000.

Brian Little has kept to his 'unchanged' policy of continuity, apart from re-introducing fit-again Mark Bosnich to replace his seven-match understudy, Michael Oakes.

The game's anticipated pattern is established from the start with Wimbledon pulling nine men behind the ball and Villa forced to pass and re-pass in search of a way through.

Worst pre-match expectations are confirmed for more than half-an-hour as Villa's approach play seems both predictable and unproductive.

Then, suddenly, Sky viewers must feel as though they've switched to an entirely different match. The turning point is a bad decision when Dwight Yorke converts a pass from Ian Taylor and is adjudged off-side, despite being the 'right' side of three defenders.

The free kick is fed to Kenny Cunningham who carelessly knocks it back towards his own goal straight into the path of Yorke who, rightly offended by the earlier decision, takes control and lashes in the goal he deserves.

Just before half-time, with Wimbledon having to change their negative approach, Dean Blackwell also loses control needlessly and Savo Milosevic pounces to gain possession, speeds towards goal and neatly side-foots the ball past the approaching Neil Sullivan.

Wimbledon attempt to take the attacking initiative in the second half, but fail to create chances against the safest defence in the Premiership.

Now Villa soak up the pressure before a 61st minute break sees Milosevic's shot, from a brilliant run and left-wing centre from Steve Staunton, deflected by the keeper for Ian Taylor to dive and head in Number three.

But for further suspect refereeing decisions the disintegrating Dons would have been overwhelmed even before a Milosevic shot deflects off Blackwell's boot and Yorke turns substitute Sasa Curcic's well-drilled right wing centre into the net to complete the unexpected rout.

"Our best performance of the season," says Brian Little as Villa look ahead to five more consecutive fixtures against the leading group. "We are right in the Championship race at this moment, that's for sure. We have to make sure that we still are by the middle of January."

Ian Taylor – first League goal of the season

Thursday 26th December 1996 • Villa Park • 3.00pm

ASTON VILLA 0 CHELSEA 2

Half-time 0-0 • Attendance 39,339

Referee Paul DANSON (Leicester)
Referee's Assistants P.M. ROBERTS and M.L. SHORT

Claret and Blue Shirts, White Shorts	Goals	Blue Shirts, Blue Shorts	Goals
1 Mark BOSNICH		30 Frode GRODAS	
3 Steve STAUNTON		2 Dan PETRESCU	
6 Andy TOWNSEND		4 Ruud GULLIT	
7 Ian TAYLOR		6 Steve CLARKE ❑	
8 Mark DRAPER ‡		8 Andy MYERS †	
9 Savo MILOSEVIC †		10 Mark HUGHES	
10 Dwight YORKE		12 Michael DUBERRY	
14 Alan WRIGHT		14 Craig BURLEY	
15 Fernando NELSON		16 Roberto DI MATTEO	
16 Ugo EHIOGU		24 Eddie NEWTON ❑	
20 Riccardo SCIMECA ❑		25 Gianfranco ZOLA	65,69

Substitutes		Substitutes	
11 Tommy JOHNSON †61		3 Terry PHELAN †61	
12 Julian JOACHIM		13 Kevin HITCHCOCK (Gk)	
13 Michael OAKES (Gk)		18 Erland JOHNSEN	
18 Carl TILER		20 Frank SINCLAIR	
26 Sasa CURCIC ‡61		22 Mark NICHOLLS	

BEFORE		P	W	D	L	F	A	pts
4	Villa	18	10	3	5	27	15	33
8	Chelsea	18	7	7	4	28	27	28

AFTER		P	W	D	L	F	A	pts
5	Villa	19	10	3	6	27	17	33
7	Chelsea	19	8	7	4	30	27	31

FACTFILE

Mark Draper passes fitness test as Villa name the same outfield ten men for fourth successive match... Run of five successive wins ends... First Chelsea goal ends spell of more than 400 minutes without conceding a goal... Chance to go joint-second is lost ... Second successive home defeat by Chelsea.

Two soft goals wreck festivities

This is to prove the Boxing Day of the big let-down, when a festive crowd fuelled by high expectations is frustrated by the failure to continue the successful run.

Chelsea arrive at Villa Park in a spell of inconsistency and Villa are expected to build on the impressive victory over Wimbledon. Sadly, the story-line goes horribly wrong...

In place of another goalscoring showpiece by Villa the 'full-house' afternoon proves to be more reminiscent of the sterile attacking displays against Helsingborg. The decisive difference is that Chelsea have a two-goal match-winner in their ranks.

Villa at their best complete their measured and controlled passing play with a cutting edge that can slice open the tightest of defences.

On other days they lack that necessary finish while, just occasionally, the best defence in the Premiership can prove vulnerable.

This is to prove the worst of the three scenarios as Chelsea's player-manager – Ruud Gullit – marshalls his team-mates shrewdly from a defensive role and Italian signing, striker, Gianfranco Zola, capitalises on two defensive lapses in the space of four minutes of farce.

For over an hour of uneventful stalemate a goalless draw looks to be the obvious outcome, with Villa failing to make an impact while looking equally unlikely to give anything away, as Chelsea are, seemingly, just as blunt as Villa up front.

What then takes place almost beggars belief. A weak-looking cross-shot by Zola looks no problem for Mark Bosnich until it takes a deflection off Ugo Ehiogu and finds its way into the net after taking yet another deflection off the hapless keeper's leg.

A goal down, but not by any means defeated at that point, yet an even worse moment for Villa is to arrive immediately on the heels of the first.

This time Bosnich stumbles and reacts slowly to a Nelson defensive header and Zola is allowed to move in unmarked for a second gift goal which settles a match of total frustration for Villa.

Even more unhappily for Brian Little the two goals have arrived minutes after he has attempted to perk his team up with a double substitution.

Sasa Curcic has replaced out-of-touch Mark Draper, while Tommy Johnson is on for the groggy Savo Milosevic whose return to an ineffectual mode is explained by a touch of the head-cold problem which has seemingly swept the entire nation.

The Serbian's poor display is a set-back since, as a new father and a more ebullient member of the squad, he has seemed set to re-establish himself positively in the side since his aborted transfer to Italian club Perugia.

"Mark could have done better with both goals," said Brian Little. "We were still in with a chance of winning the match until then."

Fernando Nelson – a sound game at wing-back

Saturday 28th December 1996 • Highbury • 3.00pm

ARSENAL 2 ASTON VILLA 2

Half-time 1-0 • Attendance 38,130

Referee Jeff WINTER (Middlesbrough)

Referee's Assistants R. BURTON and M. TINGEY

Red and White Shirts, White Shorts		Goals
24	John LUKIC	
3	Nigel WINTERBURN	
4	Patrick VIEIRA	
5	Steve BOULD	
6	Tony ADAMS	
8	Ian WRIGHT	13
9	Paul MERSON	73
10	Dennis BERGKAMP	
14	Martin KEOWN	
15	Ray PARLOUR	
19	Remi GARDE †	
Substitutes		
12	Andy LINIGHAN	
13	Vince BARTRAM (Gk)	
16	John HARTSON	
18	Steve MORROW †69	
27	Paul SHAW	

White Shirts, Claret Shorts		Goals
1	Mark BOSNICH	
3	Steve STAUNTON ❑	
6	Andy TOWNSEND	
7	Ian TAYLOR	
8	Mark DRAPER †	
9	Savo MILOSEVIC	67
10	Dwight YORKE ❑	74
14	Alan WRIGHT	
15	Fernando NELSON	
16	Ugo EHIOGU ❑	
20	Riccardo SCIMECA	
Substitutes		
11	Tommy JOHNSON †88	
12	Julian JOACHIM	
13	Michael OAKES (Gk)	
18	Carl TILER	
26	Sasa CURCIC	

BEFORE	P	W	D	L	F	A	pts
2 Arsenal	19	10	6	3	35	18	36
5 Villa	19	10	3	6	27	17	33

AFTER	P	W	D	L	F	A	pts
2 Arsenal	20	10	7	3	37	20	37
6 Villa	20	10	4	6	29	19	34

FACTFILE

Unchanged again, as Mark Draper, Ian Taylor and Savo Milosevic pass late fitness tests... Little still seeks his first win over Gunners... Milosevic's third goal in two appearances against Arsenal this season... Liverpool secure five-point lead at top by means of a Sunday victory at Southampton.

Two-goal fight-back lifts spirits

With the disappointing Chelsea result and performance still fresh in his mind Brian Little goes through a good deal of soul-searching before the visit to Highbury.

Much of this centres around the fitness or otherwise of Savo Milosevic who, the manager now admits, ought not to have played on Boxing Day because of flu symptoms.

Several players, like the majority of supporters, have been affected by colds and chest infections to some degree, but the Serbian striker confesses that he has now recovered from the worst of it.

Consequently the line-up which started against Chelsea is restored and for the first 45 minutes it looks a serious mistake with Villa still in their 'Chelsea' mode.

Arsenal, in contrast, have top place in the Premiership to go for as Liverpool wait 24 hours for their fixture at Southampton.

Under the leadership of Arsene Wenger, Gunners have been showing a more positive and confident approach this season and Villa are in danger of being swept aside.

Danger-man Ian Wright strikes after only 13 minutes as he glides onto a through ball from Dennis Bergkamp to steer the ball wide of the diving Mark Bosnich's outstretched fingers and just inside the far post.

It is no more than the home team deserve as Villa are forced onto the defensive with seemingly little chance of changing the pattern of a one-sided game.

Mark Draper

Only a miraculous goal-line intervention by Riccardo Scimeca prevents Wright scoring a second. "If we had been three or four down at half-time it would not have been out of context with the run of the game," Brian Little admits later.

Managers can earn their high salaries by means of their half-time motivational powers and this is very much one of those occasions for Brian Little.

"As a manager I have still not beaten Arsenal and there was a lot to be put right," he added.

Mercifully for the despondent travelling supporters the second-half sees a total transformation in Villa's performance with the better half of Milosevic's Jekyll and Hyde nature returning.

In the 67th minute the Yugoslavian international striker volleys the equaliser when Mark Draper heads Fernando Nelson's right-wing delivery across goal.

The action is now a two-sided thriller with Arsenal, not prepared to give way without a battle, restoring their lead within six minutes via a stunning strike by Paul Merson.

Now it is Villa's turn to confirm their resilience as Gunners fans are still rejoicing their regained lead.

Straight from the restart Mark Draper and Andy Townsend pass their way through the middle of the Arsenal defences and then neat control and accuracy by Milosevic releases Dwight Yorke for a chance he's not going to waste and the final 2-2 scoreline is completed with a shot drilled beneath the diving John Lukic.

The result fits snugly into a complicated Championship race in which all clubs concerned are busily taking points off each other.

Wednesday 1st January 1997 • Old Trafford • 8.00pm

MANCHESTER UNITED 0 ASTON VILLA 0

Half-time 0-0 • Attendance 55,133

Referee David ELLERAY (Harrow-on-the-Hill)
Referee's Assistants M.D. MESSIAS and P. WALTON

Red Shirts, White Shorts	Goals	White Shirts, Claret Shorts	Goals
1 Peter SCHMEICHEL		1 Mark BOSNICH	
2 Gary NEVILLE ❏		3 Steve STAUNTON	
3 Denis IRWIN		6 Andy TOWNSEND	
4 David MAY		7 Ian TAYLOR ❏ †	
7 Eric CANTONA		8 Mark DRAPER	
8 Nicky BUTT ‡		9 Savo MILOSEVIC ❏	
10 David BECKHAM ❏		10 Dwight YORKE	
11 Ryan GIGGS		14 Alan WRIGHT	
16 Roy KEANE		15 Fernando NELSON ❏	
19 Ronny JOHNSEN		16 Ugo EHIOGU	
20 Ole Gunnar SOLSKJAER †		18 Carl TILER ❏	
Substitutes		*Substitutes*	
9 Andy COLE †68		11 Tommy JOHNSON †84	
13 Brian McCLAIR		12 Julian JOACHIM	
15 Karel POBORSKY		13 Michael OAKES (Gk)	
17 Raimond VAN DER GOUW (Gk)		17 Lee HENDRIE	
18 Paul SCHOLES ‡90		19 Gareth FARRELLY	

BEFORE		P	W	D	L	F	A	pts
3	Man Utd	20	10	7	3	42	25	37
6	Villa	20	10	4	6	29	19	34

AFTER		P	W	D	L	F	A	pts
3	Man Utd	21	10	8	3	42	25	38
6	Villa	21	10	5	6	29	19	35

FACTFILE

Carl Tiler comes in at the back to replace Riccardo Scimeca, who was injured at Highbury... Five festive-season points out of 12 leave Villa in sixth place... Boxing Day home defeat by Chelsea was their undoing... Only one league defeat in last eight... Gareth Southgate is reported to be almost fit.

Quality display at Old Trafford

As a trial of strength and true potential, fixtures do not come more daunting than the trip to Old Trafford, especially when United are in a run of victories.

"We have to beat one of the top teams if we are to prove ourselves Championship material," stresses Brian Little as the title race gets ever more complicated.

This New Year's Day spotlight game is an 8pm kick-off to go out live on Sky while, during the afternoon, Arsenal and Newcastle have won their home games against Boro and Leeds respectively, Liverpool having lost at Chelsea.

Attention is thus firmly focussed on Old Trafford with Arsenal, now only two points behind leaders Liverpool and United, needing a victory to join Gunners in second place on points.

Carl Tiler is back in an otherwise unchanged side to replace the injured Riccardo Scimeca and Villa quickly signal their attacking intentions.

In the opening moments Ryan Giggs fails to connect properly with an excellent chance from close range. Then, in the sixth minute, Villa are denied a clear penalty when Savo Milosevic, keeping possession cleverly when surrounded by defenders, is tackled across the thigh by Roy Keane who has made no visible attempt to play the ball.

As the closely-fought, quality match unfolds, with disciplined defences restricting scoring chances despite varied and creative attacking play, referee David Elleray's 'miss' gets to look more and more expensive.

For Villa Mark Draper is a prominent figure in midfield with his industrious searching

Carl Tiler – draughted into the defence

for possession and capacity to switch the point of attack. Almost inevitably, however, it is United who control the major part of the attacking play, but they are rarely able to unhinge Villa's defence.

During the course of the entertaining 90 minutes United are in a position to score on three occasions, including the early miss by Giggs. Eric Cantona later miskicks when well-placed, allowing Mark Bosnich a routine save while Andy Cole, a second-half sub for Ole Gunnar Solskjaer, fails to get his full-force behind a low drive and again Bosnich is able to safely guard his lines.

Villa's openings are possibly less clear-cut, but they do make several during the course of an absorbing match and they well-deserve their second successive and hard-earned away point.

Andy Townsend and Draper both fire drives a touch too high while, in the second-half, another Draper shot deflects off the outflung leg of David May to clear the crossbar.

Villa's intention to go for all three points is demonstrated when Tommy Johnson replaces Ian Taylor five minutes from time. Johnson's brief is, clearly, to conjure a late winner and this he almost achieves with a shot that Peter Schmeichel is relieved to block.

Schmeichel has earlier had to make good saves from both Taylor and Milosevic, an indication that United have not had it all their own way by any means.

The one unsavoury moment in a stirring if goalless affair is a clash between Milosevic and David Beckham, following a badly-timed foul tackle by the United player on the big Serb. TV slow-motion replays suggest that Milosivic has spit at Beckham. Brian Little gives an assurance that he will investigate the matter.

Saturday 11th January 1997 • Villa Park • 3.00pm

ASTON VILLA 2 NEWCASTLE UNITED 2

Half-time 1-2 • Attendance 39,339

Referee Graham POLL (Tring)

Referee's Assistants P.V. NORMAN and D.C. RICHARDS

Claret and Blue Shirts, White Shorts		Goals	Black and White Striped Shirts, Black Shorts		Goals
1	Mark BOSNICH		15	Shaka HISLOP	
3	Steve STAUNTON		3	John BERESFORD	
4	Gareth SOUTHGATE		4	David BATTY	
6	Andy TOWNSEND		5	Darren PEACOCK	
9	Savo MILOSEVIC	52	8	Peter BEARDSLEY	
10	Dwight YORKE ‡	39	9	Alan SHEARER	16
11	Tommy JOHNSON ❑		18	Keith GILLESPIE	
14	Alan WRIGHT		19	Steve WATSON	
15	Fernando NELSON †		20	Lee CLARK	21
16	Ugo EHIOGU		26	Robbie ELLIOTT	
18	Carl TILER		27	Philippe ALBERT	
	Substitutes			*Substitutes*	
12	Julian JOACHIM ‡67		1	Pavel SRNICEK (Gk)	
13	Michael OAKES (Gk)		2	Warren BARTON	
17	Lee HENDRIE		10	Les FERDINAND	
19	Gareth FARRELLY		17	James CRAWFORD	
20	Riccardo SCIMECA †34		28	Paul KITSON	

BEFORE	P	W	D	L	F	A	pts	AFTER	P	W	D	L	F	A	pts
4 Newcastle	21	11	4	6	38	22	37	4 Newcastle	22	11	5	6	40	24	38
6 Villa	21	10	5	6	29	19	35	6 Villa	22	10	6	6	31	21	36

FACTFILE

Brian Little has signed a new five-year contract killing rumours of Newcastle interest... A third successive Premiership draw sees chance to climb table drift... Manager not satisfied with Sasa Curcic 'body language in training' and leaves him out of re-arranged cup-tie at Meadow Lane.

Keegan storm hits Villa Park

A fixture which was always to be one to set the adrenalin flowing has claimed extra national focus due to Kevin Keegan's unexpected departure from St James' Park.

News of the Newcastle manager's exit arrived only three days before the game, thus leaving the club in a state of shock and Villa facing a whiplash response.

Brian Little rightly warns his players that the Keegan affair is likely to spark off an explosive reaction and so it is to prove.

In another unsettling episode Sasa Curcic has publicly described his move to Villa Park from Bolton as a big mistake and though he has subsequently apologised to the manager for his remarks he is still not in the squad.

On the credit side Gareth Southgate is back after missing seven games and it is he, along with Tommy Johnson, who replaces the injured Mark Draper and Ian Taylor in midfield with youngsters Gareth Farrelly and Lee Hendrie on the bench.

Newcastle, under the temporary leadership of Keegan's Number 2, Terry McDermott and ex-Villa coach Arthur Cox, hit Villa from the start and are two up in 21 minutes.

Indecisive defending could be blamed each time. For the opener Steve Staunton fails to cut out a Peter Beardsley ball to Alan Shearer whose shot goes under Mark Bosnich's diving body.

The second is something of a shambles. Shearer brushes against Bosnich as the keeper is about to clear. The Australian moves a couple of paces away from the Newcastle striker, then slips and miskicks the ball straight to Lee Clark who gratefully drives it into an unguarded goal.

Now, as at St James' Park for the 4-3 thriller, Villa are confronted by a huge task and again,

both the calibre and ability of the team come shining through.

In a match of compulsive attacking action Dwight Yorke reduces the deficit when a Southgate free kick leads to Alan Wright aiming in a low centre from the left of the penalty area for Yorke to apply the finishing touch for his 13th goal of the season.

During the interval Brian Little restores Southgate to defence and moves Staunton forward, a switch which pays gratifying dividends.

The powerful Irish Republic international is the game's dominant force after the break and his link-up with Yorke supplies Savo Milosevic with a tap-in equaliser only seven minutes into the half.

Newcastle are under seige for lengthy spells and Villa's chance of securing the victory their title aspirations urgently need arrives when Milosevic is brought down by a Philippe Albert tackle which takes his legs and misses the ball.

Yorke, penalty-taker supreme, takes the ball confidently, but fails to connect properly with his kick and Shaka Hislop is presented with a simple save.

Soon afterwards Yorke is clear with a chance to atone for his miss but Hislop is given the chance to twice save again as he parries the first

shot and deflects Yorke's second attempt on the rebound.

Verdict: in an enthralling game two points lost rather than one won.

Steve Staunton – transformed the game

Tuesday 14th January 1997 • Meadow Lane • 7.45pm

NOTTS COUNTY 0 ASTON VILLA 0

Half-time 0-0 • Attendance 13,315

Referee Paul DURKIN (Portland)
Referee's Assistants J.H. LEACH and D.A. BOOTH

Black and White Striped Shirts, Black Shorts	Goals	Claret and Blue Shirts, White Shorts	Goals
1 Darren WARD		1 Mark BOSNICH	
2 Chris WILDER		3 Steve STAUNTON †	
3 Ian BARACLOUGH		4 Gareth SOUTHGATE	
4 Matthew REDMILE		6 Andy TOWNSEND ❏	
5 Gary STRODDER ❏		9 Savo MILOSEVIC	
6 Shaun DERRY ❏ #		11 Tommy JOHNSON ❏	
7 Steve FINNAN		12 Julian JOACHIM	
8 Phil ROBINSON ❏		14 Alan WRIGHT	
9 Gary MARTINDALE		16 Ugo EHIOGU	
10 Sean FARRELL ❏ †		18 Carl TILER ❏	
11 Tony AGANA ‡		20 Riccardo SCIMECA	

Substitutes		*Substitutes*	
12 Richard WALKER ‡80		13 Michael OAKES (Gk)	
13 Tony BATTERSBY †74		17 Lee HENDRIE †55	
14 Michael GALLOWAY #88		19 Gareth FARRELLY	

FACTFILE

Re-arranged from Sunday January 5th (12.00) when Meadow Lane pitch was frozen... Replay at Villa Park next Wednesday... Derby's tie at Gillingham is abandoned because of a frost-bound pitch... Villa's fourth game without a win since the 5-0 victory over Wimbledon... Fitness battle begins to field strong team at Anfield.

Julian Joachim – took over from Dwight Yorke

Bossie super save earns Cup replay

Although Dwight Yorke is missing because of a thigh injury Villa are confidently expected to make FA Cup progress at Meadow Lane, but such confidence is to prove misplaced.

County, relegated from the First Division last May, struggling in the lower reaches of the Second, and with only a caretaker manager, ought to be victims awaiting the slaughter.

Even an enforced team reshuffle caused by the absence of injured players Yorke, Mark Draper and Ian Taylor, plus the still-unsettled Sasa Curcic, leaves Villa with seemingly enough big guns to earn a fourth round tie at either Derby or Gillingham.

Yet, as an extremely disappointing game unfolds, this proves to be far from the case and a Villa Park replay in eight days time is the best Villa can manage; with a well organised County side putting up stern opposition.

Early indications are reasonable enough, if a shade untidy, with Villa repeatedly moving forward and seemingly waiting for the necessary goals to emerge.

One major problem is that the front pairing of Savo Milosevic and Julian Joachim lacks drive and purpose, while the final through ball to feed them is frequently indecisive.

The recent spell of below-freezing temperatures has left the frost, just below a soft surface, deep in the pitch which is bumpy and unpredictable, though the conditions do not constitute an excuse for Villa failing to finish off the opposition.

An example of Villa's shortcomings arrives in the 13th minute when Milosevic, presented with a shooting chance from the left-hand edge of the penalty area, puts his shot out of play at the far touchline.

The Serbian seems slow to react when given another chance, but is more menacing with a drive that narrowly clears the crossbar.

County goalkeeper Darren Ward makes saves from Ugo Ehiogu and ex-Meadow Lane forward Tommy Johnson, but the closest call of a poor match falls to the Second Division team after 36 minutes.

Former Villa man Phil Robinson opens up his ex-team-mates' defence by exchanging passes with Sean Farrell and his low left-footer looks destined for the corner of the net until Bosnich dives with great agility to turn it away.

As Villa fail to make their superior talents tell, County gain in confidence in a match which becomes increasingly competitive and which generates seven cautions.

There is one flashpoint, off-the-ball incident which sparks a fracas involving several players of both sides before Carl Tiler and Farrell are shown yellow cards.

Villa's discomfort increases when Steve Staunton has to go off with a hamstring problem to be replaced by young Lee Hendrie. The youngster contrives to lift his more experienced colleagues with a display of enthusiasm leading to further openings which are not accepted.

Notts County have defended well, Villa have preserved their place in the competition and a further, lucrative home game is now on the schedule. There have been few other plusses on a night of claret and blue frustration.

Savo in action at Meadow Lane

Saturday 18th January 1997 • Anfield • 3.00pm

LIVERPOOL 3 ASTON VILLA 0

Half-time 0-0 • Attendance 40,489

Referee Roger DILKES (Mossley)

Referee's Assistants C. BASSINDALE and D.A. BOOTH

Red Shirts, Red Shorts	Goals
1 David JAMES	
3 Bjorn Tore KVARME	
4 Jason McATEER	
5 Mark WRIGHT	
7 Steve McMANAMAN	
8 Stan COLLYMORE †	58
9 Robbie FOWLER	63
11 Jamie REDKNAPP	
20 Stig Inge BJØRNEBYE	
21 Dominic MATTEO	
23 James CARRAGHER ❏	50
Substitutes	
12 Steve HARKNESS	
13 Tony WARNER (Gk)	
19 Mark KENNEDY †75	
24 Lee JONES	
25 David THOMPSON	

White Shirts, White Shorts	Goals
1 Mark BOSNICH	
4 Gareth SOUTHGATE	
6 Andy TOWNSEND	
9 Savo MILOSEVIC	
10 Dwight YORKE	
11 Tommy JOHNSON	
14 Alan WRIGHT	
16 Ugo EHIOGU	
18 Carl TILER	
20 Riccardo SCIMECA	
26 Sasa CURCIC	
Substitutes	
12 Julian JOACHIM	
13 Michael OAKES (Gk)	
17 Lee HENDRIE	
19 Gareth FARRELLY	
24 Scott MURRAY	

BEFORE	P	W	D	L	F	A	pts
1 Liverpool	23	12	7	4	38	20	43
6 Villa	22	10	6	6	31	21	36

AFTER	P	W	D	L	F	A	pts
1 Liverpool	24	13	7	4	41	20	46
7 Villa	23	10	6	7	31	24	36

FACTFILE *Villa complete an 11-0 aggregate defeat by Liverpool in four games over the past two seasons... with another fixture against them to come... Only six points taken from 18 in the sequence of matches against the Championship challengers... Next Wednesday's Cup replay against Notts County assumes a new importance.*

Title hopes fade at Anfield

The final match of the six-match sequence against the other six teams sharing the top seven Premiership places brings the club's title route to the crossroads.

Victory, or even a draw, at Anfield would enable Villa to follow a sign reading 'still in with a chance'. In contrast, defeat leads down the 'mission impossible' road.

Brian Little is rightly able to claim beforehand that, with Steve Staunton, Mark Draper and Ian Taylor all unfit he cannot field the full-strength team he would like. However, Liverpool are also severely depleted, but prove to have greater reserves of talent.

After his spell of controversy, in which he said that joining Villa had been a serious mistake, Sasa Curcic is back in the team with advice from the manager to put his personal problems behind him and get on with playing football.

The scene is set for Villa to continue with the kind of stubborn form which saw them overwhelm Wimbledon and force draws against Arsenal, Manchester United and Newcastle.

Indeed, up to half-time there are indications that they can, at least hang on to a point and deny Liverpool consolidating their lead at the top of the table.

In the opening 45 minutes of the game Villa create a better quality of chances than Liverpool. Dwight Yorke is a 'missed chance' culprit after 33 minutes when, from a sound scoring position, he drives his shot wide.

Tommy Johnson and Savo Milosevic also, expensively, fail with openings before the break as Liverpool are unable to sound any severe warning of what is to come in the second half.

Mark Bosnich is under pressure just a couple of times in the opening half as he saves a Jason McAteer volley one-handed and then has to rely on Alan Wright's goalline clearance from Mark Wright.

Thus, the nightmare of last season when Liverpool scored three in the opening seven minutes appears to have been avoided until, in a thirteen-minute period early in the second-half, the bad dream is re-run.

First of all, on his debut , Jamie Carragher, is allowed a free header from a corner. Then Stig Inge Bjørnebye supplies the feed for Stan Collymore to head in and now Villa's normally-reliable defence is at panic stations.

Even Gareth Southgate appears to have lost his cool in Liverpool's onslaught and when Bosnich fails to hold a Jamie Redknapp shot Robbie Fowler, of all people, is supplied with an easy third goal.

"They were miles ahead of us," confesses Little. "The balance of the team wasn't right," a reference maybe to the fact that Curcic and Johnson did not blend well in midfield.

"This result is a big blow to us," he added. "I can't pretend we played anything but poorly. The first goal was a crime for us to give away and when the second went in you could see heads going down.

"I think the players are tired mentally and physically after some of the games we've had recently.

"I haven't seen them so quiet in the dressing room for a long time."

Sasa Curcic – back in first team action

Wednesday 22nd January 1997 • Villa Park • 7.45pm

ASTON VILLA 3 NOTTS COUNTY 0

Half-time 1-0 • *Attendance* 25,006

Referee Paul DURKIN (Portland)
Referee's Assistants J.P. PEARCE and M.A. WILLIAMS

Claret and Blue Shirts, White Shorts	Goals	Black and White Striped Shirts, Black Shorts	Goals
1 Mark BOSNICH		1 Darren WARD	
4 Gareth SOUTHGATE		2 Chris WILDER	
6 Andy TOWNSEND		3 Ian BARACLOUGH	
9 Savo MILOSEVIC		4 Matthew REDMILE	
10 Dwight YORKE	25,53	5 Gary STRODDER ❑	
11 Tommy JOHNSON †		6 Shaun DERRY †	
14 Alan WRIGHT		7 Steve FINNAN	
16 Ugo EHIOGU	67	8 Phil ROBINSON	
18 Carl TILER ❑		9 Gary MARTINDALE ‡	
20 Riccardo SCIMECA		10 Sean FARRELL	
26 Sasa CURCIC ❑		11 Tony AGANA #	
Substitutes		*Substitutes*	
12 Julian JOACHIM		12 Richard WALKER †60	
13 Michael OAKES (Gk)		13 Tony BATTERSBY ‡67	
17 Lee HENDRIE †70		14 Michael GALLOWAY #78	

Next stop Derby for all-Midland fourth round on Saturday... Dwight Yorke's 15th goal in the last 18 starts... Ugo Ehiogu's third goal of the season. It's his first in the FA Cup to complete a 'set' including one in the Coca-Cola Cup and one in the UEFA Cup.

High-stepping action at Villa Park

Yorke double sinks County

Two Villa team changes compared to the side for the drawn game at Meadow Lane prove decisive in charting a hazard-free course to a fourth-round tie at Derby on Saturday.

The return of Dwight Yorke up front and Sasa Curcic in midfield are to provide Villa with the improvement in shape and direction necessary to dispose of the hard-working Second Division team.

Curcic's attitude from the start confirms that he intends to put his problems behind him and make an emphatic bid for a regular place.

The attendance of 'only' 25,000 makes for a fairly low-key atmosphere for this, the first domestic cup-tie of 1996-97 at Villa Park.

Few expect a cup shock though County, with Sam Allardyce appointed manager since the Meadow Lane match, have no intention of giving Villa too easy a ride.

The opening exchanges make for limited spectator appeal and 18 minutes elapse before Tommy Johnson's left-footed volley is forced away by goalkeeper Darren Ward.

Then a dipping Curcic free-kick is a touch too high and, as Savo Milosevic supplies a feed from the left-hand side, Yorke turns the chance over the bar.

Villa are now showing a superiority which is turned into a deserved 25th-minute lead. Alan Wright centres after a surge down the left and the ball drops dangerously into the goalmouth after an aerial challenge between Milosevic and Ian Baraclough.

Yorke spots the chance and though off-balance, scoops the

Ugo Ehiogu

ball over the line, with the help of a deflection off Strodder's foot, for a lead they never look likely to relinquish.

Half-time arrives with the feeling that Villa have yet to get their act together in midfield and boss the game as they should, but the second-half removes any such doubts.

Curcic quickly becomes the game's most prominent performer despite an occasional tendency to run the ball into trouble. In the 53rd minute he picks his way from the centre circle through the back-peddling County midfield and then pierces the back-line with a forward pass which releases Yorke to drive his second goal of the game.

With Villa now in firm control Milosevic shows his left-footed wizardry with a neat bit of control followed by a smooth, swerving shot which the diving Ward tips away.

A third goal arrives in the 67th minute when Johnson drives the ball firmly at the County goal from some 20 yards as Andy Townsend tees-up the ball in a well-rehearsed free-kick. The keeper can only block the ball which is promptly headed into the net by Ugo Ehiogu's forward lunge.

Two more goals almost follow. The arrival of Lee Hendrie in place of injured Johnson sees the talented youngster trap, swivel and shoot in one slick movement, but the lad is left clutching his head in disappointment as the rising shot strikes the bar.

Milosevic has a far easier chance when he is put right clear by Yorke, but the Serb drags his left-foot shot well wide of the post.

Just before the end ten players are involved in an unseemly skirmish after a foul on Hendrie on the edge of the County penalty area and Curcic is booked for pushing.

Saturday 25th January 1997 • Baseball Ground • 3.00pm

DERBY COUNTY 3 ASTON VILLA 1

Half-time 2-0 • *Attendance* 17,977

Referee Jeff WINTER (Middlesbrough)
Referee's Assistants L.E. CABLE and P.M. ROBERTS

White Shirts, Black Shorts		Goals	Claret and Blue Shirts, White Shorts		Goals
1	Russell HOULT		1	Mark BOSNICH	
2	Gary ROWETT †		3	Steve STAUNTON	
3	Chris POWELL		4	Gareth SOUTHGATE	
7	Robin VAN DER LAAN	36	6	Andy TOWNSEND †	
8	Dean STURRIDGE	40	9	Savo MILOSEVIC	
10	Aljosa ASANOVIC		10	Dwight YORKE	
11	Ron WILLEMS	70	14	Alan WRIGHT	
15	Paul TROLLOPE		16	Ugo EHIOGU	
18	Lee CARSLEY		17	Lee HENDRIE	
22	Christian DAILLY		20	Riccardo SCIMECA	
27	Paul McGRATH		26	Sasa CURCIC	77
	Substitutes			*Substitutes*	
9	Marco GABBIADINI		13	Michael OAKES (Gk)	
14	Paul SIMPSON †20		15	Fernando NELSON †45	
21	Marino RAHMBERG		18	Carl TILER	

Tommy Johnson's thigh strain adds him to the injury list... Steve Staunton returns, as does Fernando Nelson (on the subs bench)... Disappointing start to 1997 continues... Only one win (against Notts County) in six games... Form of Lee Hendrie is a 'plus' point... Andy Townsend another injury victim.

FACTFILE

Lee Hendrie

Cup exit adds to sad New Year

Early exit from the season's third knock-out competition, following the UEFA and Coca-Cola Cup failures, leaves a feeling of anti-climax compared to the high promise of a year earlier.

Although Derby, like Villa, are short of several regular first-teamers, they put on a far better show than Villa and well deserve their passage to a fifth round home draw.

The sad fact is that, with Paul McGrath outstanding at the back for County Villa are never going to emerge from the Baseball Ground unscathed in an uninspired performance.

With Mark Draper and Ian Taylor still missing from midfield, Gareth Southgate not back to his best and Andy Townsend removed at half-time with a shoulder injury, Brian Little's team rarely functions effectively.

County's reshaped line-up (they lose wide man Jacob Laursen in the warm-up and Gary Rowett after 20 minutes) also struggles to find its shape early on. Yet, once Jim Smith's team establish a hint of form, they are able to go in at half-time leading 2-0 and with cup progress virtually already assured.

Increasingly it is McGrath who stamps his authority on the game and neither Dwight Yorke, nor the ineffective Savo Milosevic, make any meaningful impression.

The most worrying spell for Villa is the lead-up to half-time during which Derby score twice in four minutes and assume control. A Villa defence that was once the tightest in the Premiership suddenly looks as vulnerable as it did a week earlier at Liverpool.

Firstly Robbie Van De Laan, whose future at Derby had looked bleak until injuries earned him a recall, took a pass from Paul Simpson and beat the Villa defence by burying his strike past Mark Bosnich.

Then midfielder Aljosa Asanovic deceives defenders with some sparkling ball control before feeding Birmingham-born striker Dean Sturridge for the kind of clinical finish that is earning him a growing reputation.

Townsend's withdrawal means a return, as second-half sub, for Fernando Nelson, with Steve Staunton moving into midfield and as Sasa Curcic comes more into the game there is a slight and belated uplift in Villa's performance in the second half.

One encouraging feature is the promise shown by young Lee Hendrie, who looks increasingly capable of pushing for a more regular place with his skill and enthusiasm.

However, a third Derby goal when Ron Willems is allowed far too much space confirms that Brian Little will be left with a sizeable task in restoring form and confidence for the midweek Premiership visit of Sheffield Wednesday.

Curcic's goal, which takes the Derby keeper by surprise from 25 yards, proves to be too little too late and Villa are left to seek a high league finish as their only remaining route back into Europe.

Before and after the game the sporting Villa fans give the evergreen, 36-year-old McGrath the warmest of receptions and Derby boss Jim Smith comments: "He's absolutely fantastic with all his skill and experience. We would be in the mire without him."

On the day, Villa were well beaten. "There will be a lot of assessments between now and the end of the season," says Brian Little.

"We were poor in the first half and didn't earn the right to win the game in that period. We tried to shake it up after the break and if we had got one back it might have been different.

"But in all fairness we were never really in it after the first goal. They pressured us better than we pressurised them.

"Not enough of us played well and not enough of us worked hard enough and once you go 2-0 down it's difficult in any game."

Wednesday 29th January 1997 • Villa Park • 7.45pm

ASTON VILLA 0   SHEFFIELD WEDNESDAY 1

Half-time 0-0 • Attendance 26,726

Referee Paul ALCOCK (Redhill)

Referee's Assistants M.A. WILLIAMS and P.A. VOSPER

Claret and Blue Shirts, White Shorts		Goals
1	Mark BOSNICH	
3	Steve STAUNTON	
4	Gareth SOUTHGATE	
9	Savo MILOSEVIC	
10	Dwight YORKE	
14	Alan WRIGHT	
15	Fernando NELSON	
16	Ugo EHIOGU	
18	Carl TILER †	
20	Riccardo SCIMECA	
26	Sasa CURCIC ‡	

Substitutes

12	Julian JOACHIM †76
13	Michael OAKES (Gk)
17	Lee HENDRIE ‡76
19	Gareth FARRELLY
27	David HUGHES

Blue and White Shirts, Blue Shorts		Goals
1	Kevin PRESSMAN	
2	Peter ATHERTON	
3	Ian NOLAN	
4	Mark PEMBRIDGE	
6	Des WALKER	
7	Guy WHITTINGHAM	
9	David HIRST †	
10	Andy BOOTH	69
12	Graham HYDE	
14	Steve NICOL	
18	Dejan STEFANOVIC	

Substitutes

11	Regi BLINKER †84
13	Matt CLARKE (Gk)
20	Wayne COLLINS
25	Ritchie HUMPHREYS
26	Orlando TRUSTFULL

BEFORE		P	W	D	L	F	A	pts
7	Villa	23	10	6	7	31	24	36
8	Wednesday	22	7	10	5	25	27	31

AFTER		P	W	D	L	F	A	pts
7	Villa	24	10	6	8	31	25	36
8	Wednesday	23	8	10	5	26	27	34

FACTFILE

Only one win (against Notts County) in the last nine games... Six Premiership matches without a victory... Wednesday score the season's first 'double' against Villa... Wimbledon remain as the only team in the top nine whom Villa have beaten... First time on the bench for Welsh U-21 international, David Hughes.

Missed penalty leads to collapse

Two home league fixtures in four days look to provide the opportunity to wipe away the memory of the cup exit at Derby, but this is not to be as the poor run drags on.

Since the superb 5-0 blast against Wimbledon nine matches ago the club's season of high expectation has gradually gone into decline.

Mark Draper and Ian Taylor have been joined on the injury list by Andy Townsend, hurt at the Baseball Ground, and Brian Little tries another positional shuffle.

Gareth Southgate is named captain in Townsend's absence and he has Steve Staunton and Sasa Curcic alongside him in the centre of midfield.

There is a a low-key atmosphere with a crowd of 'only' 26,000, but early signs are good as Villa control the attacking play.

The two Serbs, Savo Milosevic and Curcic both work hard with the latter quick and eager to make thrusts into the Wednesday defence.

His neat, tricky ball control is such that he is floored three times with late tackles early in the game.

However the first dangerous scoring attempt comes from Milosevic when, after cleverly wrong-footing defenders with his deceptive footwork he sees his cross-shot deflected for a corner. Then the two Serbs link-up cleverly to release Sasa for a shot which is turned around a post by Pressman, diving to his left. A stroke of luck comes Villa's way when Curcic goes down under a challenge from Dejan Stefanovic and the referee awards a penalty.

Yorke, having missed his previous spot kick against Newcastle a couple of weeks earlier, strikes his shot too weakly and too close to Kevin Pressman who is able to make a diving save.

Up to now Wednesday have produced little threat and when dangerman Mark Pembridge breaks through to beat Mark Bosnich, Ugo Ehiogu intervenes smartly to clear the threat.

Just before half-time there is another glaring and frustrating miss when, as the referee waves play on after the linesman has flagged for an infringement, Milosevic knocks his give-away opening over the bar from inside the six-yard line.

Hearts around the ground sink and clearly the effect is similar among the playing ranks as Villa slowly concede their domination in the second half.

Wednesday's passing and movement off the ball has always been impressive and as their confidence grows Villa's shrinks.

The warning signs are there when a menacing Andy Booth cross-shot has to be deflected away from goal for a corner and in the 69th minute an almost-predictable lead arrives.

As in previous games there is defensive uncertainty in front of Bosnich's goal as Carl Tiler fails to clear a Guy Whittingham shot and Booth is there to tuck away the rebound.

Tiler is withdrawn along with Curcic who has become anonymous after his bright first half and the arrival of Lee Hendrie and Julian Joachim provides a minimal lift.

Fuelled now by desperation both Southgate and Milosevic test Pressman in an attempt to grasp an equaliser, but the final whistle brings the feeling that Villa are now confronted by a crisis of confidence.

Gareth Southgate – tonight took over the Villa captaincy for the first time

Saturday 1st February 1997 • Villa Park • 3.00pm

ASTON VILLA 1 SUNDERLAND 0

Half-time 1-0 • *Attendance* 32,491
Referee Stephen LODGE (Barnsley)
Referee's Assistants A.N. BUTLER and D.M. HORLICK

Claret and Blue Shirts, White Shorts		Goals	White Shirts, Black Shorts		Goals
1	Mark BOSNICH		30	Lionel PEREZ	
3	Steve STAUNTON		2	Dariusz KUBICKI †	
4	Gareth SOUTHGATE		4	Paul BRACEWELL	
9	Savo MILOSEVIC	37	7	Michael GRAY ‡	
10	Dwight YORKE		8	Richard ORD	
14	Alan WRIGHT		12	Gareth HALL	
15	Fernando NELSON ❑		15	Alex RAE	
16	Ugo EHIOGU		16	David KELLY	
18	Carl TILER		22	John MULLIN	
20	Riccardo SCIMECA		23	Darren WILLIAMS	
26	Sasa CURCIC †		33	Jan ERIKSSON ❑	

Substitutes			*Substitutes*		
12	Julian JOACHIM		9	Craig RUSSELL ‡82	
13	Michael OAKES (Gk)		13	David PREECE (Gk)	
17	Lee HENDRIE †78		18	Martin SMITH †56	
19	Gareth FARRELLY		20	Darren HOLLOWAY	
27	David HUGHES		24	Paul HECKINGBOTTOM	

BEFORE		P	W	D	L	F	A	pts	AFTER		P	W	D	L	F	A	pts
7	Villa	24	10	6	8	31	25	36	7	Villa	25	11	6	8	32	25	39
11	Sunderland	24	7	8	9	23	31	29	12	Sunderland	25	7	8	10	23	32	29

FACTFILE

"I just feel relieved," admits Brian Little... Villa are unchanged from the Owls game... First league win in seven... Savo Milosevic's first goal in six games... Revenge for Roker defeat... Players now take two weeks break due to international fixtures and hope to have one or two injured players back after that.

Savo super strike settles stalemate

The mid-week defeat by Sheffield Wednesday has turned a routine-looking Premiership match into one of supreme significance, one that Villa dare not lose.

Against such a background, the depleted team, with an entire midfield wiped out by injury, are never going to perform with any amount of enterprising freedom.

Sunderland, with their line-up of fairly anonymous, low-profile players, have settled into the Premiership well under the experienced leadership of Peter Reid.

They will not be easy to beat as the opening 15 minutes of the game are to prove. With the centre of Villa's makeshift midfield of Steve Staunton, Gareth Southgate and Sasa Curcic lacking balance and togetherness their football is bitty and fragmented.

Southgate, especially, looks uncertain is his change of role. Staunton, all heart and hard-running as ever, pumps some speculative balls forward and Curcic adopts his natural style of running with the ball, frequently into trouble.

In the opening spell both David Kelly and former Helsingborg defender Jan Eriksson, on his Premiership debut, fail to hit the target with close range headers when left temporarily unmarked by some indecisive defending.

Later, after Lionel Perez has blocked a Dwight Yorke thrust with his knees when Yorke is put through by Milosevic, after the strike partners have created the opening with a delightful exchange of passes; Ugo Ehiogu then has to intervene with a timely block when Mark Bosnich is beaten by John Mullin.

The longer Villa go without a goal the more uncertain they are going to become, but the necessary relief arrives in the shape of a 37th minute goal by Savo Milosevic.

A long goal clearance by Mark Bosnich is trapped smoothly by the Serb who is 45 yards out on the left with his back to goal. As he traps and turns, the ball rebounds in precisely the right direction for him as the move cuts out two challenging defenders.

Savo moves into possession, hungrily carries the ball forward as defenders back off and when he hits a side-foot shot from near the 18 yard line the ball takes a slight deflection off Eriksson as he closes in to block the effort, bounces away from the keeper and finds the corner of the net, leaving Perez flatfooted.

There is one of those 'world-stood-still' moments before Milosevic, realising that his seventh goal of the season is nestling in the net, rushes to the Witton side touchline for a lottery jackpot winner's celebration.

Among the ranks of Villa fans the reaction is similar to those of the scorer, with relief, joy, amusement and admiration, intermingled with premature anticipation of the first Premiership victory of the New Year.

Milosevic's colleagues are equally perked by the breakthrough they needed so desperately and by half-time there have been some slick interchanges between the two front men and a thundering long shot by Staunton.

In fact, five minutes after the goal, Yorke is only inches from a second when, after another link-up with Milosevic, the big number nine puts a smart pass across the face of goal.

The second-half is mostly a battling stalemate as Sunderland industriously deny Villa time and space to add to the lead while rarely threatening to equalise.

Eight minutes into the half there is a slightly worrying moment or two when Mullin pierces the left side of the defence, via a deft rugby style hand-off of Riccardo Scimeca, which evidently goes unnoticed by the referee, but is left with too narrow an angle for a successful conclusion and Bosnich tips his angled, rising drive over the bar.

Wednesday 19th February 1997 • Villa Park • 7.45pm

ASTON VILLA 2 COVENTRY CITY 1

Half-time 1-0 • *Attendance* 30,409

Referee Keith BURGE (Tonypandy)

Referee's Assistants J.W. PETIT and M.R. SIMS

Claret and Blue Shirts, White Shorts	Goals	Sky Blue and Navy Blue Striped Shirts, Navy Blue Shorts	Goals
1 Mark BOSNICH		1 Steve OGRIZOVIC	
3 Steve STAUNTON	78og	2 Richard SHAW	
4 Gareth SOUTHGATE ❑		4 Paul WILLIAMS ❑	
6 Andy TOWNSEND		6 Kevin RICHARDSON ‡	
7 Ian TAYLOR		7 Eoin JESS †	
8 Mark DRAPER ❑		8 Noel WHELAN ❑	
9 Savo MILOSEVIC		10 Gary McALLISTER	
10 Dwight YORKE	43,75	12 Paul TELFER	
14 Alan WRIGHT		18 Marcus HALL	
15 Fernando NELSON		25 Gary BREEN	
16 Ugo EHIOGU		28 Darren HUCKERBY	
Substitutes		*Substitutes*	
11 Tommy JOHNSON		13 John FILAN (Gk)	
12 Julian JOACHIM		14 Peter NDLOVU †71	
13 Michael OAKES (Gk)		16 Brian BORROWS	
18 Carl TILER		23 Alexander EVTUSHOK	
20 Riccardo SCIMECA		26 Gordon STRACHAN ‡81	

BEFORE		P	W	D	L	F	A	pts
7	Villa	25	11	6	8	32	25	39
15	Coventry	25	6	9	10	23	33	27

AFTER		P	W	D	L	F	A	pts
5	Villa	26	12	6	8	34	26	42
16	Coventry	26	6	9	11	24	35	27

FACTFILE

Injury crisis evaporates as the midfield returns to action... No Coventry win at Villa Park in 23 attempts... Dwight Yorke takes goals total to 17... Scoreline flatters Sky Blues as Villa cruise home... Sasa Curcic is placed on offer... Club has announced that a share flotation is to take place.

Two goal Dwight strikes again

After one of the driest Januarys on record the rains have arrived and in the build up to the kick-off the cover has to be replaced on the 'young' pitch to safeguard the game.

Despite the foul weather a gate of 30,000 is present to see Coventry City's latest attempt to win their first-ever game at Villa Park.

Brian Little is able to field what he regards his strongest team for the first time in months and has made it clear that there could be major signings come the summer if they are found wanting from now on.

In the final third of the season the strength of the squad is, effectively, 'on trial' and one likely change could be the departure of Sasa Curcic whom, the manager revealed before the kick-off, is now on offer.

Villa instantly look more solid than they have been, with the return of the midfield trio of Mark Draper, Andy Townsend and Ian Taylor. In the opening seconds Townsend strides upfield to fire a long-shot narrowly over the bar.

A couple of ineffective scoring attempts by Draper follow as the rain-soaked pitch and gusting, swirling wind make the ball difficult to either predict or control.

The 28th minute sees a Villa 'goal' disappointingly disallowed. Dwight Yorke's shot rebounds off Steve Ogrizovic, under challenge from Savo Milosevic and Ian Taylor is there to force the loose ball over the line. However, a flag has already gone up, possibly for off-side against Taylor.

Although Coventry have enjoyed a fair amount of possession their efforts have led nowhere in particular and Villa deservedly claim the lead a couple of minutes before the break.

A free-kick is fed in by Townsend from the inside-left position and Yorke, unmarked a few yards from the penalty spot, connects with a deft, beautifully accurate low header which slides in off the inside of Ogrizovic's right-hand post to nestle nicely in the far corner of the net.

Come the half-time whistle and the game is suddenly in severe danger again as the torrent intensifies into what looks like a waterfall sweeping across the already saturated pitch.

Fortunately heaven's taps are turned down again for the restart and the expensively relaid pitch reveals its newfound powers of drainage by recovering quickly.

Coventry have their first attempts on target after the break, but Bosnich is comfortably able to deal with efforts by Marcus Hall and Darren Huckerby.

Villa's second goal arrives in the 75th minute. A 20-yard pass into the area by Ugo Ehiogu finds Yorke who traps the ball, turns and drills his shot home to once again confirm his place among the Premiership's leading hit men.

A 2-0 scoreline is a fair reflection of the action, but a bizarre own goal three minutes later leaves Villa fans on the rack until the final whistle.

A hopeful ball punted forward by Noel Whelan is 'easy meat' for either Steve Staunton or the advancing Bosnich. The Irish international elects to deal with it and calmly heads it over the keeper, who is now alongside him, into his own net. Weird...

**Ian Taylor –
a fine game on his
return from injury**

Saturday 22nd February 1997 • City Ground • 3.00pm

NOTTINGHAM FOREST 0 ASTON VILLA 0

Half-time 0-0 • *Attendance* 25,239

Referee Graham BARBER (Guildford)
Referee's Assistants J.J. ROSS and P.R. SHARP

Red Shirts, White Shorts	Goals	White Shirts, Claret Shorts	Goals
1 Mark CROSSLEY		1 Mark BOSNICH	
2 Des LYTTLE ❑		3 Steve STAUNTON †	
4 Colin COOPER		4 Gareth SOUTHGATE	
5 Steve CHETTLE		6 Andy TOWNSEND	
6 Chris BART-WILLIAMS		7 Ian TAYLOR	
7 David PHILLIPS		8 Mark DRAPER	
8 Scot GEMMILL ❑		9 Savo MILOSEVIC	
9 Dean SAUNDERS		10 Dwight YORKE	
18 Alf Inge HÅLAND		14 Alan WRIGHT	
22 Bryan ROY †		15 Fernando NELSON ❑	
29 Nigel CLOUGH		16 Ugo EHIOGU	

Substitutes		*Substitutes*	
13 Alan FETTIS (Gk)		11 Tommy JOHNSON	
14 Ian WOAN †76		12 Julian JOACHIM	
17 Chris ALLEN		13 Michael OAKES (Gk)	
20 Paul McGREGOR		17 Lee HENDRIE	
25 Stephen BLATHERWICK		20 Riccardo SCIMECA †46	

BEFORE		P	W	D	L	F	A	pts
5	Villa	26	12	6	8	34	26	42
17	Forest	25	5	8	12	23	40	23

AFTER		P	W	D	L	F	A	pts
5	Villa	27	12	7	8	34	26	43
17	Forest	26	5	9	12	23	40	24

FACTFILE

Sixth away game on the trot without a win... Goal-scoring failures undermine Euro-chance... Savo Milosevic's 19th start in 24 without a goal... Steve Staunton has to leave the field with ankle ligament damage and will be out for at least two weeks... Sasa Curcic puts in a written transfer request.

Missed chances at City Ground

Enjoying the rare luxury of announcing a full-strength, unchanged line-up Brian Little looks to his team to produce three points towards a place in Europe but, unhappily, it is not to be.

Forest, under the leadership of Stuart Pearce as player-manager, had improved after Frank Clark's departure, but cup defeat by Chesterfield left them under a cloud prior to Villa's visit.

Villa begin the game as favourites after their home victories over Sunderland and Coventry, but to confirm this rating a truly convincing win is needed to raise the tempo for the final third of the season.

Early indications are encouraging as Forest play a tight, cagey game and Villa are able to dictate the shape of the attacking play.

A factor which would truly provide an all-round lift would be that of Savo Milosevic supporting Dwight Yorke in providing a regular flow of decisive goals.

In this regard effort is not a problem. The £3.5m Serbian striker makes his physical presence felt at the front of the attack in searching out chances for himself and his colleagues.

Dwight Yorke is as pacey and mobile as ever and as defence and midfield pass the ball about accurately to retain possession it is Forest who are concentrating on damage limitation.

By the final whistle, however, the only possible conclusion is, like so often in the past, that Villa have been their own worst enemies by failing to capitalise on the chances they have created.

The most obvious of these arrives after 18 minutes when a superb cameo of skill by Yorke presents Milosevic with a golden opportunity.

The West Indian, supplied with the ball by Mark Draper, beats Steve Chettle and David Phillips with his control and a deceptive shimmy and lays on the shooting chance for his strike partner. Milosevic requires a cool head and an accurate shot, but manages to conjure up neither quality as his hurried finish aggravatingly misses the target.

A little earlier Milosevic had been granted a more difficult chance when a spinning ball came his way in front of goal and that headed effort also failed to hit the target when Mark Crossley had miskicked the ball to him.

The 'missed-chance' phobia proves contagious, as Yorke moves onto an ideal delivery from Alan Wright but he, too, is unable to threaten Crossley's goal.

When Yorke misses again from a similar opening, before half-time, the feeling grows that this is to be one of those frustrating days.

Nine minutes into the second half the breakthrough appears to have arrived as the lively, thrusting Wright instigates another opening.

Yorke returns the ball back across goal and Draper's header looks to have done the trick but this time, with Crossley beaten, Chettle is well stationed to block the ball on the line.

The final straw arrives for Villa almost on the whistle when Milosevic finally gets the ball into the net and, though he is enraged by an off-side flag against Yorke, Match-of-the-Day cameras prove the ref's decision to be accurate, although whether he was interfering with play or not is clearly debatable.

Villa end the match feeling aggrieved at the loss of two points but it was not an off-side flag and the referee's whistle which did the damage, but poor finishing.

Alan Wright

Sunday 2 March 1997 • Villa Park • 4.00pm

ASTON VILLA 1 LIVERPOOL 0

Half-time 0-0 • Attendance 39,339

Referee Steve DUNN (Bristol)

Referee's Assistants D.S. BRYAN and P. WALTON

Claret and Blue Shirts, White Shorts	Goals	Ecru Shirts, Black Shorts	Goals
1 Mark BOSNICH		1 David JAMES	
3 Steve STAUNTON †		3 Bjorn Tore KVARME	
4 Gareth SOUTHGATE		4 Jason McATEER	
6 Andy TOWNSEND		5 Mark WRIGHT	
7 Ian TAYLOR	83	7 Steve McMANAMAN	
8 Mark DRAPER		8 Stan COLLYMORE ❏ †	
9 Savo MILOSEVIC		9 Robbie FOWLER	
10 Dwight YORKE		10 John BARNES	
14 Alan WRIGHT		11 Jamie REDKNAPP	
15 Fernando NELSON		20 Stig Inge BJØRNEBYE	
16 Ugo EHIOGU		21 Dominic MATTEO	
Substitutes		*Substitutes*	
11 Tommy JOHNSON		12 Steve HARKNESS	
12 Julian JOACHIM		13 Tony WARNER (Gk)	
13 Michael OAKES (Gk)		14 Neil RUDDOCK	
17 Lee HENDRIE		15 Patrik BERGER †53	
27 David HUGHES †45		19 Mark KENNEDY	

BEFORE	P	W	D	L	F	A	pts	AFTER	P	W	D	L	F	A	pts
2 Liverpool	27	15	8	4	46	20	53	2 Liverpool	28	15	8	5	46	21	53
5 Villa	27	12	7	8	34	26	43	5 Villa	28	13	7	8	35	26	46

FACTFILE

Villa's first win over Liverpool after four defeats in succession... David Hughes' debut as second-half substitute for Steve Staunton, whose ankle injury would only allow him to last the first 45 minutes... Carl Tiler, who has handed in a transfer request during the week, is not considered for this match.

Taylor strike brings relief

The shadow of a combined 0-11 scoreline in the previous four matches against the Merseysiders hangs over the live-on-Sky fixture pre-match with Villa urgently needing to reverse the trend.

Although second in the Premiership behind Manchester United, Liverpool have not been at their best in recent weeks but, to be fair, neither have Villa.

Brian Little's team selection is something of a surprise with Steve Staunton recovered from his ankle injury sufficiently to start the game and untried David Hughes chosen as sub ahead of transfer-seeking Carl Tiler.

A recent rainy spell has left the newly-laid pitch with soft, bare patches, as a sell-out crowd of just below 40,000 creates the necessary big-occasion atmosphere.

The first-half starts off with high promises, but tails off slightly in terms of entertainment value as two similar 3-5-2 formations cancel each other out. Too many final passes, affected no doubt by the conditions, go astray.

Stan Collymore hammers a shot into the Holte End stand and then misses again when Staunton and Mark Bosnich get their lines crossed, David James saves from Dwight Yorke, Andy Townsend is wide from 30 yards and not a lot else happens for the opening 43 minutes.

Then Robbie Fowler is a fraction off adding to his collection of important goals against Villa. An angled shot from the left of the goal finds Bosnich off his line and as the Liverpool fans at the far end are about to rejoice

Gareth Southgate appears a yard from the goal-line to hook the ball away.

Welsh Under-21 international David Hughes replaces Staunton at half-time to fit instantly into the back three as Villa increase their pace and passion by several notches.

Incidents pile in thick and fast now as the game improves dramatically as a spectacle and Villa are in the driving seat. Savo Milosevic is the most prominent of the forwards in keeping possession well despite some robust treatment.

Townsend, Hughes, Draper, Milosevic and Taylor all have scoring attempts and Bosnich dives to smother a cross-shot by John Barnes. The game turns on two incidents in the final fourteen minutes. Firstly Fowler gets an excellent chance from six yards, but as Bosnich rushes out to challenge him he lifts it over the cross-bar via Bosnich's right shoulder. At that moment the crowd, and no doubt the players, conclude that this time events are not going to go Liverpool's way.

Seven minutes from the end one of many Villa surges sees Townsend send an angled delivery from out on the left which beats two defenders and pierces to beyond the far post.

Debutant – David Hughes

There the industrious Taylor has arrived on one of his blind side runs to control the ball carefully, take aim and rifle the winning goal away from James' reach as the keeper advances.

The ex-Holte Ender's celebratory pose as his team mates rush in is thoroughly deserved. A well-planned and beautifully-executed goal has ended Liverpool's four-match mastery and sent a wave of relief crashing around Villa Park.

"If we can remain unbeaten in our final ten games we can qualify for Europe," says Brian Little.

Wednesday 5th March 1997 • Filbert Street • 7.45pm

LEICESTER CITY 1 ASTON VILLA 0

Half-time 0-0 • Attendance 20,626

Referee Graham POLL (Tring)
Referee's Assistants M.L. SHORT and P.A. VOSPER

Blue Shirts, White Shorts	Goals	White Shirts, Claret Shorts	Goals
13 Kasey KELLER		1 Mark BOSNICH	
2 Simon GRAYSON		4 Gareth SOUTHGATE	
5 Steve WALSH		6 Andy TOWNSEND	
6 Mustafa IZZET		7 Ian TAYLOR	
7 Neil LENNON		8 Mark DRAPER †	
10 Garry PARKER		9 Savo MILOSEVIC ‡	
11 Emile HESKEY #		10 Dwight YORKE	
12 Mark ROBINS †		14 Alan WRIGHT	
17 Spencer PRIOR ‡		15 Fernando NELSON	
18 Matt ELLIOTT		16 Ugo EHIOGU ❏	
24 Steve GUPPY ❏		27 David HUGHES ❏	
Substitutes		*Substitutes*	
1 Kevin POOLE (Gk)		11 Tommy JOHNSON †74	
4 Julian WATTS ‡59		12 Julian JOACHIM ‡74	
8 Scott TAYLOR #62		13 Michael OAKES (Gk)	
9 Steve CLARIDGE †45	66	17 Lee HENDRIE	
21 Jamie LAWRENCE		24 Scott MURRAY	

BEFORE		P	W	D	L	F	A	pts	AFTER		P	W	D	L	F	A	pts
5	Villa	28	13	7	8	35	26	46	5	Villa	29	13	7	9	35	27	46
11	Leicester	26	9	6	11	32	38	33	9	Leicester	27	10	6	11	33	38	36

FACTFILE

Leicester complete double over Villa... No wins over Leicester in four attempts since Brian Little's move (two draws, two defeats)... David Hughes' full debut after one appearance as substitute... Villa turn down an attempt from Sheffield United to take Carl Tiler on loan, insisting on a permanent deal only.

No punch or goals at Filbert Street

The visit to Filbert Street, bearing in mind Brian Little's acrimonious departure, inevitably has an additional undercurrent and this one falls into the same category.

With Steve Staunton still injured, David Hughes, the Welsh Under-21 international who was introduced as sub against Liverpool, makes his full senior debut.

The Filbert Street match-day programme features an item in manager Martin O'Neill's notes asking the crowd to show respect to Brian Little and adds provocatively 'what you wish to do if and when Mark McGhee visits us with Wolves is entirely at your own discretion.'

In the event the Villa manager gets a relaxed welcome, unlike in the past, though there is to come a time when a section chants 'Brian, Brian, what's the score...?'.

Villa are the superior attacking side in a promising first half, enjoying greater possession with some slick passing movements, although there is little sign of their making the breakthrough they need.

Indeed, the most threatening moment is conjured up by Leicester, when a sixth minute delivery by Simon Grayson is met by a Matt Elliott header and looks set for the top corner until Mark Bosnich leaps to claw it away.

Savo Milosevic shows some neat control and frequently inter-changes well with Dwight Yorke, but the end-product is not there.

A Dwight Yorke drive is charged down by the impressive Matt Elliott, a Mark Draper free kick skids through threateningly and a cross-goal pass by Ian Taylor frustratingly finds Yorke too far forward.

Early in the second-half Fernando Nelson is close with a 20-yard drive, but soon the tide changes and Leicester, who have done well in the two cups and have climbed the table, grasp the initiative.

Bosnich makes two more fine saves, both from the industrious Elliott, one from a rasping drive and the other from a close-range header as Villa survive dangerously.

But, from the second of the two saves, a spectacular affair, the ball rebounds invitingly for Steve Claridge to force it over the line.

Clearly Villa are not going to pull back without at least trying something different and Draper and Milosevic are withdrawn to be replaced by substitutes Tommy Johnson and Julian Joachim with 15 minutes to go.

By now, however, hard-working, determined Leicester have established a grip which they do not intend to relinquish as Villa continue to fail to find a cutting edge.

When Ugo Ehiogu shoots straight at Kasey Keller with six minutes remaining it is only the second Villa shot of the second half, a pale offering from a team with rapidly diminishing hopes of a return to Europe.

"We tailed off as the game went on," confesses Brian Little. "We started well but couldn't go on from there. Some of our lads are disappointed at not getting a point, but I thought we could have lost 5-0.

"We've got players who can be good for one game, but they have to be good week in, week out."

Mark Bosnich – fine form in goal

Saturday 15th March 1997 • Villa Park • 3.00pm

ASTON VILLA 0 WEST HAM UNITED 0

Half-time 0-0 • Attendance 35,992

Referee David ELLERAY (Harrow-on-the-Hill)
Referee's Assistants M.D. MESSIAS and D.C. RICHARDS

Claret and Blue Shirts, White Shorts	Goals	Ecru Shirts, Claret Shorts	Goals
1 Mark BOSNICH		1 Ludek MIKLOSKO	
4 Gareth SOUTHGATE		2 Tim BREACKER	
6 Andy TOWNSEND		3 Julian DICKS ❑	
7 Ian TAYLOR		4 Steve POTTS	
8 Mark DRAPER †		7 Ian BISHOP	
10 Dwight YORKE		9 Paul KITSON	
12 Julian JOACHIM ‡		10 John HARTSON	
14 Alan WRIGHT		16 John MONCUR ❑	
15 Fernando NELSON		17 Stan LAZARIDIS ❑	
16 Ugo EHIOGU		26 Frank LAMPARD ❑ †	
27 David HUGHES		28 Slaven BILIC	
Substitutes		*Substitutes*	
11 Tommy JOHNSON ‡74		8 Marc RIEPER	
13 Michael OAKES (Gk)		13 Hugo PORFIRIO	
17 Lee HENDRIE †71		14 Iain DOWIE	
23 Neil DAVIS		21 Les SEALEY (Gk)	
24 Scott MURRAY		27 Rio FERDINAND †32	

BEFORE		P	W	D	L	F	A	pts
5	Villa	29	13	7	9	35	27	46
17	West Ham	28	7	7	14	27	39	28

AFTER		P	W	D	L	F	A	pts
6	Villa	30	13	8	9	35	27	47
17	West Ham	29	7	8	14	27	39	29

FACTFILE

Tommy Johnson rejects a £2m move back to Derby in run-up to West Ham visit... Savo Milosevic injured whilst on duty with Yugoslavia, he could be out for three weeks... Staunton and Scimeca still struggling for fitness... Eight points dropped in three of last four games... Only one goal scored in last four matches.

Sterile stalemate in home bore

A perceptive difference has been emerging between the manager's aspirations of a high Premiership finish and the public's perception of what the disappointing team are likely to achieve.

Supporters have become uneasy about several uninspired displays in recent times other than in beating Liverpool in the last home game.

The remaining target of a place in Europe demands that most of the last nine games, especially those at home, are won.

Seven European places will be on offer, of which three out of four in the UEFA Cup will be decided on Premiership placings. How far the qualifications go down the Premiership table depends on who wins the two domestic cups. A top-five place is the safest target.

In his programme notes Brian Little specifies six wins out of nine as the requirement and, presumably, no defeats.

Relegation-threatened Hammers arrive with their expensive new strike force of John Hartson and Paul Kitson and in the middle of a spell of results which has kept them out of the bottom three.

Another near-capacity Villa Park attendance reflects the strength of the support but, as a mediocre game unfolds, 'disappointment' is to become the name of this particular game.

There has been criticism of Savo Milosevic and his shortage of goals yet, in his absence through injury on this occasion, the Serb's ability to hold the ball up and create openings for others is clearly missed.

Julian Joachim gets the vote to replace him but, like Dwight Yorke, makes little impact up front. Behind them there is little penetration from midfield, where Ian Taylor's usual hunger for hard-running is the feature.

Neither Mark Draper nor Andy Townsend dominate the play or create good openings and mid-way through the second-half Lee Hendrie replaces Draper and Tommy Johnson goes on for Joachim.

In a match of few meaningful chances at either end the two clearest are created by West Ham, who are deprived of the two additional points by the brilliance of Mark Bosnich.

Just before half-time the Australian dives to rescue Villa when Hartson is presented with what looks a simple tap in from a few yards out.

This is followed, in the second half, by the in-form keeper surging of his line, after Gareth Southgate has stumbled, giving Kitson a free run-in on goal, to dive at the striker's feet, again when a goal looks inevitable.

True Villa enjoy far more of the possession and the approach play thus causing the odd skirmish in West Ham's goalmouth, but they seldom look able to produce the first of those six wins on the manager's shopping list.

Their best chances falling to the two substitutes late in the game, firstly the hard-working Lee Hendrie makes a run into the six-yard box getting onto the end of a left-wing cross from Yorke, but just slightly over-runs the ball and his effort is blocked by Miklosko. Then it is Johnson's turn to meet a left wing cross on the near post, but an excellent covering tackle by Bilic prevents a goal.

After a lively spell in the second half, the Hammers revert to their earlier tactics of getting everyone behind the ball and are well content with a point when the final whistle goes.

"The points we have dropped recently have been big points. But we definitely cannot allow the season to just peter out," he insists. "It can't happen and it won't happen because we are chasing a place in Europe.

"We have important players who are just not playing as well as they are capable of. Today we just did not have individuals who could affect the game."

Saturday 22nd March 1997 • Ewood Park • 3.00pm

BLACKBURN ROVERS 0 ASTON VILLA 2

Half-time 0-0 • *Attendance* 24,274

Referee Alan WILKIE (Chester-le-Street)

Referee's Assistants C. BASSINDALE and A.J. GREEN

Blue and White Halved Shirts, White Shorts		Goals	Claret and Blue Shirts, Claret Shorts		Goals
1	Tim FLOWERS		1	Mark BOSNICH	
3	Jeff KENNA		3	Steve STAUNTON	
4	Tim SHERWOOD		6	Andy TOWNSEND ❏	
5	Colin HENDRY ❏		7	Ian TAYLOR	
6	Graeme LE SAUX		8	Mark DRAPER	
8	Kevin GALLACHER		9	Savo MILOSEVIC †	
9	Chris SUTTON †		10	Dwight YORKE	79
11	Jason WILCOX		14	Alan WRIGHT ❏	
17	Billy McKINLAY		15	Fernando NELSON	
20	Henning BERG		16	Ugo EHIOGU	
23	Garry FLITCROFT #		20	Riccardo SCIMECA	
	Substitutes			*Substitutes*	
10	Lars BOHINEN #69		11	Tommy JOHNSON †59	64
12	Nicky MARKER		12	Julian JOACHIM	
13	Shay GIVEN (Gk)		17	Lee HENDRIE	
16	Per PEDERSEN †6 ‡		27	David HUGHES	
21	Georgios DONIS ‡55		30	Adam RACHEL (Gk)	

BEFORE		P	W	D	L	F	A	pts	AFTER		P	W	D	L	F	A	pts
6	Villa	30	13	8	9	35	27	47	5	Villa	31	14	8	9	37	27	50
12	Blackburn	30	8	12	10	33	30	36	12	Blackburn	31	8	12	11	33	32	36

FACTFILE

Villa's first Premiership win at Ewood Park... Andy Townsend booking brings suspension... Transfer talk rife as Brian Little combs market... Gareth Southgate joins the England squad... Tommy Johnson (£2.4m), Carl Tiler (£650,000) and Phil King (Free) leave the club on transfer deadline day.

Back to fifth in the Premiership

Brian Little is still talking in positive terms about the chances of qualifying for the UEFA Cup and by the final whistle this optimism seems justified.

Ewood Park has not been a happy hunting ground for Villa in the Premiership, while Blackburn's recent home form confirms the fixture's degree of difficulty.

In a happier fitness report both Riccardo Scimeca and Steve Staunton are now available, while Savo Milosevic has also survived a late test on a thigh strain.

The manager is deeply involved in talks with many clubs regarding possible transfers in and out, and the indications are that a new team-building operation is underway.

Carl Tiler is the target of Sheffield United for a fee of up to £850,000, but the details had not been finalised when the weekend's deadline arrived.

Blackburn start off the game in disastrous fashion when striker Chris Sutton crashes heads with Ugo Ehiogu and is removed permanently from the action.

Soon it is evident that the home team are lacking in drive thus enabling Villa to create the better chances up to the break. Without improving substantially on recent disappointing displays they are seldom in danger of going behind.

After an hour of fairly indecisive forward play Milosevic is replaced by Tommy Johnson who, remember, could by now have been playing for Derby County against Spurs had he accepted the recent transfer opportunity.

Johnson's first chance to shine is spoiled by poor control, but after less than five minutes on the field he accepts a precision pass from Alan Wright out on the left touch-line, cuts out

Colin Hendry with a fine first touch and drives the ball left-footed beyond Flowers' reach and into the bottom left-hand corner of the net.

This is the signal for Rovers to virtually collapse without trace and Villa to step up another gear in pursuit of the three points.

Unlike in other games, where little has gone right, Villa are blessed with a welcome stroke of fortune ten minutes from time in the form of a rare slip by Henry, who fails to control a flick-on by Tommy Johnson.

This conveniently puts Dwight Yorke in possession, the worst possible scenario for the home team, as the Villa striker takes the ball round Flowers and tucks away his 18th goal of the season from wide of the left hand post.

Apart from the odd, fleeting moment Villa have not been in significant danger and while it has not been the most entertaining of games, as the manager readily concedes, the result is all-important.

As Chelsea lose at Middlesbrough, Sheffield Wednesday draw with Leeds at home and Newcastle subsequently draw with Wimbledon Villa's apparent descent of the table is stemmed.

"There is still something missing in our play," Brian Little concedes. "But not too much.

"If you're strong and not giving very much away that's not too bad. A few more victories and we can secure a European place."

Super-sub Tommy Johnson

Saturday 5th April 1997 • Villa Park • 3.00pm

ASTON VILLA 3 EVERTON 1

Half-time 1-1 • Attendance 39,339

Referee Jeff WINTER (Middlesbrough)
Referee's Assistants P. V. NORMAN and K. PIKE

Claret and Blue Shirts, White Shorts		Goals
13	Michael OAKES	
3	Steve STAUNTON †	49
4	Gareth SOUTHGATE	
7	Ian TAYLOR ‡	
8	Mark DRAPER	
9	Savo MILOSEVIC	40
10	Dwight YORKE	53
14	Alan WRIGHT	
15	Fernando NELSON	
16	Ugo EHIOGU	
19	Gareth FARRELLY	
	Substitutes	
12	Julian JOACHIM	
24	Scott MURRAY	
26	Sasa CURCIC ‡81	
27	David HUGHES †55	
30	Adam RACHEL (Gk)	

Amber and Blue/Black striped Shirts, Black Shorts		Goals
1	Neville SOUTHALL	
4	David UNSWORTH ‡	13
5	Dave WATSON ❑	
6	Terry PHELAN	
7	Graham STUART	
9	Duncan FERGUSON	
10	Gary SPEED	
15	Claus THOMSEN	
18	Joe PARKINSON	
19	Marc HOTTIGER †	
21	Craig SHORT ❑	
	Substitutes	
13	Paul GERRARD (Gk)	
23	Michael BRANCH †54	
25	Michael BALL	
27	Richard DUNNE ‡59	
35	John HILLS	

BEFORE		P	W	D	L	F	A	pts
5	Villa	31	14	8	9	37	27	50
13	Everton	31	9	9	13	37	45	36

AFTER		P	W	D	L	F	A	pts
5	Villa	32	15	8	9	40	28	53
14	Everton	32	9	9	14	38	48	36

FACTFILE

Of the Villa players on international duty only Riccardo Scimeca is unavailable for selection... Still no Villa Park win for Everton in five years of Premiership... Villa catch Newcastle on points... Villa chairman Doug Ellis expresses anger as council defer main stand improvement plan.

Full house sees second half rout

Everton arrive at Villa Park for their first game since the surprise departure of Joe Royle as manager, leaving the team fighting for survival points under the guidance centre-back Dave Watson as caretaker-boss.

Villa are without injured Mark Bosnich and suspended Andy Townsend. The midfield vacancy is filled by Gareth Farrelly, on his first full appearance of the season while Savo Milosevic is back, in good shape, after scoring the winning goal for Yugoslavia in mid-week.

Badly depleted Everton, who have won only twice in 15 Premierships starts, are without the likes of Nick Barmby, Earl Barrett and Paul Rideout and they make their intentions clear from the opening minutes.

A defensive blockade as springboard for sudden attacking thrusts is the Watson plan, plus an extra dose of aggression as the new Everton leader ploughs right through Dwight Yorke in the opening minutes. Amazingly there is no free kick, let alone a well-justified yellow card and from then on the crowd is firmly on the referee's back as he continues to be too lenient with indiscriminate challenges.

Villa are clearly unsettled by Everton's tough methods and after 13 minutes find themselves a goal down. Defensively, Villa have looked equally ill-at-ease, as illustrated when Duncan Ferguson powers through the middle, leaving Steve Staunton stranded after a misplaced pass from the left wing puts Everton in possession.

Ferguson releases Graham Stuart for a clear shot on goal, but from his first time effort, Michael Oakes thrills Villa supporters with an athletic dive to his left and a one-handed save.

Unhappily for Villa, however, it proves merely to be a temporary reprieve as the resulting corner leads to Ferguson nodding down a chance for David Unsworth to deliver the lead at the second attempt.

Until five minutes before the break Villa's attempts to pull-back are less than impressive. Then Draper's left wing corner gets through to the far post, via Ian Taylor's boot, for Milosevic, who has had two good previous opportunities to score, to nod the equaliser.

This proves to be the turning point, especially as Staunton supplies the lead at the start of the second half. From a free kick for a foul on Yorke just outside the penalty area he finds the net with a low swerving shot, just inside Southall's right hand post.

Everton's Plan A, has now been ruined. With nothing left to defend it is now their turn to attempt to pull back, but there is seemingly no Plan B for Villa to worry about.

"I thought they began to look a little tired," says Brian Little, reflecting afterwards on the extent to which Villa assumed control.

The third goal is tucked away with consummate ease by Dwight Yorke as a Ugo Ehiogu assist from Farrelly's right wing delivery falls ideally for him. By 90 minutes the scoreline in Villa's favour could have been doubled.

"Europe is definitely there for us," adds the manager. "It's in our own hands. If we don't take it we have only ourselves to blame."

Gareth Farrelly watches Mark Draper embroiled in an aerial duel

Wednesday 9th April 1997 • Selhurst Park • 7.45pm

WIMBLEDON 0 ASTON VILLA 2

Half-time 0-1 • *Attendance 9,015*

Referee ROGER DILKES (Mossley)

Referee's Assistants K.J. HAWKES and M.R. SIMS

Dark Blue Shirts, Dark Blue Shorts	Goals	White Shirts, Claret Shorts	Goals
13 Paul HEALD		13 Michael OAKES	
3 Alan KIMBLE		4 Gareth SOUTHGATE	
9 Efan EKOKU		6 Andy TOWNSEND	
12 Chris PERRY		7 Ian TAYLOR	
17 Brian McALLISTER ❑		8 Mark DRAPER	
18 Neal ARDLEY †		9 Savo MILOSEVIC	26
19 Stewart CASTLEDINE		10 Dwight YORKE	
20 Mick HARFORD		14 Alan WRIGHT ❑	78
21 Duncan JUPP		15 Fernando NELSON	
23 Jason EUELL		16 Ugo EHIOGU	
24 Peter FEAR ❑		27 David HUGHES	
Substitutes		*Substitutes*	
1 Neil SULLIVAN (Gk)		1 Mark BOSNICH (Gk)	
14 Jon GOODMAN		12 Julian JOACHIM	
15 Alan REEVES		19 Gareth FARRELLY	
22 Andy CLARKE †84		24 Scott MURRAY	
26 Carl CORT		26 Sasa CURCIC	

BEFORE		P	W	D	L	F	A	pts	AFTER		P	W	D	L	F	A	pts
5	Villa	32	15	8	9	40	28	53	4	Villa	33	16	8	9	42	28	56
8	Wimbledon	31	12	10	9	42	38	46	8	Wimbledon	32	12	10	10	42	40	46

FACTFILE

Mark Bosnich fit again, but returns on the subs' bench... Villa complete Premiership double over Dons... First-ever Premiership win over Wimbledon at Selhurst Park... Third successive win and only one defeat in nine... Alan Wright's first goal of the season... Lowest Premiership crowd of the season.

Weakened Dons battle in vain

Selhurst Park is not normally one of Villa's favourite grounds but on this occasion the trip is undertaken in the knowledge that Wimbledon have mixed priorities.

The suspicion is that, with Sunday's FA Cup semi-final date against Chelsea looming, it will not be easy for Joe Kinnear's admirable team to concentrate their minds solely on this game.

Previous slips in the Premiership have already dictated that a high league finish is now off the agenda, thus adding even greater significance to the cup.

This much is indicated by the team line-up which shows eight changes from the weekend defeat at Tottenham and is littered with less-familiar names.

Villa, in contrast, have merely retained David Hughes in the back three, where he replaced Steve Staunton on Saturday and recalled Andy Townsend in place of the transfer-seeking Gareth Farrelly.

The signs are good for Villa from the earliest minutes when both Dwight Yorke and Savo Milosevic break free of the Dons' defence.

Yorke is quickly snuffed before he can get in a scoring attempt, though the £3.5m Serb manages a shot which is smothered by Paul Heald.

The attendance of fewer than 10,000 fans is, in fact, boosted by Villa's travelling contingent but the lukewarm atmosphere nonetheless contrasts sharply with the house-full feeling at Villa Park last Saturday.

Savo Milosevic

The lead arrives in just under the half-hour and, as in the Everton game, the supplier is Milosevic, a healthy development, indeed.

An opening is provided by Mark Draper, who was sadly off his game last Saturday. This time his pass arrows beautifully into an inviting space for Milosevic to move forward confidently, hold off Brian McAllister's challenge and bury the ball wide of Heald.

So often in the past the big Serb has lost his cool in such moments. More like this on a consistent basis would save Brian Little a seven-figure fee!

The goal, from Villa's point of view at least, added a sparkle to an otherwise rather dull affair in which Dons are restricted to their usual quota of honest endeavour.

For much of the second-half Villa are forced to cling on doggedly to their slender lead as Wimbledon concentrate on a high-ball game backed by much physical effort.

Efan Ekoku is close to an equaliser inside the hour while Yorke misses a promising chance. A second goal is required to haul the scoreline out of reach and Alan Wright duly obliges twelve minutes from time. After Townsend and Yorke have linked up to Wimbledon's confusion the latter heads the ball to the wing-back who slams in a volley from 18 yards which leaves Heald groping.

"At the moment we are looking at ourselves, Newcastle United and Sheffield Wednesday competing for the two UEFA Cup places," says Brian Little. "In an ideal world you would look to one of our teams winning one of the European competitions, which would ease our situation, but its not something we can rely on."

Saturday 12th April 1997 • Baseball Ground • 3.00pm

DERBY COUNTY 2 ASTON VILLA 1

Half-time 2-0 • *Attendance* 18,071

Referee Paul DANSON (Leicester)

Referee's Assistants M. HALL and A.J. MARTIN

White Shirts, Black Shorts		Goals	Claret and Blue Shirts, White Shorts		Goals
1	Russell HOULT		13	Michael OAKES	
2	Gary ROWETT	21	4	Gareth SOUTHGATE	
3	Chris POWELL ❑		6	Andy TOWNSEND ❑	
7	Robin VAN DER LAAN †	36	7	Ian TAYLOR	
8	Dean STURRIDGE		8	Mark DRAPER †	
10	Aljosa ASANOVIC ‡		9	Savo MILOSEVIC	
12	Ashley WARD #		10	Dwight YORKE	
15	Paul TROLLOPE		14	Alan WRIGHT	
16	Jacob LAURSEN		15	Fernando NELSON ❑	
22	Christian DAILLY ❑		16	Ugo EHIOGU	
27	Paul McGRATH		27	David HUGHES ‡	
	Substitutes			*Substitutes*	
4	Darryl POWELL †79		12	Julian JOACHIM ‡73	84
13	Martin TAYLOR (Gk)		19	Gareth FARRELLY	
14	Paul SIMPSON		24	Scott MURRAY	
23	Mauricio SOLIS ‡79		26	Sasa CURCIC †61	
26	Paulo WANCHOPE #79		30	Adam RACHEL (Gk)	

BEFORE		P	W	D	L	F	A	pts	AFTER		P	W	D	L	F	A	pts
4	Villa	33	16	8	9	42	28	56	4	Villa	34	16	8	10	43	30	56
12	Derby	33	9	12	12	39	50	39	11	Derby	34	10	12	12	41	51	42

FACTFILE

Steve Staunton and Riccardo Scimeca still sidelined so David Hughes makes his fourth start of the season... Second defeat of the year at Derby... Press speculate on possible Mark Bosnich sale... UEFA Cup-place rivals Newcastle United and Sheffield Wednesday play out a draw on Sunday.

Another dark day at Derby

Villa's final appearance at the Baseball Ground as Derby prepare to move to their new stadium at Pride Park next season proves to be one of the season's most lamentable occasions.

Just as in the FA Cup exit in January Villa are comprehensively upstaged by their Midland rivals, though this defeat is prefaced by a disturbing episode behind the scenes.

The pre-match team sheet had been completed by Brian Little, naming Michael Oakes to retain the jersey vacated by Mark Bosnich when he injured a hamstring while with Terry Venables' Australia squad.

Oakes had deputised admirably against both Everton and Wimbledon and the Villa manager felt that Bosnich had not yet been able to train sufficiently to comfortably make his return.

However, Little is told at 1.55pm that the extrovert Aussie, obviously upset at not being recalled to the team, has staged a walk-out.

Members of the public later report having seen Bosnich leave the stadium with fitness coach Paul Barron, who was clad in his match gear, in feverish pursuit while visibly but vainly urging the keeper to return.

Against this background Villa's impressive surge towards an assured UEFA Cup place, peters out in one of the season's least-impressive performances.

There is no suggestion that the Bosnich drama is entirely to blame for Villa's failures on the field, though to go AWOL in the build-up to the action does inevitably tend to undermine the harmony of the dressing room.

After an uninspired opening 20 minutes by Villa, Derby's Birmingham-born Dean Sturridge, livelier and more effective than anyone in the Villa ranks, creates the chance for Gary Rowett's first goal of the season.

The best Villa can offer in reply are missed chances by Savo Milosevic, a sitter, and Dwight Yorke as Sturridge makes a second goal for Robin Van Der Laan.

With ex-Villa favourite Paul McGrath outstanding in the Derby defence Villa make little impression and the ineffectiveness of Mark Draper is reflected when, once again, he is replaced by Sasa Curcic in the second half.

County have the three points in their sights to confirm Premiership survival and this, on the day, appears to be a greater motivating force than does a European place for Villa.

After arriving as a 73rd minute substitute for David Hughes, Julian Joachim capitalises on a mix-up between Russell Hoult and Rowett to score from Yorke's flick-on.

The goal is too little too late but, nonetheless, all Villa are going to get out of a very bad day at the office for Brian Little.

"Mark was to be on the bench again and the next thing I know, at five-to-two, I am told he has left the ground," says the Villa manager afterwards, in thinly-veiled annoyance.

"A lot of people in the dressing room were let-down (by Bosnich) today," he adds. "I will see him on Monday and sort it out. It may be a disciplinary matter."

Julian Joachim

Saturday 19th April 1997 • Villa Park • 3.00pm

ASTON VILLA 1 TOTTENHAM HOTSPUR 1

Half-time 0-0 • Attendance 39,339

Referee Martin BODENHAM (Looe)

Referee's Assistants L.E. CABLE and P.A. VOSPER

Claret and Blue Shirts, White Shorts	Goals		White Shirts, Dark Blue Shorts	Goals
13 Michael OAKES		1 Ian WALKER	
3 Steve STAUNTON		2 Dean AUSTIN	
4 Gareth SOUTHGATE †		3 Justin EDINBURGH ❏	
6 Andy TOWNSEND		4 David HOWELLS ‡	
7 Ian TAYLOR		5 Colin CALDERWOOD	
8 Mark DRAPER ‡		10 Teddy SHERINGHAM	
9 Savo MILOSEVIC		12 Jason DOZZELL	
10 Dwight YORKE	81	19 Paul McVEIGH †	
14 Alan WRIGHT		23 Sol CAMPBELL	
15 Fernando NELSON ❏		24 Ramon VEGA	54
16 Ugo EHIOGU		27 Andy SINTON	
Substitutes		*Substitutes*	
1 Mark BOSNICH (Gk)		13 Espen BÅRDSEN (Gk)	
12 Julian JOACHIM		14 Stuart NETHERCOTT ‡89	
24 Scott MURRAY		21 Danny HILL	
26 Sasa CURCIC ‡65		20 Neale FENN †82	
27 David HUGHES †45		33 Garry BRADY	

BEFORE	P	W	D	L	F	A	pts	AFTER	P	W	D	L	F	A	pts
5 Villa	34	16	8	10	43	30	56	5 Villa	35	16	9	10	44	31	57
9 Spurs	34	12	6	16	40	46	42	9 Spurs	35	12	7	16	41	47	43

Steve Staunton back from injury, David Hughes relegated to the substitutes bench... Five dropped points in two games undermines Euro-bid... Need for new striker is obvious once again... Sixth-placed Sheffield Wednesday's win narrows Premiership gap to one point.

Yorke strikes as Euro bid falters

An afternoon that begins with the stadium's centenary-party atmosphere is to end with no better than a sigh of relief and a lingering air of apprehension over European prospects.

The day's programme of events, to commemorate the opening of Villa Park on Easter Saturday 1897, was not meant to include a cliff-hanger of a game to avoid defeat.

On paper the visit of Spurs had looked the most favourable of the remaining four fixtures from which Brian Little had stressed that three victories were required.

The London club, with ten of their 17 away fixtures lost and a mediocre recent record in all games, arrive with 13 players unavailable and several key performers missing.

Villa, in contrast, while continuing with Michael Oakes in goal and Mark Bosnich on the bench, are at full strength in kicking-off as firm favourites.

Soon, however, it emerges that Spurs' boss Gerry Francis has a damage-limitation plan for his sorely-weakened line up, namely to gather bodies behind the ball in depth and leave Villa to break through if they can.

With this format established Spurs have just one scoring attempt before half-time, a header by Vega in the seventh minute, from David Howells' free kick, which clears the bar.

Dwight Yorke's similar, earlier effort has suffered the same fate, while a 30-yard shot by Alan Wright is tipped over by Ian Walker and a couple of cleverly-executed Savo Milosevic flicks land safely into the keeper's arms.

Five minutes before the break a heavy aerial collision between Gareth Southgate and Dean Austin results in the Villa defender failing to re-appear in the second half.

It seems a matter of time before Villa secure their breakthrough, but the reverse proves to be the case as a token-looking Spurs counter-attack results in Vega heading Teddy Sheringham's right-wing delivery past David Hughes, the replacement for Southgate, and Oakes.

Now a touch of increased urgency is added to Villa's game as they find themselves chasing a draw instead of cruising to the anticipated victory. The service from midfield has not been anywhere near sharp enough and mid-way through the half Sasa Curcic replaces the injured Mark Draper to step up the pace.

The equaliser duly arrives nine minutes from time as Villa dominate the shape of the game. Steve Staunton has let fly with a steaming cross shot that Walker cannot hold and the rebound falls invitingly for Yorke for his 20th goal of the season.

Walker saves well from Curcic and Yorke, while Oakes has to dive acrobatically to his right to push away a cross-shot by Sheringham in an all-action finish to a disappointing match.

"It is difficult to break down teams who play in this way, especially when you are missing the half-chances that come your way," admits Brian Little afterwards.

"In the end we were pleased to get something out of it and although we know Sheffield

Wednesday are a threat to our European chances they still have to win their match in hand to overtake us."

Dwight Yorke

Tuesday 22nd April 1997 • Elland Road • 7.45pm

LEEDS UNITED 0   ASTON VILLA 0

Half-time 0-0 • *Attendance 26,897*

Referee Graham BARBER (Guildford)

Referee's Assistants P.M. ROBERTS and P. WALTON

White Shirts, White Shorts	Goals	Claret and Blue Shirts, Claret Shorts	Goals
1 Nigel MARTYN		1 Mark BOSNICH	
2 Gary KELLY		3 Steve STAUNTON	
3 Tony DORIGO ❑		4 Gareth SOUTHGATE	
4 Carlton PALMER		6 Andy TOWNSEND ❑ †	
5 Lucas RADEBE		7 Ian TAYLOR	
6 David WETHERALL		9 Savo MILOSEVIC ❑	
9 Ian RUSH		10 Dwight YORKE	
11 Lee BOWYER ❑		14 Alan WRIGHT	
17 Derek LILLEY		15 Fernando NELSON	
18 Gunnar HALLE		16 Ugo EHIOGU	
25 Pierre LAURENT †		26 Sasa CURCIC	
Substitutes		*Substitutes*	
7 Lee SHARPE		12 Julian JOACHIM	
8 Rod WALLACE †62		13 Michael OAKES (Gk)	
15 Mark BEENEY (Gk)		19 Gareth FARRELLY †45	
20 Ian HARTE		24 Scott MURRAY	
30 Robert MOLENAAR		27 David HUGHES	

BEFORE		P	W	D	L	F	A	pts	AFTER		P	W	D	L	F	A	pts
5	Villa	35	16	9	10	44	31	57	5	Villa	36	16	10	10	44	31	58
10	Leeds	35	11	10	14	27	37	43	9	Leeds	36	11	11	14	27	37	44

FACTFILE

Mark Draper out with hamstring injury... Goals shortage again undermines Villa progress... Seven points dropped out of the last nine... Defeat for Wednesday at Blackburn keeps Villa's nose in front... Brian Little is keeping an eye on Jon Dahl Thomasson, a 20-year-old Danish international attacking midfield player.

Chances wasted as points drift

The last lap of the race for the final available place of four in the UEFA Cup is now in it's crucial final stage with Villa and David Pleat's Sheffield Wednesday side competing for fifth position in the Premiership.

Ground was lost last Saturday when the Owls closed the gap by two points, in addition to their having a match in hand.

Tonight, as Villa look for three points at Elland Road and a treble over Leeds this season, Wednesday play Blackburn Rovers, who need points to keep away from relegation danger, at Ewood Park.

Brian Little restores Mark Bosnich in goal, to hopefully close a controversial chapter, while Sasa Curcic continues in place of the injured Mark Draper.

On paper, Leeds' threat looks minimal, George Graham's side having scored only 27 goals in 35 Premiership fixtures, and this proves to be the case as Villa dominate the attacking pattern throughout the game.

As a highly-frustrating and one-sided contest unfolds, Bosnich's return proves to be mostly as a mere spectator observing his side's failure to score the one goal they need at the other end, despite a hat-full of goal opportunities.

Travelling supporters find it to be largely a re-run of last Saturday's first half against Spurs when Villa dictated the majority of the play but could not finish it all off.

Among several chances of varying quality the nearest Villa approach to the break-through they need is when a seemingly in-offensive hook by Savo Milosevic forces Nigel Martyn to scramble hastily across his line to clear at the expense of a corner.

Andy Townsend and Ugo Ehiogu both shoot straight at the Leeds goalkeeper and when David Wetherall's mis-hit back-pass leaves the home goal exposed, Milosevic and Dwight Yorke get in each other's way.

The second-half is mainly a reflection of the first. Steve Staunton's 20-yard free-kick curls too high and when Milosevic meets Alan Wright's centre from the left his shot skids to safety off Wetherall.

Ehiogu shoots wide when reasonably placed and substitute Gareth Farrelly, on for the injured Andy Townsend, joins the fray with a low drive which Martyn collects safely.

The England-squad keeper then confirms his growing reputation by tipping away a well-struck angled drive by Milosevic after Yorke had skilfully played the Serb in on goal with a deft back-heel pass.

Having failed for the second successive match to finish off a game which they had virtually monopolised, Villa find themselves under a flurry of Leeds pressure late on.

A point away from home would have produced greater satisfaction had Villa taken the full allocation from Spurs last Saturday, as the manager readily concedes.

"We should have won," said Brian Little, echoing the feelings of all but the most partisan home supporters. "We regard this as two points lost. Now we are focussing on winning our last two games which would mean Sheffield Wednesday having to win three."

Fernando Nelson

Saturday 3rd May 1997 • Riverside Stadium • 3.00pm

MIDDLESBROUGH 3 ASTON VILLA 2

Half-time 2-0 • Attendance 30,074

Referee Paul ALCOCK (Redhill)

Referee's Assistants D.S. BABSKI and I. BLANCHARD

Red Shirts, White Shorts		Goals
25	Ben ROBERTS	
5	Nigel PEARSON	
6	EMERSON	
8	Robbie MUSTOE	
9	Mikkel BECK †	33
10	JUNINHO ❑	
11	Fabrizio RAVANELLI	20,90pen
14	Curtis FLEMING ❑	
17	Clayton BLACKMORE	
18	Gianluca FESTA	
21	Craig HIGNETT	
	Substitutes	
2	Neil COX	
3.	Derek WHYTE	
4	Steve VICKERS	
20	Philip STAMP †67	
24	Chris FREESTONE	

White Shirts, Claret Shorts		Goals
1	Mark BOSNICH ‡	
3	Steve STAUNTON ❑ ■80	
4	Gareth SOUTHGATE	
6	Andy TOWNSEND ❑	
7	Ian TAYLOR ❑	
9	Savo MILOSEVIC #	75
10	Dwight YORKE	
14	Alan WRIGHT	
15	Fernando NELSON	
16	Ugo EHIOGU	58
26	Sasa CURCIC †	
	Substitutes	
12	Julian JOACHIM †57	
13	Michael OAKES (Gk) ‡75	
19	Gareth FARRELLY #85	
20	Riccardo SCIMECA	
27	David HUGHES	

BEFORE		P	W	D	L	F	A	pts
5	Villa	36	16	10	10	44	31	58
19	Boro	34	9	9	16	44	54	33

AFTER		P	W	D	L	F	A	pts
5	Villa	37	16	10	11	46	34	58
19	Boro	35	10	9	16	47	56	36

FACTFILE

Sheffield Wednesday defeat keeps Villa on UEFA Cup course... FA Cup finalists Chelsea also in contention... Ten points dropped out of last 12 undermines Villa's Euro-bid... Ravanelli spoken to by the referee at half-time... Reports of post-match scuffles in the tunnel following dubious penalty decision.

Fight-back foiled at the Riverside

The disruptive, stop-start season has produced another sizeable gap between fixtures, for internationals, prior to the final, fateful, deciding matches of the campaign.

Establishing continuity of performance has been difficult from the outset and the draws with Spurs and Leeds now seem light years in the past.

Those who have been forecasting all through that the issues would go 'right to the wire' are being proved correct with several clubs locked in the last-ditch scramble for survival points.

Figures of up to £10m are constantly quoted as being the cost of relegation and the graphic reason that the endangered clubs battle more ferociously than ever for points.

Middlesbrough, where Brian Little once served as a coach, are one of the clubs most severely threatened, thus leaving no doubt that European points will not be easily surrendered.

Although the atmosphere at the Riverside Stadium is intimidating, it is Villa who force the pace in search of a morale-lifting lead. What they distinctly do NOT need is uncertainty in defence, but this, sadly, proves to be their lot as Ravanelli and Beck post a two-goal lead in the opening 34 minutes.

In each case Mark Bosnich appears to be below his usual high standard and when he is replaced by Michael Oakes in the second-half, his recurring knee problem is believed to be the cause of his uncertainty.

Middlesbrough's opener arrives when Craig Hignett's delivery finds Ravanelli and the Italian's goal is helped by the fact that Bosnich seems to have committed himself too far too soon, leaving crucial space to be exploited and the striker with an open goal. For Boro it is a case of one chance, one goal.

Their second goal features similar defensive disorder as Curtis Fleming's pass beats Steve Staunton for Mikkel Beck to go around the again-stranded Bosnich.

By half-time Villa players and fans are feeling that they are getting the worst of referee Paul Alcock's debatable decision-making, including a penalty appeal turned down.

From the start of the second half Villa seize the attacking initiative even more firmly than before and are rewarded by two goals to level the scoreline. Firstly, a long throw by Nelson is knocked down by Savo Milosevic for Ugo Ehiogu to steer in his fourth goal of the season with a shot into the roof of the net from close range.

Then, a poor pass by Ravanelli enables Andy Townsend to get possession and flight a perfect through ball for the £3.5m Serbian striker to advance on goal, cool as you like, and place the equaliser wide of the keeper.

Now a victory is well on the cards, but an angry, disjointed finish with defensive shape again discarded frustratingly hands the points to Bryan Robson's side.

Villa distinctly lose their cool when the referee ignores a blatant hack by Juninho on Alan Wright. In the scene that follows Juninho, Townsend and Staunton are booked. The fracas should end there, but Staunton foolishly continues the verbal exchange and out comes the red card.

Seeing the oppositon reduced to ten men gives Boro a vital lift, helped by a hotly-debated injury-time penalty award when late substitute Gareth Farrelly is judged by referee Danson to have pulled back Craig Hignett.

Catching the unexpected lifeline in a safe pair of hands, Ravanelli beats Oakes to send Villa home pointless. Many blame the referee for Villa's downfall though, in public at least, not Brian Little.

He can recognise self-inflicted wounds when he sees them.

Sunday 11th May 1997 • Villa Park • 4.00pm

ASTON VILLA 1 SOUTHAMPTON 0

Half-time 1-0 • *Attendance* 39,339

Referee Gary WILLARD (Worthing)

Referee's Assistants D.A. BOOTH and J.H. HOLBROOK

Claret and Blue Shirts, White Shorts	Goals		Yellow and Blue Striped Shirts, Blue Shorts	Goals
1 Mark BOSNICH			33 Maik TAYLOR	
3 Steve STAUNTON			2 Jason DODD	
4 Gareth SOUTHGATE			3 Francis BENALI	
6 Andy TOWNSEND			4 Jim MAGILTON	
7 Ian TAYLOR			8 Mike EVANS	
9 Savo MILOSEVIC			18 Matthew OAKLEY	
10 Dwight YORKE			19 Richard DRYDEN	11og
14 Alan WRIGHT			20 Robbie SLATER	
15 Fernando NELSON			22 Claus LUNDEKVAM	
16 Ugo EHIOGU			30 Egil ØSTENSTAD †	
20 Riccardo SCIMECA			32 Ulrich VAN GOBBEL	
Substitutes			*Substitutes*	
8 Mark DRAPER			1 Dave BEASANT (Gk)	
12 Julian JOACHIM			7 Matthew LE TISSIER †71	
13 Michael OAKES (Gk)			10 Neil MADDISON	
19 Gareth FARRELLY			15 Alan NEILSON	
26 Sasa CURCIC			29 Eyal BERKOVIC	

BEFORE		P	W	D	L	F	A	pts
5	Villa	37	16	10	11	46	34	58
16	Saints	37	10	11	16	50	55	41

AFTER		P	W	D	L	F	A	pts
5	Villa	38	17	10	11	47	34	61
16	Saints	38	10	11	17	50	56	41

FACTFILE

First win in five games earns top-five finish... Riccardo Scimeca back in defence after missing six games through injury... Steve Staunton moves into midfield... "You need a big book of excuses if you miss Europe", Brian Little concedes... Summer comings and goings on the cards.

One own goal hits Villa target

All of the remaining Premiership fixtures have been switched to Sunday to avoid any clubs gaining advantage from knowing precisely the result required.

The Villa Park visitors are one of four clubs who are attempting to avoid relegation with Nottingham Forest, while Villa are seeking the fifth Premiership place that would earn a return to the UEFA Cup.

Both clubs actually need just one point to achieve their respective objectives and, with a large following from the South Coast, yet another full house is recorded.

Brian Little could be excused for having mixed feelings about the most appropriate game plan. On the one hand the principle of seeing the season out in a blaze of goals must be tempting; on the other, the risk of giving goals away has to be avoided at all costs.

To lose that European return when only one home point is required to secure it would end the season in the depths of gloom. Villa clearly have to play with sensible caution and the fact that Steve Staunton is in midfield, while Mark Draper and Sasa Curcic occupy places on the bench, suggests that no risks will be taken.

However, any fears Villa might have about failing to secure their safe passage into Europe virtually disappears after only 11 minutes when Richard Dryden scores an own goal.

A beautifully-flighted low centre from the excellent Nelson on the right creates momentary panic in front of the Southampton goal and, in attempting to cut it out, the former Birmingham City

Steve Staunton

defender merely deflects the ball past his own goalkeeper.

The welcome lead puts Villa in a position of strength, but possibly devalues the match as a spectacle, since the home team now have merely to avoid any mistakes for another 79 minutes to see the season out satisfactorily.

Far more onus is placed on Southampton who could find themselves losing their Premiership place if Sunderland, Middlesbrough and Coventry were all to win their away games.

A complication has been introduced to the scenario by Coventry's game at White Hart Lane having kicked off fifteeen minutes behind the others due to traffic congestion in the North London area.

Graeme Souness has demonstrated his own initial mood of safety-first by leaving Matt Le Tissier on the bench and, once a goal down, Saints try all they know to get back onto level terms.

In the second-half Mark Bosnich defends the favourable scoreline with two magnificent saves, one from a deflected free-kick by Le Tissier, now on as a substitute, the other from Robbie Slater.

In the 89th minute Le Tissier manages to get the ball into the net but is adjudged to have fouled Bosnich and by now Villa's objective has been achieved with a couple of points to spare. The final whistle does not instantly relieve Southampton's tension, however, until the news comes through that both Sunderland and Middlesbrough have lost and are down.

This news prompts an even more joyful end-of-season celebration for the Saints fans than for Villa's who, nevertheless, happily applaud their team on a pre-arranged lap of the pitch. It had been a difficult and changeable nine months, but there was an eventual reward for resilience.

Monday 29th July 1996 • Bescot Stadium • 7.45pm

WALSALL 0 ASTON VILLA 2

Half-time 0-1 • Attendance 7,080

Referee Terry HOLBROOK (Walsall)
Referee's Assistants S. CASTLE and M. COOPER

Red Shirts, Black Shorts		Goals	Navy Blue Shirts, Light Blue Shorts		Goals
1	Jimmy WALKER		1	Michael OAKES	
2	Wayne EVANS		2	Ian TAYLOR	34
3	Ray DANIEL		3	Alan WRIGHT #	
4	Adrian VIVEASH		4	Ugo EHIOGU ‡‡	
5	Franc BERGER †		5	Paul McGRATH ‡	
6	Derek MOUNTFIELD		6	Gareth SOUTHGATE	
7	Fabio NIGRA ‡		7	Steve STAUNTON	
8	Darren BRADLEY		8	Mark DRAPER †	
9	Kyle LIGHTBOURNE #		9	Tommy JOHNSON ††	
10	Kevin WILSON		10	Dwight YORKE ##	60
11	Andreas SCHOLL §		11	Andy TOWNSEND §	

	Substitutes			*Substitutes*	
12	Chris MARSH †70		12	Carl TILER ‡45	
14	George LAWRENCE ‡70		14	Julian JOACHIM #45	
15	Rod McDONALD #70		15	Riccardo SCIMECA ‡‡78	
16	Charlie NTAMARK §78		17	Gareth FARRELLY ††72	
			18	Lee HENDRIE §62	
			19	Scott MURRAY †25	
			20	Franz CARR ##82	

FACTFILE

Fernando Nelson is forced to delay his debut in Villa colours as a persistent thigh strain keeps him out of action... Mark Bosnich and Savo Milosevic are also out of action due to injury... Former Villa team-mates, Brian Little and Chris Nicholl face each other as managers for the first time... Villa use all seven substitutes in an attempt to give run-outs to as many of the squad as possible.

Taylor and Yorke set up victory

This was as hard and competitive a match as Brian Little could have asked for as he starts his build-up to the new season.

Walsall introduced four trialists into their squad, Germans Franz Berger and Andreas Scholl, together with Argentinian midfielder Fabio Nigra who has been playing in Italy and has had a spell with Lazio. On the bench was ex-Southampton striker George Lawrence, who has been playing in Malta.

Villa picked a strong squad, but were without the services of Fernando Nelson, Mark Bosnich and Savo Milosevic through injury.

Walsall started the match strongly, with both Germans prominent. In the third minute Berger hit a strong left-foot shot just wide of the post when well placed and a minute later, Nigra shot over the bar, also from a good position.

But it was not long before the Villa players started to get into their stride and soon had the Saddlers back peddling and from here on in they were forced to defend for long periods.

Villa's first clear-cut chance came when Jimmy Walker made a good save from a shot by Mark Draper, having to dive low to divert what seemed a certain goal. Shortly after it was Ugo Ehiogu's turn to get in on the act when he sent in a vicious shot from over 30 yards which Walker did well to tip over the bar.

Paul McGrath was then unlucky to see a header narrowly skim the bar and Dwight Yorke almost scored with a header following a left wing cross from Steve Staunton.

The inevitable goal finally arrived in the 34th minute following a fine move, in which Yorke, collecting the ball wide out on the left, laid it back for Staunton to deliver an accurate cross beyond the far post for the incoming Scott Murray to head back across the face of goal and

Ian Taylor had the simple task of placing a close-range header past the helpless keeper.

The earlier enforced substitution of Draper through injury and the other changes made at half-time did nothing to upset Villa's progress and they carried on in the second half as they had done in the first.

Some patient approach work from Villa led to an early chance for Tommy Johnson, who forced a save from Walker, diving low to scramble the ball to safety.

Skipper Andy Townsend was unlucky to see his left-foot shot hit the outside of a post, firing in from an acute angle, before, on the hour, Yorke settled matters with Villa's second goal.

It was Julian Joachim who set up the goal with a 50-yard run along the right-hand touchline, followed by a low cross into the path of Yorke who calmly tucked away a left-foot shot.

Walsall had never let their heads drop and came back strongly in the final stages as Villa took their foot off the pedal.

George Lawrence and Rod McDonald put efforts wide of the target before Lawrence forced a save out of Michael Oakes.

Paul McGrath

Wednesday 31st July 1996 • Sincil Bank • 7.30pm

LINCOLN CITY 0 ASTON VILLA 1

Half-time 0-0 • Attendance 3,377

Referee Peter JONES (Loughborough)

Referee's Assistants J. WASSON and D. STEANS

Red and White Striped Shirts, Black Shorts	Goals	Navy Blue Shirts, Light Blue Shorts	Goals
1 Barry RICHARDSON		1 Michael OAKES	
2 Jason BARNETT		2 Scott MURRAY	
3 Terry FLEMING †		3 Steve STAUNTON #	
4 Mark TODD ‡		4 Ugo EHIOGU	
5 Steve HOLMES #		5 Paul McGRATH ‡	
6 Kevin AUSTIN		6 Carl TILER §	
7 Gareth AINSWORTH		7 Ian TAYLOR	
8 Mark HONE ††		8 Lee HENDRIE ††	
9 Gijsbert BOS §		9 Julian JOACHIM †	
10 Stephen BROWN ‡‡		10 Dwight YORKE ##	
11 Worrell STERLING		11 Tommy JOHNSON ‡‡	

Substitutes		*Substitutes*	
12 Jonathan WHITNEY †45		12 Riccardo SCIMECA ‡45	
13 John DENNIS ‡45		13 Adam RACHEL (Gk)	
14 John ROBERTSON #45		14 Alan WRIGHT #45	
15 Gerald DOBBS ††73		15 Gareth SOUTHGATE §45	
16 Carl LAWRENCE §64		16 Gareth FARRELLY ††45	82
17 Udo ONWERE ‡‡73		17 Phil KING ‡‡75	
		18 Franz CARR †43	
		19 Neil DAVIS ##75	

Mark Draper, Savo Milosevic, Fernando Nelson and Mark Bosnich are all suffering from minor injuries and so are not to be risked at Sincil Bank... Nelson's debut delayed again... 18-year-old Lee Hendrie gets a place in the starting line-up... Only reserve keeper Adam Rachel does not get a game.

Farrelly volleys super winner

Monday's workout at Bescot was followed up at Sincil Bank by yet another hard-fought encounter against a well-organised and capable opposition.

John Beck has a reputation for turning out sides which are difficult to beat and his Lincoln City outfit proved no exception to the rule.

Villa dominated the possession from the start and as early as the seventh minute Dwight Yorke finished off a good passing move by putting Julian Joachim through on the keeper, only for Barry Richardson to stop the resulting shot with his legs.

Villa's next chance was not long coming, this time from a Steve Staunton corner, Carl Tiler

Matchwinner – Gareth Farrelly

getting the initial header and Ugo Ehiogu, in an attempt to divert the ball into the back of the net, succeeding only in angling his effort wide.

Villa continued to have the lion's share of the possession and Joachim nearly capitalised when he tested Richardson again from 22 yards.

As the first-half wore on the Imps' keeper continued to be the busiest player on the pitch, having to save, in quick succession, rasping shots from the edge of the box from both Staunton and Lee Hendrie.

Just before the half-time break Villa suffered another injury set-back when Joachim, who had not long before clipped the post with a glancing header, trod on the ball and had to limp off to be replaced by Franz Carr.

In spite of several changes of personnel by both sides at half-time, the pattern of the game did not change in the second half. Villa having all the possession and Lincoln putting up solid resistance; putting their extra height and physical presence to good use.

Twenty minutes into the half Gareth Farrelly almost gave the visitors the lead with a fine effort which Richardson was pleased to see go narrowly wide of the target.

Shortly afterwards Yorke, given a clear chance to score, managed only to blast his shot well wide of the target.

The deadlock was finally broken in the 82nd minute when Farrelly, who recently won his first full cap for the Republic of Ireland against Portugal, scored a goal of exceptional quality.

A left wing cross from Alan Wright reached defender Jonathan Whitney, who could only direct his attempted clearance as far as Farrelly, who was waiting beyond the far post.

It was an extremely acute angle, but Farrelly waited for the ball to come down before hitting a scorching volley back into the goal and past the astonished Imps keeper.

This was a good workout for Villa and with the exception of Joachim's unfortunate injury, proved to be a useful exercise.

Saturday 3rd August 1996 • Racecourse Ground • 3.00pm

WREXHAM 2 ASTON VILLA 2

Half-time 0-1 • *Attendance 3,501*

Referee Terry LUNT (Ashton-in-Makerfield)

Referee's Assistants M. JONES and M. DEAN

Red Shirts, White Shorts		Goals	Navy Blue Shirts, Light Blue Shorts		Goals
1	Andy MARRIOTT		1	Michael OAKES	
2	Mark McGREGOR		2	Ian TAYLOR	
3	Phil HARDY		3	Alan WRIGHT	
4	Gareth OWEN		4	Ugo EHIOGU	
5	Brian CAREY	56	5	Paul McGRATH	
6	Barry JONES		6	Gareth SOUTHGATE	
7	Martyn CHALK		7	Steve STAUNTON	
8	Kevin RUSSELL		8	Mark DRAPER	
9	Karl CONNOLLY		9	Tommy JOHNSON	39
10	Steve WATKIN		10	Dwight YORKE	66
11	Bryan HUGHES	74	11	Andy TOWNSEND	
	Substitutes			*Substitutes*	
12	Deryn BRACE		12	Scott MURRAY	
13	Mark CARTWRIGHT (Gk)		13	Stuart BROCK (Gk)	
14	Jason SOLOMON		14	Lee HENDRIE	
15	Wayne PHILLIPS		15	Gareth FARRELLY	
16	Dave BRAMMER		16	Franz CARR	
			17	Richard WALKER	
			18	Darren BYFIELD	
			19	Ben PETTY	
			20	David HUGHES	

FACTFILE

Andy Townsend and Mark Draper return after slight injuries... Fernando Nelson, Savo Milosevic and Mark Bosnich still sidelined, although all are progressing well and Carl Tiler and Phil King have now joined the injury list with knee and thigh problems respectively.

Neither side made any substitutions during the game.

Battling Robins earn a draw

Villa went into this game at the Racecourse ground looking for their third consecutive warm-up win. But it was not to be as Wrexham gave Villa their most stringent test yet and came from behind twice to force a draw.

Villa were first into their stride and opened brightly, forcing the Robins back onto the defensive.

As early as the fifth minute Villa earned a corner and Steve Staunton's inswinging cross was desperately pushed out from under the bar by keeper Andy Marriott. A minute later, from a flick-on by Paul McGrath, Ugo Ehiogu saw his effort cleared off the line after beating Marriott to the ball.

The visitors' early domination was broken in the 20th minute when only a timely last-ditch tackle by the immaculate McGrath prevented Karl Connolly from scoring.

And six minutes later Michael Oakes was called into action when he took the ball off the head of Martyn Chalk following a teasing left-wing cross from Martin Russell.

But after this brief spell of pressure from the home side Villa went back onto the offensive for Johnson to test Marriott with a smart header which the keeper kept out in style and from the ensuing corner Andy Townsend hit the outside of the post from 20 yards.

Johnson was not to be outdone, however, and in the 39th minute he put Villa into the lead. From a partially cleared corner Ugo Ehiogu laid the ball off to Alan Wright who got in a powerful shot which was blocked and Johnson gratefully rammed home the rebound.

Villa started the second half in attacking mode with Dwight Yorke leaving three Reds defenders stranded before forcing another good save from the keeper.

Ian Taylor then hit a shot narrowly over the bar after being set up by Yorke; before Wrexham put themselves back into the game with an equaliser from Brian Carey when he headed home from a corner.

However, Wrexham's joy was short-lived as ten minutes later, in the 66th minute, Yorke restored Villa's lead when Taylor put in a cross from the right which the keeper could only palm out to Draper on the edge of the box and his ball back into the danger area was headed in by the striker, stooping to score.

This goal served to inspire the Robins and they put Villa under pressure for a lengthy spell before they deservedly equalised again the the 74th minute.

Mark McGregor put over a tantalising cross from the right and Bryan Hughes glanced a header over Oakes and into the net.

Four minutes from time the Villa keeper was brought into action again when he blocked a long-range shot from Steve Watkin.

Michael Oakes

Tuesday 6th August 1996 • Boundary Park • 7.45pm

OLDHAM ATHLETIC 0 ASTON VILLA 3

Half-time 0-1 • Attendance 2,237

Referee Scott MATHEWSON (Stockport)
Referee's Assistants E. EVANS and P. GRANGE

Green and Navy Blue Shirts, Navy Blue Shorts		Goals
1	Jon HALLWORTH	
2	Gunnar HALLE	
3	Carl SERRANT	
4	Nick HENRY #	
5	Craig FLEMING	
6	Steve REDMOND	
7	Paul RICKERS	
8	Richard GRAHAM	63og
9	Sean McCARTHY	
10	Lee RICHARDSON †	
11	Martin PEMBERTON ‡	

Substitutes

12	Scott McNIVEN #81	
13	Nicky BANGER	
14	Toddy ORLYGGSON †45	
15	David BERESFORD	
16	Stuart BARLOW ‡45	

Claret and Blue Shirts, White Shorts		Goals
1	Michael OAKES	
2	Scott MURRAY	
3	Alan WRIGHT	
4	Gareth SOUTHGATE ‡	
5	Ugo EHIOGU	
6	Steve STAUNTON †	
7	Ian TAYLOR	
8	Mark DRAPER #	
9	Franz CARR ††	
10	Dwight YORKE ‡‡	40,59
11	Gareth FARRELLY §	

Substitutes

12	Carl TILER †45	
13	Adam RACHEL (Gk) ##83	
14	Paul McGRATH ‡45	
15	Andy TOWNSEND #45	
16	Lee HENDRIE §45	
17	Tommy JOHNSON ††45	
18	Lee BURCHELL ‡‡77 ##	

FACTFILE

Villa's last full scale pre-season warm-up game is to mark the retirement from the game of ex-Villa favourite, Ian Olney... England Under-21 international Olney is 26-years-old and came through the club's junior ranks before being sold to Oldham for £700,000 in July 1992 (a record fee for the Latics)... Bosnich, Savo and Nelson still unable to play, Tiler returns from a knee injury.

Dwight double clinches victory

Villa declared themselves more than happy to provide the opposition in Ian Olney's Testimonial game. Manager Brian Little stating: "When we were asked to go up I had little hesitation in agreeing to it. It slotted in with our pre-season schedule and I have every sympathy with Ian after what has happened, I should know after all."

Ian has not played since he received that dreaded knee injury in November 1993 at Upton Park. He did attempt a come-back last season, but it lasted only 40 minutes. Unfortunately, he is not fit enough to take part in tonight's game; but it is estimated he will benefit to the tune of around £15,000 on the night.

Five minutes into the match it was necessary for Oldham to change their strip, their normal colours of red and blue hoops clashing with Villa's claret and blue, so they changed to their second strip.

The game opened in much the same vein as the previous games, with Villa having the bulk of possession, but meeting stiff resistance from a determined Latics' rearguard.

The visitors were passing the ball around with calm assurance, but without really being able to break down a packed defence. The best effort of the early exchanges was a well struck left-footed shot from Gareth Farrelly which was just wide of the target.

Villa's dominance finally paid off five minutes from half-time when Franz Carr received possession, took the ball down the right and centred for Ian Taylor to head back across goal, where Dwight Yorke was on hand to score from close range.

The second half opened quietly, but with Villa still managing to retain most of the territorial advantage. The match was wrapped up in a four minute spell 14 minutes into the half when Yorke took full advantage of a mistake by Oldham centre-back, Richard Graham, who hit an attempted clearance straight at the Villa No. 10, who took the ball past Graham and scored with a left-foot shot past the advancing keeper, Jon Hallworth.

Two minutes later Yorke put Tommy Johnson through on goal and his powerful shot rebounded off an upright. Then, following a run to the by-line by Scott Murray, it was Graham again, who volleyed into his own net from six yards from the wing-back's cross.

Oldham then had their best spell of the game and with 15 minutes to go Sean McCarthy was unlucky to see his effort come back off a post.

This was a confident performance from the claret and blues and will put them in good heart for the first match of the season against Sheffield Wednesday next week.

Substitute Lee Burchell was injured in the 83rd minute of the game and as Villa had used all the other substitutes, reserve keeper Adam Rachel came on as an outfield player for the last seven minutes of the game.

Ian Olney

Tuesday 13th May 1997 • Spartan Stadium • 7.45pm

SAN JOSÉ CLASH 1 ASTON VILLA 1

Half-time 1-1 • *Attendance* 13,522

Referee Tim WEYLAND

Referee's Assistants Jorge REYES and Javier PADILLA

Green and Black Striped Shirts, White Shorts	Goals		Claret and Blue Shirts, White Shorts	Goals
1 Tom LINER		1	Mark BOSNICH	
2 Oscar DRAGUICEVICH		2	Gary CHARLES †	
5 Michael EMENALO		3	Alan WRIGHT	
7 Dominic KINNEAR		4	Riccardo SCIMECA	
9 Lawrence LOZZANO		5	Ugo EHIOGU	37
12 Troy DAYAK		6	David HUGHES	
13 Shawn MEDVED †	44	7	Ian TAYLOR ❏	
14 Daniel GUZMAN		8	Mark DRAPER ‡	
15 Istvan URBANYI		9	Julian JOACHIM	
17 Tim MARTIN		10	Dwight YORKE	
21 Eddie LEWIS		11	Scott MURRAY	
Substitutes			*Substitutes*	
4 Curt ONALFO		12	Darren BYFIELD ‡75	
6 Ben IROHA		13	Michael OAKES (Gk)	
8 Jeff BAICHER †72		14	Ben PETTY	
10 Christopher SULLIVAN		15	Neil DAVIS †64	
19 Tayt IANNI		16	Lee COLLINS	

FACTFILE

Villa, without most of their international players, forced the early pace in an entertaining game, but not surprisingly began to tire as the game went on, not having sufficient time to recover from their long journey. Villa went ahead when, following neat work by David Hughes and Dwight Yorke, Ugo Ehiogu blasted a shot in from six yards. As Villa eased off towards the end of the first-half, the Clash equalised from a rare attack when Shawn Medved scored with a header from near the penalty spot. Villa cruised through an evenly contested second-half. Gary Charles played for just over an hour and came through unscathed.

Wednesday 21st May 1997 • Pasadena Rose Bowl • 7.45pm

LOS ANGELES GALAXY 1 ASTON VILLA 1

Half-time 0-0 • Attendance 8,759

Referee Josh PATLACK

Referee's Assistants Roger ITAYA and Juan HERNANDEZ

White Shirts with Black Trim, Black Shorts	Goals	Claret and Blue Shirts, White Shorts	Goals
22 Kevin HARTMAN		1 Mark BOSNICH	
2 Danny PENA		2 Scott MURRAY	
4 Robin FRASIER †		3 Alan WRIGHT	
6 Dan CALICHMAN ‡		4 Ugo EHIOGU	
10 Mauricio CIENFUEGOS §		5 David HUGHES	
15 Steve JOLLEY		6 Riccardo SCIMECA	
16 Greg VANNEY		7 Ian TAYLOR	
17 Ante RAZOV ††		8 Mark DRAPER	
20 John JONES #		9 Julian JOACHIM †	
21 Paul CALIGUIRI		10 Dwight YORKE	
29 Eduardo HURTADO		11 Stan COLLYMORE	75

Substitutes		*Substitutes*	
1 David FRAMEI (Gk)		12 Gary CHARLES	
3 Mark SEMIOLI †45		13 Michael OAKES (Gk)	
5 Martin MACORO		14 Ben PETTY	
8 Brad WILSON		15 Darren BYFIELD †67	
11 Harut KAMPETY		16 Neil DAVIS	
12 Gulliermo JARA ‡45			
13 Cobi JONES #45			
14 Chris ARMAS §45			
16 Brian TAYLOR			
19 WELTON ††45	59		

Stan Collymore joined the Villa party last Thursday 15th May after his club record signing (£7m) on Tuesday 13th May.

FACTFILE

Stan Collymore marked his Villa debut with a headed goal in the 75th minute, courtesy of a Mark Draper cross. This cancelled out a goal by the Brazilian, Welton, who scored at the second attempt from six yards. "I'd hate to play Villa when they're serious", commented Galaxy coach, Lothar Osiander.

Tuesday 23rd July 1996 • The Bush • 7.30pm

PELSALL VILLA 1 ASTON VILLA 1

Attendance 450

Referee Mark COOPER (Walsall)

Referee's Assistants T. PARKES and D. KUZMANOVIC

Red and Black Shirts, Black Shorts	Goals	Claret and Blue Shirts, White Shorts	Goals
1 Neil JONES		1 Adam RACHEL	
2 Hardip SINGH		2 Jonathan MILEY	
3 Neil COLES		3 Ben PETTY	
4 Chris HODGES		4 Lee COLLINS	
5 Adrian HORNE		5 Carl TILER	
6 Mike MASON		6 David HUGHES	
7 Paul NEWMAN ‡		7 Lee BURCHELL	
8 Steve LYONS		8 Leslie HINES †	
9 Matt CARTWRIGHT		9 Darren BYFIELD §	46
10 Mazhar IQBAL #		10 Richard WALKER ‡	
11 Bryen HUMPHREYS †		11 Tommy JASZCZUN #	
Substitutes		*Substitutes*	
12 Stuart EDWARDS †45		12 Brendan BAKER ‡61	
13 Steve BEECH		13 Stuart BROCK (Gk)	
14 M. MOSELEY		15 Lee HENDRIE †47	
15 Rob ASHFIELD ‡45		16 Scott MURRAY #70	
16 Neil HOLMES		17 Neil DAVIS §70	
17 Dave STEPHENS #45			

Pelsall Villa's goal details not recorded.

FACTFILE

For the second year running Villa sent a team to The Bush to play Pelsall, but unlike last year, when they ran out 7-2 winners, this match was much more evenly contested and ended all-square. Pelsall put up a fine performance to hold Villa and although having most of the play, Villa had only a goal from Darren Byfield to show for their efforts. But Pelsall deserved their share of the honours.

Saturday 27th July 1996 • Stonebridge Road • 3.00pm

GRAVESEND & NORTHFLEET 1 ASTON VILLA 2

Half-time 0-0 • *Attendance* 1,041

Referee Ray ELLINGHAM

Referee's Assistants G. HEARE and D. CANNON

Red Shirts, White Shorts		Goals	Navy Blue Shirts, Light Blue Shorts		Goals
1	Lee TURNER		1	Stuart BROCK	
2	Mark LEAHY		2	Ben PETTY ‡	
3	Paul LAMB †		3	Nelson CAMERO †	
4	Matt GUBBINS		4	Lee COLLINS	
5	Peter MORTLEY		5	Riccardo SCIMECA	
6	Jimmy JACKSON	80	6	Carl TILER	
7	Ian GIBBS		7	Gareth FARRELLY	
8	Dave ARTER		8	Neil DAVIS	60pen
9	Colin BLEWDEN		9	Lee BURCHELL #	
10	Clint GOODING		10	Franz CARR	
11	Richard NEWBERY ‡		11	Lee HENDRIE	
	Substitutes			*Substitutes*	
12	Lee SPILLER †16		12	Jonathan MILEY ‡67	
14	Darren BALLPITT ‡75		13	Matthew GEORGE	
15	Graham WELLS		14	Leslie HINES #84	
16	Tristan HODGES		15	Tommy JASZCZUN †53	63
			16	Brendan BAKER	

Villa sent a reserve strength side to Stonebridge Road to further cement the relationship set up between the clubs during Gravesend & Northfleet's visit to Villa Park in the third round of the FA Cup last season... Nelson Camero, a trialist from South Africa, played at left-wing-back and Carl Tiler came safely through another 90 minutes in his fight for full fitness after his injury problems... Villa won a close fought encounter, goals from Neil Davis (penalty) and Tommy Jaszczun giving Villa a two goal cushion before the Fleet pulled one back ten minutes from time through Jimmy Jackson.

FACTFILE

Thursday 1st August 1996 • The Lamb • 3.00pm

TAMWORTH 0 ASTON VILLA 3

Half-time 0-1 • Attendance 1,482

Referee B. MILLERSHIP

Referee's Assistants R. ORCHARD and N. PETRICCA

Red Shirts, Red Shorts	Goals	Navy Blue Shirts, Light Blue Shorts	Goals
1 Mark PHILLIPS		1 Adam RACHEL	
2 Brendan BEDERY		2 Ben PETTY §	
3 Mick SHAW		3 Tommy JASZCZUN	
4 Chris KEOGH		4 Lee COLLINS	53
5 Jon HOWARD		5 Riccardo SCIMECA #	
6 Paul BROGAN		6 Carl TILER †	
7 David FOY †		7 Gareth FARRELLY ††	54
8 Ian BROWN ‡		8 Neil DAVIS ‡	
9 Lee WILSON		9 Lee BURCHELL	8
10 Mark WHITEHOUSE #		10 Darren BYFIELD ‡‡	
11 Gary SMITH		11 Lee HENDRIE	

Substitutes		*Substitutes*	
12 Dennis MULHOLLAND		12 Jonathan MILEY #70	
14 Ian BENNETT †45		13 Stuart BROCK (Gk)	
15 Michael WILLIAMS ‡45		14 Leslie HINES §70	
16 Adrian BADDAMS #45		15 Richard WALKER ‡21	
		16 Alan LEE ‡‡83	
		17 Alan KIRBY ††82	
		18 David HUGHES †13	

FACTFILE

Unlucky Carl Tiler has to leave the field after suffering a jarred knee... Lee Hendrie is in the side to face Tamworth, who are managed by his father, Paul Hendrie... Lee Burchell gave Villa the lead direct from a free-kick... In the second half Lee Collins increased the lead and within a minute a 20-yard drive from Gareth Farrelly had completed the scoring.

Wednesday 7th August 1996 • Keys Park • 7.30pm

HEDNESFORD TOWN 0 ASTON VILLA 0

Half-time 0-0 • Attendance 1,075

Referee A.G. WILEY (Burntwood)

Referee's Assistants N. HANCOX and A.M. GARRATT

White Shirts, Black Shorts	Goals	Claret and Blue Shirts, White Shorts	Goals
1 Scott COOKSEY		1 Stuart BROCK	
2 Paul CARTY		2 Ben PETTY	
3 Keith RUSSELL		3 Tommy JASZCZUN	
4 Wayne SIMPSON		4 Lee COLLINS	
5 Steve ESSEX		5 David HUGHES	
6 Andy COMYN		6 Carl TILER	
7 Bernard McNALLY		7 Gareth FARRELLY §	
8 Colin LAMBERT		8 Franz CARR †	
9 Steve TAYLOR		9 Riccardo SCIMECA #	
10 Gary FITZPATRICK		10 Darren BYFIELD ††	
11 Joe O'CONNOR		11 Lee HENDRIE ‡	
		Substitutes	
12 John COTTERILL		12 Richard WALKER †60	
13 Richard DANDY		13 Phillip ELIAS (Gk)	
14 Kevin COLLINS		14 Leslie HINES ‡65	
15 Leighton DERRY		15 Alan LEE §82	
16 Tyron STREET		16 Richard BURGESS ††82	
17 Gavin PICK		17 Alan KIRBY #78	
18 Luke YATES			
19 Steve PALMER			
20 Gavin BRANT			

FACTFILE

A strong Villa side including Carl Tiler, Franz Carr, Riccardo Scimeca, Gareth Farrelly and Lee Hendrie were held to a draw by a determined Pitmen side who put up a determined defensive display to keep dominant Villa at bay.

Monday 12th August 1996 • The Oval • 7.30pm

BEDWORTH UNITED 1 ASTON VILLA 3

Half-time 1-3

Referee Keren BARRATT (Coventry)

Referee's Assistants K. RYE and S. ALLARDYCE

Green and White Striped Shirts, White Shorts		Goals	Navy Blue Shirts, Light Blue Shorts		Goals
1	Wayne STARKEY		1	Stuart BROCK	
2	Matt WILEMAN ‡		2	Ben PETTY	39
3	Sean McGRORY		3	Tommy JASZCZUN ††	
4	Peter WILKINS †		4	Lee COLLINS	
5	Simon WILLIAMS		5	David HUGHES	
6	Andy PENNY		6	Carl TILER †	
7	Tom DALY	2	7	Gareth FARRELLY	
8	Morton TITTERTON		8	Darren BYFIELD §	
9	John SYMONDS		9	Riccardo SCIMECA	
10	Rob BEARD		10	Franz CARR #	14
11	Mark SMITH		11	Lee HENDRIE ‡	1

Substitutes			*Substitutes*		
12	Tony CLARKE ‡79		12	Richard WALKER #70	
14	Alan MALLABUNE †75		14	Alan KIRBY †45	
15	Alan RICHARDS		15	Leslie HINES ‡65	
			16	Richard BURGESS §87	
			17	Alan LEE ††87	

Stuart Brock

> **FACTFILE**
>
> *Carl Tiler continues his rehabilitation programme after a long lay-off... Two goals in the first two minutes get the game off to a flying start... Villa are two goals up by the break and an evenly contested second-half remains goalless.*

Wednesday 14th August 1996 • Belvoir Drive • 7.30pm

LEICESTER Y.M.C.A. 1 ASTON VILLA 7

Half-time 1-4

Referee Not Recorded

Referee's Assistants Not Recorded

Red and Black Halved Shirts, Black Shorts	Goals	Claret and Blue Shirts, White Shorts	Goals
1 David GRAHAM		1 Matthew GEORGE	
2 Scott BROWN		2 Bradley BLACKBURN	
3 Scott CHARLES		3 Leslie HINES	78pen
4 Andy POTTER		4 Lee COLLINS	79
5 Mark KING		5 Ben PETTY	
6 Mark WOOD		6 David HUGHES	42og
7 Chris HUGHES		7 Alan KIRBY	
8 Gareth KING		8 Darren BYFIELD ‡	40
9 Matt WILSON		9 Richard WALKER	22
10 Sean MURTHA		10 Michael BLACKWOOD †	6,36
11 Steve JACKSON		11 Tommy JASZCZUN	
Substitutes		*Substitutes*	
12 Lee COX		12 Richard BURGESS †45	
14 Andy HOOPER		14 Alan LEE ‡70	82
15 Alex WHITTAKER			
16 Scott SMITH			
17 Jason RILEY			
18 Scott ROBINSON			

Richard Walker

A young Villa side cruised to a comfortable win over Leicester Y.M.C.A., the result was never in doubt after the visitors went into a sixth minute lead... Three goals to the good at half-time, Villa cruised through the second half and scored another three goals without reply, Leicester's only score being an own goal by David Hughes.

Tuesday 12th November 1996 • Ostlers Lane • 7.00pm

STONY STRATFORD TOWN 0 ASTON VILLA 6

Half-time 0-4 • *Attendance* 475

Referee Ron JAMES (Bletchley)

Referee's Assistants T. JEYES and C. CHERRY

White Shirts, Navy Blue Shorts	Goals	Claret and Blue Shirts, White Shorts	Goals
1 Adam PEACH †		1 Adam RACHEL	
2 Andy WARD		2 Jonathan MILEY	
3 Mick LEMON		3 Leslie HINES	1 goal
4 Peter MILLER		4 Lee COLLINS	
5 John TREW		5 Ben PETTY	
6 Paul BEVIS		6 David HUGHES	
7 Lee BROUGHTON		7 Lee HENDRIE	
8 Keith GOODRIDGE		8 Lee BURCHELL	
9 Lee CAMPBELL		9 Richard WALKER	1 goal
10 Nigel BURDETT		10 Darren BYFIELD	2 goals
11 Carl DEAN		11 Alan KIRBY	1 goal

Substitutes		*Substitutes*	
12 Ian SWANSTON ††		12 Scott MURRAY	
13 Darren BENDALL §		13 Stuart BROCK (Gk)	1 goal
14 Ian STARBROOK #			
15 Matty HERBERT ‡‡			
16 Paul LOVELAND ‡			
19 Kenny THOMPSON (Gk) †45			

Darren Byfield

THE MANAGEMENT TEAM

When it became known in mid-season that coach John Gregory was to try his hand as a manager again, at Wycombe Wanderers, it could have appeared as a major blow to Villa's managerial threesome.

The Brian Little-Allan Evans-Gregory trio, all ex-Villa players, was an ideal set-up to run the show at the Bodymoor Heath training ground, bearing in mind their collective expertise and experience, plus their extensive working knowledge of each other.

However, what could have been a body blow was quickly proven to be no more than a hiccup as the manager shrewdly re-shaped his manpower resources.

The chief-coach role was shifted from the departed Gregory to fellow-coach KEVIN MacDONALD, whose experience as part of a Championship-winning Liverpool side was qualification enough for the role.

MacDonald had also worked extensively with BRIAN LITTLE and ALLAN EVANS at Leicester City and had been at Villa Park himself long enough to know the ropes.

Then, to fill the gap now existing in the coaching set-up he switched chief scout MALCOLM BEARD to the role of reserve team manager and coach to work in partnership with Kevin MacDonald and TONY McANDREW, whose specialist duties continued to be with the youth team where his record is outstanding.

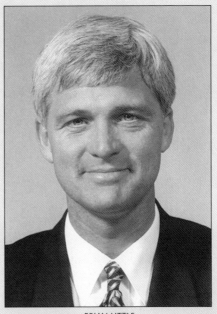

BRIAN LITTLE

Evidence as to the extent of the success of their working practices came with the progress of the likes of Michael Oakes, Riccardo Scimeca, Lee Hendrie, Gareth Farrelly and Adam Rachel, plus the introduction for his first-team baptism of David Hughes.

Like the other youngsters before him, the tall Welsh Under-21 defender arrived into

ALLAN EVANS

KEVIN MacDONALD

MALCOLM BEARD

TONY McANDREW

the senior squad looking thoroughly well prepared by the collective in-put of the coaching staff.

Beard's switch from the chief coach role led to another little shuffle in the pack, namely the move by PETER WITHE from youth development officer to chief scout.

The former Villa Championship and European Cup-winning striker was given the brief to comb this country, the continent and if necessary the world, to form a database of knowledge concerning the best players in every position.

In being offered the chief scout job Peter Withe was thus alerted to have his passport at the ready for a good deal of European travel.

This left open the youth development job and there waiting, already in-house, working part-time, was the club's former youth officer, BRYAN JONES.

Bryan had returned to the fold to help out Peter Withe in the increasingly important and far-flung task of trawling young schoolboy talent. He thus undertook the full-time responsibility of keeping up the supply of young talent with relish.

As a result of the staff revamp the important and widespread job behind the scenes continued unhindered, despite the departure of John Gregory, who had been such an important component.

The fitness, health and rehabilitation responsibilities remained in the extremely safe hands of long-serving physiotherapist, JIM WALKER and former goalkeeper PAUL BARRON.

While the physio's role is that of, sometimes with the help of the club doctor, correctly diagnosing and treating injuries the fitness coach concentrates on just that: physical fitness.

The pair work very closely together when injured players are able to progress from solely being on the treatment table, since the two functions are essentially very inter-related.

Diet and sensible life-style come closely into the general subject of fitness, health and well-being and Jim Walker and Paul Barron work with the rest of the managerial-coaching staff to carefully implement club policy in this area.

The way that the fixture scheduling has become so unpredictable in recent years, with matches switched to accommodate international weekends, TV and other calls, has meant that proper preparation, enabling players to peak at the right time, has become far more complicated and scientific than in the past.

Villa's backroom team is well constructed and properly qualified to meet football's latest challenge.

JIM WALKER   *PAUL BARRON*   *BRYAN JONES*   *PETER WITHE*

VILLA PARK'S ONE-HUNDRED YEAR CELEBRATIONS

The centenary of the opening of Villa Park, on Easter Saturday 1897, was celebrated at the home game against Tottenham Hotspur on April 19th, one hundred years to the nearest Saturday.

To avoid the important milestone passing unnoticed two hours of activities both inside and outside of the ground were staged to give the fixture a carnival atmosphere.

Out on the pitch a procession of former players from several past decades was introduced to the crowd after a match in period costume between Villa Old Stars and the Old Stars of Blackburn Rovers, who were the opponents on the opening day of the stadium.

For entertainment between the events there was a marching and musical presentation by the excellent band of the West Midlands Fire Service.

Meanwhile, a procession comprising vintage cars from the 1890s, bicycles, a fire engine, a brewery dray and a charabanc finished on display in Aston Park.

They were preceded by circus-style tumblers, clowns and stilt-walkers, as crowds lined Witton Lane and Trinity Road to sample the spectacle and the 'big-day' atmosphere.

The fixture attracted the season's sixth sell-out attendance of 39,339, while several previous attendances had also been close to that figure.

Unfortunately the actual game did not match the occasion with a severely-weakened Spurs team defending in depth and denying Villa attacking space in earning a 1-1 draw, which undermined Villa's prospects of a UEFA Cup place.

HISTORICAL FLASHBACK: The first match at Villa Park saw Villa beat Blackburn Rovers 3-0 with the first goal at the new stadium being scored by Johnny Campbell, a Scot from Celtic.

First goal of the second hundred years was an equaliser by Dwight Yorke, a West Indian from Trinidad & Tobago.

The Villa Old Stars line up prior to their match against a Blackburn Rovers former players team. The players, from left to right, back row: Bobby Thompson, Des Bremner, Ken McNaught, Fred Turnbull, Frank Carrodus, Jimmy Cumbes, Gary Shaw, 'Chico' Hamilton. Front row: Andy Blair, Colin Gibson, Gary Williams, Bobby McDonald, Sammy Morgan, Tommy Hughes and Tony Morley.

Villa Park shines in the sun as football comes home

Despite earlier misgivings about the state of the Villa Park playing surface it was, in fact, in fine shape for the European Championship matches staged at the ground.

Both the stadium and the City of Birmingham came through the summer football festival with flying colours as visitors from Scotland, Holland and Switzerland flooded in.

After the group matches and the quarter final, details of which are listed here, shoals of letters arrived praising just about every aspect of the presentation by the club and the city. The only reports of arrests were for drink-related high spirits as a warm, friendly, holiday atmosphere prevailed between colourfully-dressed rival fans.

A new pitch was laid at Villa Park in the short period between Euro 96 and the start of the football season but the worst drought conditions since records began held back its growth and another new playing surface, using a revolutionary system, was put down in the summer of 1997.

Holland's Ronald de Boer keeps Swiss defender Ramon Vega at arm's length as their sides meet at Villa Park

Details of Euro '96 games played at Villa Park

GROUP A 11.06.96
HOLLAND 0 SCOTLAND 0
Referee: Sundell (Sweden)
HOLLAND: Van der Sar, Reiziger, Blind, Bogarde, De Boer R. (Winter 68), Davids, Seedorf, Witschge (Cocu 78), Taument (Kluivert 63), Bergkamp, Cruyff.
SCOTLAND: Goram, McKimmie (Burley 85), Calderwood, Hendry, Boyd, Gallacher (McKinlay B.), McCall, McAllister, Collins, Booth (Spencer 46), Durie.

GROUP A 13.06.96
SWITZERLAND 0 HOLLAND 2
Scorers: Cruyff 66, Bergkamp 79
Referee: Ouzounov (Bulgaria)
SWITZERLAND: Pascolo, Jeanneret (Comisetti 68), Vega, Henchoz, Quentin, Hottiger, Sforza, Vogel, Türkyilmaz, Grassi, Chapuisat.
HOLLAND: Van der Sar, Reiziger, Blind, Bogarde, De Boer R. (Davids 80), Winter, Seedorf (De Kock 26), Witschge, Cruyff (Kluivert 84), Bergkamp, Hoekstra.

GROUP A 18.06.96
SCOTLAND 1 SWITZERLAND 0
Scorer: McCoist 36
Referee: Krondl (Czech Republic)
SCOTLAND: Goram, Burley, Calderwood, Hendry, Boyd, Collins, McCall, McAllister, McKinlay T. (Booth 60), McCoist (Spencer 84), Durie.
SWITZERLAND: Pascolo, Hottiger, Vega, Henchoz, Quentin (Comisetti 80), Vogel, Koller (Wicky 46), Sforza, Türkyilmaz, Bonvin, Chapuisat.

QUARTER FINAL 23.06.96
PORTUGAL 0 CZECH REPUBLIC 1
Scorer: Poborsky 53
Referee: Krug (Germany)
PORTUGAL: Vitor Baía, Secretário, Fernando Couto, Hélder, Dimas, Figo (Cadete 83), Oceano (Folha 65), Paulo Sousa, Rui Costa, Sá Pinto (Domingos 46), João Pinto.
CZECH REPUBLIC: Kouba, Hornak, Kadlec, Suchoparek, Latal, Poborsky, Bejbl, Nemecek (Berger 90), Nemec, Smicer (Kubik 85), Kuka.

Back row, left to right: Scott Murray, Phil King, Neil Davis, Gareth Farrelly, Carl Tiler, Riccardo Scimeca, Darren Byfield, Lee Hendrie, Fernando Nelson.

Middle row: Paul Barron (Fitness Coach), Paul McGrath, Gareth Southgate, Ugo Ehiogu, Michael Oakes, Mark Bosnich, Ian Taylor, Gary Charles, Tommy Johnson, Jim Walker (Physio).

Front row: Julian Joachim, Steve Staunton, Franz Carr, Mark Draper, Allan Evans (Assistant Manager), Brian Little (Manager), John Gregory (Coach), Savo Milosevic, Dwight Yorke, Andy Townsend, Alan Wright.

MARK BOSNICH

Born Fairfield, Australia, 13th January 1972. *Joined Villa* February 1992 from Sydney Croatia. *Villa debut* v Luton Town, Lge (a) 25/4/92.

Although interrupted by injuries, another season of goalkeeping brilliance by the extrovert Aussie as his dedication to fitness, agility and correct preparation produced its results in terms of outstanding performances.

Having begun the season with a knee injury he later, in October, underwent cartilage surgery.

On 11th June '97, whilst playing in a World Cup qualifying match for Australia against the Solomon Islands in Sydney, Mark scored a last minute goal from the penalty spot to round off a 13-0 rout for the Aussies. This was his first goal in professional football.

Career Record:

Season	Club	League Apps	Gls Ag	Cups Apps	Gls Ag
89-90	Man. United	1	-	-	-
90-91	Man. United	2	2	-	-
91-92	Aston Villa	1	1	-	-
92-93	Aston Villa	17	12	1	-
93-94	Aston Villa	28	28	12 (1)	11
94-95	Aston Villa	30	44	4	5
95-96	Aston Villa	38	35	13	7
96-97	Aston Villa	20	16	4	4
Villa record		134	136	34 (1)	27
TOTAL		137	138	34 (1)	27

★ *Australian international.*

● NOTE: *Career records of goalkeepers Mark Bosnich (above) and Michael Oakes (p126) list number of goals conceded in the goals columns.*

● NOTE: *All international records are up to the end of the English domestic season (11th May 1997).*

GARY CHARLES

Born London, 13th April 1970. *Joined Villa* January 1995 from Derby County, £1m. *Villa debut* as sub v. Nottingham Forest, Lge (a), 21/1/95.

The horrific, career-threatening ankle injury sustained in April, 1996, kept Charles out of the team for the entire season. However, behind the scenes and working hard at Bodymoor Heath, he made steady progress and made several reserve appearances late in the season.

The former England cap was determined to start challenging for a recall in 1997-98, though new signing Fernando Nelson had effectively taken over his right wing-back role.

Career Record:

Season	Club	League Apps	Gls	Cups Apps	Gls
87-88	Nottingham F.	-	-	-	-
88-89	Nottingham F.	1	-	1	-
(loan)	Leicester City	5 (3)	-	-	-
89-90	Nottingham F.	- (1)	-	- (2)	-
90-91	Nottingham F.	9 (1)	-	7	1
91-92	Nottingham F.	30	1	12 (2)	-
92-93	Nottingham F.	14	-	1	-
93-94	Derby County	43	1	8 (1)	-
94-95	Derby County*	18	2	7	-
	Aston Villa	14 (2)	-	-	-
95-96	Aston Villa	34	1	13	-
96-97	Aston Villa	-	-	-	-
Villa record		48 (2)	1	13	-
TOTAL		168 (7)	5	49 (5)	1

* N.B. Cup figures for Derby Co. 94-95 only include Anglo-Italian and Coca-Cola Cup competitions

★ *Full England international (2 caps).*
Also capped at Under-21 level.

SASA CURCIC

Born Belgrade,
14th February 1972.
Joined Villa August 1996
from Bolton W, £4m.
Villa debut v Derby
County, Lge (h)
24/8/96.

A club record signing when Villa pay
Bolton £4m for the former Partizan
Belgrade, Serbian team-mate of Savo
Milosevic right at the start of the season.

It proved, however, to be a difficult
season for him as he struggled to fit in.

Undoubted skill on the ball and pacey
dribbling prowess were sometimes
undermined a touch by his tendency to
run into trouble and lose possession.

After losing his place he becomes
disenchanted with his move and
following talks behind the scenes it is
revealed that Curcic has had personal
problems since his move.

He apologised to the club for publicly
bemoaning his move and buckled down
to fight for his place back, while the club
agreed to his request for a move if a
suitable offer were to come along.

The deadline passed without such a
move and efforts were made to integrate
the Yugoslavia World Cup squad
member more successfully.

Career Record:

Season	Club	League Apps	Gls	Cups Apps	Gls
90-93	OFK Belgrade				
93-94	Partizan Belgrade	32 (1)	8		
94-95	Partizan Belgrade	30 (1)	6		
95-96	Partizan Belgrade	10	2		
95-96	Bolton W.	28	4	5	3
96-97	Aston Villa	17 (5)	-	3	1
TOTAL		117 (7)	20	8	4

Yugoslav International (13 caps, 1 goal).

NEIL DAVIS

Born Bloxwich,
15th August 1973.
Joined Villa May 1991
from Redditch United.
Villa debut as sub v
Nottingham Forest,
FA Cup (a), 13/3/96.

The former Redditch forward found it
difficult to sustain a place in the first-
team squad and in October went to
Wycombe Wanderers for a three month
loan spell with ex-Villa Park coach John
Gregory, who moved there as manager.

Back at Villa Park, Davis was named as
one of the subs for the 0-0 home draw
with West Ham and turned down the
chance of a £100,000 move to FA Cup
quarter-finalists, Wrexham.

Career Record:

Season	Club	League Apps	Gls	Cups Apps	Gls
91-92	Aston Villa	-	-	-	-
92-93	Aston Villa	-	-	-	-
93-94	Aston Villa	-	-	-	-
94-95	Aston Villa	-	-	-	-
95-96	Aston Villa	- (2)	-	- (1)	-
96-97	Aston Villa	-	-	-	-
loan	Wycombe W.	13	-	-	-
Villa record		- (2)	-	- (1)	-
TOTAL		13 (2)	-	- (1)	-

INTO THE MILLENNIUM

During the weeks leading up to the
1996/97 season, four players, namely:
**Alan Wright, Ian Taylor, Lee
Hendrie** and **Dwight Yorke**, joined
other members of the senior squad, who
had already put pen to paper, by signing
long-term contracts with the club.

This will see them playing for Villa to
the start of the new Millennium and,
hopefully, for a few years after that!

MARK DRAPER

Born Derby, 11th November 1970. *Joined Villa* July 1995 from Leicester City, £3.25m. *Villa debut* v Manchester Utd, Lge (h), 19/8/95.

Having worked his way to the fringe of the England squad the former Notts County and Leicester midfield player stuggled to reproduce his most consistent and creative form.

Draper was on the bench for the World Cup qualifier in Moldova in September. However, it quickly emerged that he and Sasa Curcic did not blend well as a pair and he suffered a psychological set-back when he was sent-off in the thrilling 4-3 defeat at St. James' Park.

Draper withstood the challenge of Curcic, however, to retain his place as a regular until another set-back arrived in the shape of a seven-match absence for a hernia operation at the start of the year.

At his best Draper continued to be Villa's most accomplished playmaker.

Career Record:

Season	Club	League Apps	Gls	Cups Apps	Gls
88-89	Notts County	16 (4)	3	3 (1)	-
89-90	Notts County	29 (5)	3	6	1
90-91	Notts County	41 (4)	9	12 (1)	1
91-92	Notts County	32 (3)	1	4 (1)	2
92-93	Notts County	44	11	5	1
93-94	Notts County	44	13	15	4
94-95	Leicester City	39	5	4	-
95-96	Aston Villa	36	2	13	3
96-97	Aston Villa	28 (1)	-	3 (1)	-
Villa record		64 (1)	2	16 (1)	3
TOTAL		309 (17)	47	65 (4)	12

★ *England Under-21 international.*

UGO EHIOGU

Born Hackney, London, 3rd November 1972. *Joined Villa* July 1991 from West Bromwich Albion, £40,000. *Villa debut* v Arsenal, Lge (h), 24/8/91.

A consistent high level of performance has made Ehiogu a fixture in the back three as visiting attackers to Villa Park have largely found it unproductive ground. The former England under-21 captain plays equally well whoever his back-line partners happen to be with his decisive tackling and strength in the air.

Only he, along with Alan Wright, was able to keep his ever-present record stretching on through the season, as his name automatically went onto the team sheet, match after match.

Although not a high-scoring defender he does add his height and power to attacking set-pieces.

He began the season disapppointed at missing England's European Championship squad, having been on the full England Tour of the Far East and coming on as a sub in China.

Career Record:

Season	Club	League Apps	Gls	Cups Apps	Gls
90-91	W.B.A.	- (2)	-	-	-
91-92	Aston Villa	4 (4)	-	1 (1)	-
92-93	Aston Villa	1 (3)	-	1	-
93-94	Aston Villa	14 (3)	-	- (2)	-
94-95	Aston Villa	38 (1)	3	9	1
95-96	Aston Villa	36	1	13	1
96-97	Aston Villa	38	3	7	1
Villa record		131 (11)	7	31 (3)	3
TOTAL		131 (13)	7	31 (3)	3

★ *England international at Full (1 cap) and Under-21 levels.*

GARETH FARRELLY

Born Dublin,
28th August 1975.
Joined Villa August 1992
as YTS. September 1992
on professional forms.
Villa debut As sub v
Peterborough Utd, CCC
(h), 20/9/95.

The Irish Republic youngster became frustrated at not making a regular breakthrough into the first-team and asked for a move before the transfer deadline.

Unable to talk him into signing a new, long-term contract, Brian Little reluctantly agreed to listen to offers, but the deadline passed without a move being forthcoming.

The Villa manager remained convinced that, should he elect to stay, that a fine future beckoned at Villa Park for a player on the fringe of full international honours, having won his first cap.

However, competition for midfield places promised to be stiffer than ever with signings imminent during the summer.

Career Record:

Season	Club	League Apps	Gls	Cups Apps	Gls
92-93	Aston Villa	-	-	-	-
93-94	Aston Villa	-	-	-	-
94-95	Aston Villa	-	-	-	-
95-96	Aston Villa	1 (4)	-	- (1)	-
96-97	Aston Villa	1 (2)	-	-	-
TOTAL		2 (6)	-	- (1)	-

★ *Republic of Ireland full international (3 caps), also Youth and Under-21 international.*

LEE HENDRIE

Born Birmingham,
18th May 1977.
Joined Villa July 1993 as
YTS trainee. July 1994
on professional forms.
Villa debut As sub v
Queens Park Rangers
Lge (a), 23/12/95.

The Birmingham-born youngster from a footballing family has been serving his apprenticeship, largely as a first-team sub though he won his first England Under-21 cap as a substitute against Croatia in the Spring of 1996.

Having made his debut as a substitute in December 1995 he spent 1996-97 establishing himself as a regular member of the squad.

Hendrie has undoubted natural skills, including the neat control and precision shooting revealed during his occasional appearances.

It was FA Cup fourth round day, at Derby, before he made a first full appearance, but there seems little doubt that, with patience, he will get more such opportunities.

Career Record:

Season	Club	League Apps	Gls	Cups Apps	Gls
94-95	Aston Villa	-	-	-	-
95-96	Aston Villa	2 (1)	-	-	-
96-97	Aston Villa	- (4)	-	1 (2)	-
TOTAL		2 (5)	-	1 (2)	-

★ *England Under-21 international.*

CAPTAINS FANTASTIC

On 11th February 1997 Steve Staunton took over the captaincy of the Republic of Ireland from Andy Townsend, who was injured, for the game against Wales in Cardiff, which ended in a 0-0 draw. Steve had done the job once before, against Portugal in 1995.

DAVID HUGHES

Born Wrexham,
1st February 1978.
Joined Villa as associate
schoolboy April 94; full
professional 1st July 96.
Villa debut as sub v
Liverpool, Lge (h),
2/3/97.

The Welsh under-21 centre-back became
the latest of a long line of promising
Villa youngsters to progress to the first
team when he made his debut as a
substitute for the injured Steve Staunton
at half-time in the 1-0 win over
Liverpool at Villa Park.

This was followed by his full debut at
Leicester and his home debut against
West Ham, during which time he
revealed great calmness and maturity,
another great find in the Scimeca mould.

His readiness for first-team action was
another tribute to the quality of the club
youth scheme. Signed a new four year
contract with club at the end of May '97.

Career Record:

Season	Club	League Apps	Gls	Cups Apps	Gls
96-97	Aston Villa	4 (3)	-	-	-

★ *Welsh Under-21 international.*

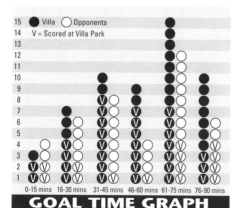

15	● Villa	○ Opponents			
14	Ⓥ = Scored at Villa Park				

GOAL TIME GRAPH

0-15 mins   16-30 mins   31-45 mins   46-60 mins   61-75 mins   76-90 mins

JULIAN JOACHIM

Born Peterborough,
12th September 1974
Joined Villa February
1996 from Leicester City,
£1.5m.
Villa debut as sub v
Wimbledon, Lge (a),
24/2/96.

After signing from Leicester City in
February 1996, he completed his first
year or so at the club without being able
to secure a regular place.

Although a regular substitute and very
highly regarded by the manager, dating
back to their days together at Filbert
Street, his chances were strictly limited.

One of the goals in the 2-1 win at
Coventry in November was his season's
first highlight and when he scored at the
Baseball Ground in April it was too late
to rescue the losing scoreline.

At the age of 22, and with a fair
amount of first team experience, he is
regarded as still having time to fulfil his
early-teenage potential.

Career Record:

Season	Club	League Apps	Gls	Cups Apps	Gls
92-93	Leicester City	25 (1)	10	5 (1)	4
93-94	Leicester City	27 (9)	11	5 (2)	1
94-95	Leicester City	11 (4)	3	2	-
95-96	Leicester City	12	2	2	-
	Aston Villa	4 (7)	1	-	-
96-97	Aston Villa	3 (12)	3	2	-
Villa record		7 (19)	4	2	-
TOTAL		82 (33)	30	16 (3)	5

★ *England Youth and Under-21 International
(8 caps).*

TOMMY JOHNSON

Born Newcastle,
15th January 1971
Joined Villa January 1995
from Derby County,
£1.9m.
Villa debut v QPR,
Lge (h), 14/1/95.

The popular Geordie's £2.4m move to Celtic in April ended his two-year Villa spell during which his all-out effort and dressing room presence was highly regarded. Unfortunately, things did not always quite work out for him at Villa Park in terms of his actual role, a situation best summed up by his own comment that: "I still don't know what is my best position."

When Celtic's bid came in, soon after the player had rejected a bid from his former club, Derby County, Brian Little felt it was a progressive career move for the player, especially as signings were on the cards, come the close season.

Career Record:

Season	Club	League Apps	Gls	Cups Apps	Gls
88-89	Notts Co.	6 (4)	4	1 (1)	-
89-90	Notts Co.	34 (6)	18	9 (2)	2
90-91	Notts Co.	29 (8)	16	7 (3)	5
91-92	Notts Co.	31	9	7 (1)	3
	Derby Co.	12	2	2	1
92-93	Derby Co.	34 (1)	8	16	2
93-94	Derby Co.	31 (6)	13	7 (1)	6
94-95	Derby Co.	14	7	5	2
	Aston Villa	11 (3)	4	- (1)	-
95-96	Aston Villa	17 (6)	5	7 (1)	3
96-97	Aston Villa	10 (10)	4	4 (1)	1
Villa record		38 (19)	13	11 (3)	4
TOTAL		229 (44)	90	65 (11)	25

* N.B. Cup figures for Derby Co. 94-95 only include Anglo-Italian and Coca-Cola Cup competitions.

★ *England Under-21 international.*

PHIL KING

Born Bristol,
28th December 1967
Joined Villa August 1994
from Sheffield
Wednesday, £250,000
Villa debut as sub v
Everton, Lge (a) 20/8/94.

After his injury-plagued previous season, and a brief loan spell with West Bromwich Albion, King was again unable to make the first team in 1996-97.

Service in the Reserves, with no promotion prospects, led to his being granted a free transfer.

Towards the end of March he was transferred to Swindon Town, managed by ex-Villa man Steve McMahon, on a two-year contract.

Career Record:

Season	Club	League Apps	Gls	Cups Apps	Gls
84-85	Exeter City	15 (1)	-	1 (1)	-
85-86	Exeter City	9 (2)	-	1	-
86-87	Torquay U.	24	3	5	-
	Swindon T.	20 (1)	-	-	-
87-88	Swindon T.	44	1	14	-
88-89	Swindon T.	34 (3)	2	7	-
89-90	Swindon T.	14	1	3	-
	Sheff Wed.	25	-	4	-
90-91	Sheff Wed.	43	-	13	-
91-92	Sheff Wed.	38 (1)	1	8	-
92-93	Sheff Wed.	11 (1)	1	3	-
93-94	Sheff Wed.	7 (3)	-	3	-
(loan)	Notts Co.	6	-	2	-
94-95	Aston Villa	13 (3)	-	7	-
95-96	Aston Villa	-	-	-	-
(loan)	W.B.A.	4	-	1	-
96-97	Aston Villa	-	-	-	-
Villa record		13 (3)	-	7	-
TOTAL		307 (15)	9	72 (1)	-

PAUL McGRATH

Born Ealing, London,
4th December 1959.
Joined Villa August 1989
from Man. United,
£400,000.
Villa debut v Nott'm F.,
Lge (a), 19/8/89.

After negotiating a new one-year deal to continue his Villa Park career McGrath became unsettled at being on the bench in the opening nine matches.

His only appearance was as substitute in the away leg against the Swedish club Helsingborg in the UEFA Cup.

In September he was transferred to Derby County, whom he then helped to consolidate their newly gained position in the Premiership.

Career Record:

Season	Club	League Apps	League Gls	Cups Apps	Cups Gls
81-82	Man. United	-	-	-	-
82-83	Man. United	14	3	1 (1)	-
83-84	Man. United	9	1	3	-
84-85	Man. United	23	-	7	2
85-86	Man. United	40	3	8	1
86-87	Man. United	34 (1)	2	4 (1)	-
87-88	Man. United	21 (1)	2	2	1
88-89	Man. United	18 (2)	1	5 (1)	-
89-90	Aston Villa	35	1	12	-
90-91	Aston Villa	35	-	9	-
91-92	Aston Villa	41	1	7	-
92-93	Aston Villa	42	4	8	1
93-94	Aston Villa	30	-	14	-
94-95	Aston Villa	36 (4)	-	9	-
95-96	Aston Villa	29 (1)	2	8 (2)	-
96-97	Aston Villa	-	-	- (1)	-
Villa record		248 (5)	8	67 (3)	1
TOTAL		407 (9)	20	97 (6)	5

★ *Republic of Ireland full international (83 caps, 8 goals).*

SAVO MILOSEVIC

Born Bijeljina, Yugoslavia,
2nd September 1973.
Joined Villa June 1995
from Partizan Belgrade,
£3.5m.
Villa debut v Manchester
United, Lge (h) 19/8/95.

Another season of highs and lows from the enigmatic £3.5m Serbian who was all set up to join Italian club Perugia just after the start of the season.

He missed eight of the opening sixteen matches, enabling Tommy Johnson to bid for a regular place, but the goals supply was disappointing.

When the Perugia move fell through Milosevic returned to the fold with renewed enthusiasm towards the end of November.

Once again his educated left foot, ability to go past opponents, to shield the ball and to make some superb passes caught the eye, as did his habit of missing too many good chances.

Milosevic became Yugoslavia's leading scorer in their World Cup qualifying bid, including a hat-trick against the Faroe Islands.

Career Record:

Season	Club	League Apps	League Gls	Cups Apps	Cups Gls
92-93	Partizan Belgrade	20 (11)	14		
93-94	Partizan Belgrade	32	20		
94-95	Partizan Belgrade	35	30		
95-96	Aston Villa	36 (1)	12	12	2
96-97	Aston Villa	29 (1)	9	5 (1)	-
Villa record		65 (2)	21	17 (1)	2
TOTAL		152 (13)	85	17 (1)	2

★ *Yugoslav full international (20 caps, 11 goals).*

SCOTT MURRAY

Born Aberdeen,
26th May 1974.
Joined Villa March 1994
from Fraserburgh,
£35,000.
Villa debut v Middles-
brough, Lge (h) 19/3/96.

The Scottish-born player who deputised for Gary Charles at the end of the previous season lost his place due to the close-season signing of Fernando Nelson.

He remained on the first-team fringe, however, having played in the opening game at Hillsborough before Nelson was introduced.

Later he was sub against Leicester City at Filbert Street and West Ham at Villa Park.

Career Record:

Season	Club	League Apps	Gls	Cups Apps	Gls
93-94	Aston Villa	-	-	-	-
94-95	Aston Villa	-	-	-	-
95-96	Aston Villa	3	-	-	-
96-97	Aston Villa	1	-	-	-
Villa record		4	-	-	-

DEPARTURES

PAUL BROWNE returned to his native Scotland to join Raith Rovers on 3/7/96 after turning down a new contract with Villa. Browne, a strong central defender, made two appearances in the first team after coming through the youth ranks.

FRANZ CARR went to Italian Serie A side, Reggiana on a free transfer on 23/10/96. The speedy winger had been unable to gain a regular place in the Villa side.

FOUR first-year professionals were released by the club at the end of the 1996/97 season. They are: Stuart Brock, Lee Burchell, Jonathan Miley and Richard Burgess.

FERNANDO NELSON

Born Porto, Portugal,
5th November 1971.
Joined Villa July 1996
from Sporting Lisbon,
£1.75m.
Villa debut as sub v
Derby County, Lge (h)
24/8/96.

Portuguese international, signed during the close season for £1.75m from Sporting Lisbon, the right-side wing-back arrived heavily recommended by ex-England boss, Bobby Robson.

Nelson, as he likes to be called, was the replacement for the sorely-injured Gary Charles and, after a brief 'breaking-in' period, he settled down to make the job his own.

Quick and nimble and with well-developed awareness of his dual-role, Nelson's forward thrusts and thoughtful crosses have been a feature of the season.

In the style that Brian Little favours, with three centre backs and two wide, all-purpose midfielders, Nelson performs a similar service on the right to that of Alan Wright on the other side.

Career Record:

Season	Club	League Apps	Gls	Cups Apps	Gls
90-91	SC Salgueiros	22 (2)	-		
91-92	Sporting Lisbon	2	-		
92-93	Sporting Lisbon	13 (2)	-		
93-94	Sporting Lisbon	33	1		
94-95	Sporting Lisbon	33	1		
95-96	Sporting Lisbon	32	1		
96-97	Aston Villa	33 (1)	-	4 (1)	-
TOTAL		168 (5)	3	4 (1)	-

★ *Portuguese full international (5 caps).*

No details available of cup matches played in Portugal.

MICHAEL OAKES

Born Northwich, 30th October 1973. *Joined Villa* July 1991 as a non-contract player, February 1992 on professional forms *Villa debut* v Wigan Ath., CCC (a), 5/10/94.

The England Under-21 international is, without doubt, one of the best second-string goalkeepers in the country.

Safe, reliable, strong and athletic, it is always a problem for Brian Little to demote him to the bench after spells deputising for Mark Bosnich.

When the Australian was unfit at the start of the season with a knee injury he enjoyed his best spell of ten successive first-team appearances, including both European matches, after making his full Premiership debut on the opening day.

He returned for a further spell of half-a-dozen matches when Bosnich was out again and then the problem of 'two-good 'uns-for-one position' reared its head with Bosnich's walk-out at Derby as Oakes kept his place.

Career Record:

| Season | Club | League | | | Cups | |
		Apps	Gls	Ag	Apps	Gls Ag
91-92	Aston Villa	-	-		-	-
92-93	Aston Villa	-	-		-	-
93-94	Aston Villa	-	-		-	-
(loan)	Scarborough	2	*		-	-
(loan)	Tranmere	-	-		-	-
94-95	Aston Villa	-	-		1	-
95-96	Aston Villa	-	-		-	-
96-97	Aston Villa	18 (2)	18		3	2
Villa record		18 (2)	18		4	2
TOTAL		20 (2)	18		4	2

★ *England Under-21 international.*

* Goals conceded whilst on loan at Scarborough not known.

RICCARDO SCIMECA

Born Leamington Spa, 13th June 1975. *Joined Villa* July 1991 as YTS trainee. July 1993 on professional forms. *Villa debut* As sub v Manchester United, Lge (h), 19/8/95.

The progress achieved by the local-born son of an Italian restaurant family was continued in his second season in the first team squad.

After starting the season as resident substitute he then made fourteen full appearances, in defence and midfield, though interrupted by illness and injury.

It was the obvious promise of such calm, accomplished young players that enabled Brian Little to release the likes of Paul McGrath and Carl Tiler in the knowledge that young replacements were on hand.

Regular England Under-21 defender, he was made captain of the side to play Italy Under-21s at Ashton Gate in February, Scimeca has all the attributes for a lengthy, successful career at the top. Named Supporters' Young Player of the Year in May 1996.

Career Record:

| Season | Club | League | | Cups | |
		Apps	Gls	Apps	Gls
93-94	Aston Villa	-	-	-	-
94-95	Aston Villa	-	-	-	-
95-96	Aston Villa	7 (10)	-	3 (2)	-
96-97	Aston Villa	11 (6)	-	4 (1)	-
TOTAL		18 (16)	-	7 (3)	-

★ *England Under-21 international (5 caps).*

Because of their involvement in the UEFA Cup, Villa were exempt from the two-legged second round of the Coca-Cola Cup; coming in at the third round stage, in which they were drawn away to Leeds.

GARETH SOUTHGATE

Born Watford,
3rd September 1970.
Joined Villa June 1995
from Crystal Palace,
£2.5m.
Villa debut v Manchester
United, Lge (h), 19/8/95.

The crushing experience of missing a crucial penalty for England in the European Championship shoot-out against Germany thrust him into a high-profile start to the season.

This led to slightly below-par early-season form but, like the true professional he is, the versatile defender gradually put it behind him. Scored the winning goal in his first home match of the season, against Blackburn Rovers, partially purging his England miss.

A couple of injury spells added to what proved to be a somewhat hot-and-cold year for a player who has been tipped to be a future captain of England.

Has signed a new four-and-a-half year contract with the club.

Career Record:

Season	Club	League Apps	Gls	Cups Apps	Gls
88-89	Crystal Palace	- -	-	- -	-
89-90	Crystal Palace	- -	-	- -	-
90-91	Crystal Palace	1	-	1 (1)	-
91-92	Crystal Palace	26 (4)	-	9	-
92-93	Crystal Palace	33	3	6	2
93-94	Crystal Palace	46	9	7	3
94-95	Crystal Palace	42	3	15	2
95-96	Aston Villa	31	1	12	1
96-97	Aston Villa	28	1	6	-
Villa record		*59*	*2*	*18*	*1*
TOTAL		207 (4)	17	56 (1)	8

★ *Full England international (14 caps), making his debut as a substitute against Portugal at Wembley, 12/12/95.*

STEVE STAUNTON

Born Drogheda, Ireland,
19th January 1969.
Joined Villa August 1991
from Liverpool, £1.1m.
Villa debut v Sheff. Wed.
League (a), 17/8/91.
Scored the winner.

The Irish Republic defender was constantly being linked with a possible bid from his former club, Liverpool but, in reality he remained a crucial part of Brian Little's plans.

In the early days of the season his form in the back three alongside Gareth Southgate and Ugo Ehiogu consigned Paul McGrath to the bench and led to his compatriot's departure.

A couple of brief injury spells interrupted a fine season but, in whatever role, he was an inspirational figure in terms of the competitive example he constantly set.

Career Record:

Season	Club	League Apps	Gls	Cups Apps	Gls
86-87	Liverpool	-	-	-	-
87-88	Liverpool	-	-	-	-
(loan)	Bradford City	7 (1)	-	3	-
88-89	Liverpool	17 (4)	-	8	1
89-90	Liverpool	18 (2)	-	4 (2)	3
90-91	Liverpool	20 (4)	-	9	2
91-92	Aston Villa	37	4	6	-
92-93	Aston Villa	42	2	9	-
93-94	Aston Villa	24	3	9	-
94-95	Aston Villa	34 (1)	5	8	-
95-96	Aston Villa	11 (2)	-	3 (3)	1
96-97	Aston Villa	30	2	5	-
Villa record		*178 (3)*	*16*	*40 (3)*	*1*
TOTAL		240 (14)	16	64 (5)	7

★ *Full Republic of Ireland international (67 caps, 5 goals).*

IAN TAYLOR

Born Birmingham,
4th June 1968.
Joined Villa December
1994 in straight swop
deal with Guy Whitting-
ham from Sheffield Wed.
Villa debut v Arsenal,
League (a), 26/12/94.

The Birmingham-born midfielder's
delight at playing for the club he once
supported as a Holte Ender continued to
be reflected in his wholehearted
performances.

Sasa Curcic's arrival initially led to
additional challenge for midfield places,
but Ian, a different kind of player, soon
regained his place for another season of
consistency.

Brian Little continued to admire his
capacity to work the field unceasingly
from penalty area to penalty area.

Although not scoring the goals he
expects from his forward thrusts the one
goal of the game against Liverpool at
Villa Park on March 2nd, ended the
growing monopoly of the Anfield side
and kept Villa in the Euro-chase.

Career Record:

Season	Club	League Apps	Gls	Cups Apps	Gls
92-93	Port Vale	41	15	15	4
93-94	Port Vale	42	13	8	3
94-95	Sheff. Wed.	9 (5)	1	2 (2)	1
	Aston Villa	21	1	2	-
95-96	Aston Villa	24 (1)	3	7 (2)	2
96-97	Aston Villa	29 (5)	2	3	1
Villa record		*74 (6)*	*6*	*12 (2)*	*3*
TOTAL		166 (11)	35	37 (4)	11

CARL TILER

Born Sheffield,
11th January 1970.
Joined Villa October
1995 from Nottingham
Forest, £750,000.
Villa debut v Everton,
Lge (h), 28/10/95.

The former Nottingham Forest centre
back never really settled at Villa Park
after being seriously injured in his first
game and wisely accepted the chance to
join Sheffield United's promotion
campaign.

Brian Little accepted Howard Kendall's
£850,000 offer as it became obvious that
young David Hughes was moving into
the first-team frame.

Tiler made a dozen full appearances
during the season, including a similar
number as substitute, but was never a
settled part of the back three.

After an unfortunate start at the club,
in terms of injury, he basically had little
chance to play himself back into form
and the move was a sensible one for
him.

Career Record:

Season	Club	League Apps	Gls	Cups Apps	Gls
88/89	Barnsley	4 (1)	-	-	-
89-90	Barnsley	18 (3)	1	2 (2)	-
90-91	Barnsley	45	2	9	-
91-92	Nott'ham F.	24 (2)	1	7 (1)	-
92-93	Nott'ham F.	37	-	9	-
93-94	Nott'ham F.	3	-	-	-
94-95	Nott'ham F.	3	-	1	-
(loan)	Swindon Town	2	-	-	-
95-96	Aston Villa	1	-	-	-
96-97	Aston Villa	9 (2)	1	3	-
Villa record		*10 (2)*	*1*	*3*	*-*
TOTAL		146 (8)	5	31 (3)	-

★ *England Under-21 international.*

Born Maidstone, 27th July 1963.
Joined Villa July 1993 from Chelsea, £2.1m.
Villa debut v Queens Park Rangers, Lge (h), 14/8/93.

The Irish Republic stalwart continued as Villa's on-the-field leader as a virtual regular, minor injuries and a suspension apart.

Townsend was the subject of a firm bid from Celtic to move to Glasgow, but Brian Little was adamant that his hard-working midfielder was an essential part of the Villa line-up.

Although not the goalscorer he can sometimes be his first of the season earned a draw against his former club, Chelsea at Stamford Bridge and his second beat Southampton 1-0 at The Dell in December.

Career Record:

Season	Club	League Apps	League Gls	Cups Apps	Cups Gls
84-85	Southampton	5	-	-	-
85-86	Southampton	25 (2)	1	5 (5)	-
86-87	Southampton	11 (3)	1	2 (1)	-
87-88	Southampton	36 (1)	3	5	-
88-89	Norwich	31 (5)	5	7 (1)	2
89-90	Norwich	35	3	9	-
90-91	Chelsea	34	2	11	3
91-92	Chelsea	35	6	10	1
92-93	Chelsea	41	4	7	3
93-94	Aston Villa	32	3	15	1
94-95	Aston Villa	32	1	8	1
95-96	Aston Villa	32 (1)	2	12	1
96-97	Aston Villa	34	2	7	-
Villa record		130 (1)	8	42	3
TOTAL		383 (12)	33	98 (7)	12

★ *Republic of Ireland international (65 caps, 7 goals).*

Born Ashton-under-Lyme, 28th September 1971.
Joined Villa March 1995 from Blackburn Rovers, £900,000.
Villa debut v West Ham Utd, Lge (h), 18/3/95.

The smallest player in the squad in terms of physical stature, but somewhere near the top in terms of skill, experience and competitive spirit.

There are few Premiership players better equipped than the former Blackburn Rovers defender in the modern role of an attacking wing-back. In a season of injuries, form fluctuations and suspensions Wright achieved the considerable feat of remaining an automatic choice and an ever-present.

Such is his self-belief that he has not given up on his ambition to complete a full-set of England caps from schoolboy level having been chosen as a squad player.

Career Record:

Season	Club	League Apps	League Gls	Cups Apps	Cups Gls
87-88	Blackpool	- (1)	-	-	-
88-90	Blackpool	14 (2)	-	3 (1)	-
89-90	Blackpool	20 (4)	-	9 (3)	-
90-91	Blackpool	45	-	12	-
91-92	Blackpool	12	-	5	-
	Blackburn R.	32 (1)	1	5	-
92-93	Blackburn R.	24	-	9	-
93-94	Blackburn R.	7 (5)	-	2	-
94-95	Blackburn R.	4 (1)	-	- (1)	-
	Aston Villa	8	-	-	-
95-96	Aston Villa	38	2	13	-
96-97	Aston Villa	38	1	7	-
Villa record		84	3	20	-
TOTAL		242 (14)	4	65 (5)	-

★ *England Under-21 International.*

DWIGHT YORKE

Born Canaan, Tobago, 3rd November 1971. *Joined Villa* December 1989 from Signal Hill in Tobago, £120,000. *Villa debut* v C.Palace, Lge (a), 24/3/90.

There was a degree of pressure on the cheerful Trinidad & Tobagan international after his outstanding season in 1995-96, when he was Supporters' Player of the Year and the also the Midland Football Writers' choice. Can he keep it up? asked some of the sceptics. Although subjected to the uncertainty of who would be his strike partner, Yorke got into his stride after failing to score in his opening nine games.

A hat-trick in the 4-3 defeat at Newcastle set him off and then the goals began to flow again, so that once again he proved himself to be one of the Premiership's greatest dangermen.

A final tally of 20 put him among the leading six in the Premierhip's top hit men. Despite widespread interest in his talents from home and abroad he signed a new deal to keep him him Villa Park at least until the year 2,000.

Career Record:

Season	Club	League Apps	Gls	Cups Apps	Gls
89-90	Aston Villa	- (2)	-	-	-
90-91	Aston Villa	8 (10)	2	3	-
91-92	Aston Villa	27 (5)	11	8	6
92-93	Aston Villa	22 (5)	6	6 (2)	1
93-94	Aston Villa	2 (10)	2	- (2)	1
94-95	Aston Villa	33 (4)	6	6	2
95-96	Aston Villa	35	17	13	8
96-97	Aston Villa	37	17	6	3
TOTAL		164 (36)	61	42 (4)	21

★ *Full international with Trinidad & Tobago (35 caps, 15 goals).*

STAN COLLYMORE

A new club signing record was set on Tuesday May 13th when Stan Collymore was signed from Liverpool for £7m.

Brian Little remained behind to complete the deal when the club party travelled to the USA for the post-season tour.

Cannock-born, Collymore started his career on Walsall's YTS scheme and subsequently signed for Wolves, Stafford Rangers in the Vauxhall Conference, Crystal Palace (£100,000), Southend (£80,000), Nottingham Forest (£2.2m) and Liverpool (British Record £8.5m).

Collymore took his place on top of the club's 'Record Signing' table in the Premiership as follows:

£7m **Stan Collymore** (Liverpool)
MAY 1997

£4m **Sasa Curcic** (Bolton Wanderers)
AUGUST 1996

£3.5m **Savo Milosevic** (Partizan Belgrade)
JUNE 1995

£3.25m **Mark Draper** (Leicester City)
AUGUST 1995

£2.5m **Gareth Southgate** (Crystal Palace)
JULY 1995

£2.3m **Dean Saunders** (Liverpool)
SEPTEMBER 1992

ASTON VILLA WELCOME STAN THE MAN COLLYMORE

The club's stock market flotation took place on Thursday, April 17th, 1997 when the company valuation was placed at £125.9m, below the original forecast of £140m.

Shares were priced at £11 each, with a minimum investment of £440. Trading was earmarked to begin on May 7th.

Flotation sponsors were the Birmingham-based stockbrokers, Albert E Sharp, while the legal advisers were the Birmingham law firm, Edge & Ellison.

The club chairman Mr Doug Ellis and his family retained a stake of thirty-eight per cent, worth approximately £48m. A part of the family holding was sold for £4m.

Of the 1.8 million new shares to be put on sale to raise £15.22m for ground and team redevelopment, most were being placed with institutional investors and were three times over-subscribed.

Preference for share purchase from 454,545 on public offer was given to staff, including players and the existing 20,000 shareholders, though 40 shares at £11 each was the minimum deal available.

More than 8,000 investors who paid £5 per share at the 1968 share issue saw the value of their individual shares grow to £1,100, though 646 of them were not traced at the time of the new flotation.

The offer document issued described the club as one of the six biggest in the country and the biggest in the Midlands.

"The club has been run as a business not as a fantasy," said Mr Ellis. Over the preceding six years the club generated profits of £23.4m and at the time of the float had no debts.

When the share offer closed it was found to be almost three times over-subscribed.

In tandem with the flotation the board was increased to seven by the appointment of three new members, namely:

MARK ANSELL a 46-year-old Executive Financial Director and chartered accountant who was formerly Head of Corporate Finance with Deloitte & Touche, Midlands.

DAVID OWEN (Non-Executive Director), a 56-year-old Senior Corporate Partner of Edge & Ellison, solicitors, who for seven years had already served the club as chairman of the Aston Villa Promotions Association.

TONY HALES (Non-Executive Director), the 48-year-old Chief Executive of Allied Domecq plc who, between 1987-89, was Managing Director of Ansells Ltd.

Sadly, the enlarged board was then depleted by the loss of club doctor and director **Dr. David H. Targett**, who died a week after Villa's final fixture of the season.

Aged 65, he passed away after brain surgery in the Queen Elizabeth Hospital. He had been the club's medical officer for 25 years and a director since 1983.

Dr Targett was also the Midland Boxing Board of Control medical officer and worked for West Midland Police. He left a widow, Ann, three sons and a daughter.

ANNUAL BALANCE SHEET 1995-96

The club's AGM at the Sports and Leisure Centre on August 15th 1996 announced a profit, before transfer fees, of £5.9m, with a total turnover of almost £19m. After transfer dealings and tax there was a loss on the year of £63,000. Commercial income was £6.8m.

At the meeting Mr Tony Alderson retired as a director and succeeded the retiring Mr Harold Musgrove as club president.

GATES RECORD

There were seven capacity attendances of 39,339 during the season 1996-97.

These were against Manchester United, Chelsea, Newcastle, Liverpool, Everton, Spurs and Southampton.

This took the average home league attendance above the 36,000 mark for the first time since 1975-76 (38,874) and only the second time since 1951-52 (38,940).

The average for the Championship-winning year in 1980-81 was 33,641.

FA CARLING PREMIERSHIP STATISTICS 1996-97

		Home					Away					Total				
	Pl	W	D	L	F	A	W	D	L	F	A	W	D	L	F	A	Pts
1 Manchester United	38	12	5	2	38	17	9	7	3	38	27	21	12	5	76	44	75
2 Newcastle United	38	13	3	3	54	20	6	8	5	19	20	19	11	8	73	40	68
3 Arsenal	38	10	5	4	36	18	9	6	4	26	14	19	11	8	62	32	68
4 Liverpool	38	10	6	3	38	19	9	5	5	24	18	19	11	8	62	37	68
5 **Aston Villa**	38	11	5	3	27	13	6	5	8	20	21	17	10	11	47	34	61
6 Chelsea	38	9	8	2	33	22	7	3	9	25	33	16	11	11	58	55	59
7 Sheffield Wednesday	38	8	10	1	25	16	6	5	8	25	35	14	15	9	50	51	57
8 Wimbledon	38	9	6	4	28	21	6	5	8	21	25	15	11	12	49	46	56
9 Leicester City	38	7	5	7	22	26	5	6	8	24	28	12	11	15	46	54	47
10 Tottenham Hotspur	38	8	4	7	19	17	5	3	11	25	34	13	7	18	44	51	46
11 Leeds United	38	7	7	5	15	13	4	6	9	13	25	11	13	14	28	38	46
12 Derby County	38	8	6	5	25	22	3	7	9	20	36	11	13	14	45	58	46
13 Blackburn Rovers	38	8	4	7	28	23	1	11	7	14	20	9	15	14	42	43	42
14 West Ham United	38	7	6	6	27	25	3	6	10	12	23	10	12	16	39	48	42
15 Everton	38	7	4	8	24	22	3	8	8	20	35	10	12	16	44	57	42
16 Southampton	38	6	7	6	32	24	4	4	11	18	32	10	11	17	50	56	41
17 Coventry City	38	4	8	7	19	23	5	6	8	19	31	9	14	15	38	54	41
18 Sunderland	38	7	6	6	20	18	3	4	12	15	35	10	10	18	35	53	40
19 Middlesbrough*	38	8	5	6	34	25	2	7	10	17	35	10	12	16	51	60	39
20 Nottingham Forest	38	3	9	7	15	27	3	7	9	16	32	6	16	16	31	59	34

* Middlesbrough deducted 3 points by the Premier League for failing to turn up for a fixture at Blackburn Rovers

ROLL OF HONOUR

Champions: Manchester United
Runners-up: Newcastle United
Relegated: Sunderland, Middlesbrough and Nottingham Forest
FA Cup winners: Chelsea
Coca-Cola Cup winners: Leicester City

FACTS & FIGURES

Of the 380 games played in the Premiership, 162 resulted in home wins, 99 in away wins and 119 draws. A total of 970 goals were scored at an average of 2.55 per game, with 559 being scored by the home clubs and 411 by the visitors

Most goals: 76, Manchester United
Most home goals: 54, Newcastle United
Most away goals: 38, Manchester United
Least goals: 28, Leeds United
Least home goals: 15,
Leeds United and Nottingham Forest

Least away goals: 12, West Ham United
Least goals conceded: 32, Arsenal
Least home goals conceded: 13,
Aston Villa and Leeds United
Least away goals conceded: 14, Arsenal
Most goals conceded: 60, Middlesbrough
Most home goals conceded: 27, Nott'm Forest
Most away goals conceded: 36, Derby County

Highest goals aggregate: 120, Manchester United
Lowest goals aggregate: 66, Leeds United

Best home record: 42pts, Newcastle United
Best away record: 34pts, Manchester United
Worst home record: 18pts, Nottingham Forest
Worst away records: 13pts,
Sunderland and Middlesbrough

Highest home scores:
Everton 7 Southampton 1, 16.11.96
Newcastle United 7 Tottenham 1, 28.12.96

Highest away scores:
Leeds United 0 Manchester United 4, 7.9.96
Nott'm Forest 0 Manchester United 4, 26.12.96
Sunderland 0 Tottenham 4, 4.3.97

GOALSCORERS & ATTENDANCES

LEADING SCORERS
(Including Cup & European games)

31 Robbie Fowler (Liverpool)
31 Fabrizio Ravanelli (Middlesbrough)
30 Ian Wright (Arsenal)
28 Alan Shearer (Newcastle United)
21 Les Ferdinand (Newcastle United)
20 **Dwight Yorke** (Aston Villa)
19 Ole Gunnar Solskjaer (Manchester United)
16 Stan Collymore (Liverpool)
16 Matthew Le Tissier (Southampton)
15 Steve Claridge (Leicester City)
15 Juninho (Middlesbrough)
14 Dennis Bergkamp (Arsenal)
14 Eric Cantona (Manchester United)
14 Mark Hughes (Chelsea)
14 Egil Østenstad (Southampton)
14 Dean Sturridge (Derby County)
13 Andy Booth (Sheffield Wednesday)
13 Marcus Gayle (Wimbledon)

Four goals in a game:
Robbie Fowler (Liverpool) v M'boro 14.12.96

Three goals in a game:
Fabrizio Ravanelli (M'boro) v L'pool 17.8.96
Kevin Campbell (Forest) v Coventry 17.8.96
Ian Wright (Arsenal) v Sheff. Wed. 16.9.96
Dwight Yorke (A. Villa) v Newcastle, 30.9.96
Egil Østenstad (Soton) v Man U, 26.10.96
Gary Speed (Everton) v Soton, 16.11.96
Alan Shearer (Newcastle) v Leicester 2.2.97
Ian Marshall (Leicester) v Derby 22.2.97
Steffen Iversen (Spurs) v Sunderland 4.3.97
Fabrizio Ravanelli (M'boro) v Derby 5.3.97
Kevin Gallacher (Blackburn) v W'don. 15.3.97
Paul Kitson (West Ham) v Sheff. Wed. 3.5.97

QUICK OFF THE MARK
Villa's fastest goal of the season came courtesy of a 4th minute strike by Dwight Yorke in the 4-3 Premiership defeat by Newcastle United at St James' Park on 30th September 1996.

THE GATE LEAGUE

	Total	Best	Lowest	Average
Manchester Utd	1,046,547	55,314	54,178	55,081
Liverpool	757,547	40,892	36,126	39,871
Arsenal	718,558	38,264	33,461	37,819
Newcastle Utd	692,866	36,582	36,143	36,467
Everton	687,612	40,177	30,368	36,190
Aston Villa	684,520	39,339	26,726	36,027
Leeds United	610,585	39,981	25,860	32,136
Tottenham	590,276	33,040	22,943	31,067
Middlesbrough	564,541	30,215	29,485	29,713
Chelsea	524,722	28,418	24,027	27,617
Sheffield Wed	488,565	38,943	16,390	25,714
Blackburn Rovers	473,999	30,476	19,214	24,947
Nottingham Forest	467,151	29,181	17,525	24,587
West Ham Utd	441,661	25,064	19,105	23,245
Sunderland	398,497	22,512	18,642	20,974
Leicester City	383,490	21,134	17,562	20,184
Coventry City	373,190	23,085	15,273	19,642
Derby County	339,885	18,287	17,022	17,889
Wimbledon	287,637	25,786	7,979	15,139
Southampton	286,986	15,253	14,418	15,105

Highest attendance:
55,314, Manchester Utd v Wimbledon, 29.1.97

Lowest attendance:
7,979, Wimbledon v Leeds Utd, 16.4.97

MIDLAND MELVILLE YOUTH LEAGUE

	P	W	D	L	F	A	Pts
Nottingham F.	34	23	6	5	77	32	75
Wolves	34	23	4	7	88	42	73
Notts County	34	20	7	7	70	49	67
Aston Villa	34	19	5	10	60	40	62
Coventry City	34	17	9	8	54	42	60
Leicester City	34	18	5	11	67	42	59
Stoke City	34	17	5	12	63	38	56
Birmingham City	34	16	5	13	53	41	53
Walsall	34	14	8	12	58	58	50
Port Vale	34	14	7	13	56	48	49
Peterborough U.	34	13	4	17	54	68	43
Grimsby Town	34	11	9	14	35	40	42
West Brom. A.	34	13	3	18	46	63	42
Derby County	34	11	6	17	54	54	39
Lincoln City	34	8	8	18	35	64	32
Northampton T.	34	8	5	21	34	65	29
Mansfield Town	34	4	7	23	26	60	19
Shrewsbury Town	34	5	3	26	43	114	18

FIRST TEAM APPEARANCES & GOALSCORERS

	LEAGUE		FA CUP		LGE CUP		UEFA CUP		TOTAL	
	Apps	Gls	Apps	Gls	Apps	Gls	Apps	Gls	Apps	Gls
Mark BOSNICH	20	-	3	-	1	-	-	-	24	-
Sasa CURCIC	17 (5)	-	2	1	1	-	-	-	20 (5)	1
Mark DRAPER	28 (1)	-	-	-	1 (1)	-	2	-	31 (2)	-
Ugo EHIOGU	38	3	3	1	2	-	2	-	45	4
Gareth FARRELLY	1 (2)	-	-	-	-	-	-	-	1 (2)	-
Lee HENDRIE	- (4)	-	1 (2)	-	-	-	-	-	1 (6)	-
David HUGHES	4 (3)	-	-	-	-	-	-	-	4 (3)	-
Julian JOACHIM	3 (12)	3	1	-	1	-	-	-	5 (12)	3
Tommy JOHNSON	10 (10)	4	2	-	1	-	1 (1)	1	14 (11)	5
Paul McGRATH	-	-	-	-	-	-	- (1)	-	- (1)	-
Savo MILOSEVIC	29 (1)	9	3	-	- (1)	-	2	-	34 (2)	9
Scott MURRAY	1	-	-	-	-	-	-	-	1	-
Fernando NELSON	33 (1)	-	- (1)	-	2	-	2	-	37 (2)	-
Michael OAKES	18 (2)	-	-	-	1	-	2	-	21 (2)	-
Riccardo SCIMECA	11 (6)	-	3	-	1 (1)	-	-	-	15 (7)	-
Gareth SOUTHGATE	28	1	3	-	1	-	2	-	34	1
Steve STAUNTON	30	2	2	-	1	-	2	-	35	2
Ian TAYLOR	29 (5)	2	-	-	2	1	1	-	32 (5)	3
Carl TILER	9 (2)	1	2	-	1	-	-	-	12 (2)	1
Andy TOWNSEND	34	2	3	-	2	-	2	-	41	2
Alan WRIGHT	38	1	3	-	2	-	2	-	45	1
Dwight YORKE	37	17	2	2	2	1	2	-	43	20
Own goals	-	2	-	-	-	-	-	-	-	2

Unused Substitutes:
Julian Joachim 25, Michael Oakes 21, Gareth Farrelly 16, Adam Rachel 16, Lee Hendrie 12,
Riccardo Scimeca 11, Carl Tiler 9, Paul McGrath 8, Scott Murray 8, Sasa Curcic 6,
Tommy Johnson 6, David Hughes 5, Mark Bosnich 3, Stuart Brock 2, Mark Draper 2,
Neil Davis 1, Fernando Nelson 1, Ian Taylor 1.

Goalscorers in friendly games:
First team: Dwight Yorke 4, Stan Collymore 1, Ugo Ehiogu 1, Gareth Farrelly 1,
Tommy Johnson 1, Ian Taylor 1, Own goals 1.
Reserves: Darren Byfield 4, Michael Blackwood 2, Lee Collins 2, Les Hines 2, Richard Walker 2,
Stuart Brock 1, Lee Burchell 1, Franz Carr 1, Neil Davis 1, Gareth Farrelly 1, Lee Hendrie 1,
Tommy Jaszczun 1, Alan Kirby 1, Alan Lee 1, Ben Petty 1.

VILLA FACTS & FIGURES 1996-97

HIGHEST AND LOWEST

Highest home attendance: 39,339 (7 times)
v Manchester United 21/9/96, v Chelsea
26/12/96, v Newcastle United 11/1/97,
v Liverpool 2/3/97, v Everton 5/4/97,
v Spurs 19/4/97, v Southampton 11/5/97
Lowest home attendance: 25,006
v Notts County (FAC3R) 22/1/97
Highest away attendance: 55,133
v Manchester United 1/1/97
Lowest away attendance: 7,573
v Wimbledon (CCC4) 26/11/96
Biggest victory:
5-0 v Wimbledon (Home) 22/12/96
Heaviest defeat:
0-3 v Liverpool (Away) 18/1/97
Most goals in a match:
3 - Dwight Yorke v Newcastle (Away) 30/9/96
Most goals against:
2, Les Ferdinand (Newcastle) 30/9/96.
2, Gianfranco Zola (Chelsea) 26/12/96.
2, Fabrizio Ravanelli (Middlesbrough) 3/5/97.

Clean Sheets: 22
Failed to score in: 14
Villa scored first: 21
Scored first and won: 17
Scored first and drew: 3
Scored first and lost: 1
Opponents scored first: 17
Lost after opponents scored first: 12
Drew after opponents scored first: 3
Won after opponents scored first: 2
Highest League position: 2nd
Lowest League position: 15th

SEQUENCE RECORDS

Most matches undefeated:
8, Aug 21 - Sep 24
Most home matches undefeated:
7, Aug 21 - Nov 2 and Feb 1 - May 11
Most away matches undefeated:
6, Dec 4 - Jan 14
Most wins in succession:
4, Nov 30 - Dec 22
Most home wins in succession:
3, Feb 1 - Mar 2
Most away wins in succession:
2, Dec 4 - Dec 7 and Mar 22 - Apr 9
Longest run without a win:
7, Sep 7 - Oct 12

Longest run without a home win:
3, Sep 7 - Sep 21
Longest run without an away win:
7, Dec 28 - Mar 5
Most defeats in succession:
2, Sep 30 - Oct 12 and Jan 25 - Jan 29
Goals for in successive matches:
7, Aug 17 - Sep 15
Goals against in successive matches:
3, Sep 7 - Sep 15 and Nov 16 - Nov 26
Longest run without scoring:
256 minutes, Sep 15 - Sep 30
Longest run without conceding a goal:
471 minutes, Nov 26 - Dec 26
Most consecutive appearances:
100 - Alan Wright, 29/4/95 - 11/5/97
Ever Presents: Ugo Ehiogu and Alan Wright

DEBUTANTS

Three players made their Villa debuts this
season, they were: Sasa Curcic, David Hughes
and Fernando Nelson. Michael Oakes made
his Premiership debut two seasons after his
first senior outing in a Coca-Cola Cup tie
against Wigan Athletic.

PENALTIES

Villa were awarded five penalties during the
season, three were converted and two were
missed. Tommy Johnson scored against
Derby County (24/8/96) Lge, (h); Dwight
Yorke against Leeds Utd (23/10/96) CCC3,
(a); Dwight Yorke against Middlesbrough
(30/11/96) Lge, (h). Yorke had two spot-kicks
saved: v Newcastle Utd (11/1/97) Lge, (h)
saved by Shaka Hislop and v Sheffield Wed.
(29/1/97) Lge, (h) saved by Kevin Pressman.

Penalties conceded were: Gary Parker for
Leicester City (16/11/96) Lge (h); Fabrizio
Ravanelli for Middlesbrough (3/5/97) Lge (a).
One penalty was missed when Mark Bosnich
saved from Sunderland's David Kelly
(26/10/96) Lge, (a), but Paul Stewart scored
from the rebound.

RED CARDS

Villa received two red cards, both on trips to
the North-East during the 1996-97 season.
They were for Mark Draper at Newcastle and
Steve Staunton at Middlesbrough. No oppos-
ing players were sent off in games with Villa.

Two popular players from around the World War II era died during the season. Defender Frank Moss made his debut in the season before the war, while both he and Vic Potts figured in the first season after the war and thereafter.

VIC POTTS

Popular immediate post-war right back, Vic Potts, died aged 81 in October 1996.

Aston-born and an outstanding local schools player, he became a firm favourite as the right back alongside the legendary George Cummings between 1945 and 1948.

This was near the end of his career, however, the six years of World War II having intervened. Otherwise his total number of Villa appearances, which was restricted to 72, should have been many more.

At the start of his career he was missed by Villa, although on their doorstep, and joined Tottenham Hotspur whom he continued to serve well after his playing days, as a scout. After his retirement from football he resided in Sutton Coldfield until his death a few months after his former Villa colleague, Eric Houghton.

FRANK MOSS

A few days after the end of the 1996-97 season the club's early post-war centre-half, Frank Moss, died in a nursing home in Looe, Cornwall. He was 79.

Frank's late father, Frank senior, and his brother Amos, who survived him, both also played for Aston Villa FC. Aston-born Frank junior made 314 appearances for the club between 1938 and 1955 despite the six years of war, during which time he was on active service in the Royal Navy.

His playing career as a battling centre-half was virtually ended in a tackle by Manchester United's Duncan Edwards in December 1954.

He became a newsagent in Kingstanding, Birmingham, and later moved to a similar business in Looe.

Former Players' Association and Old Stars XI

Towards the end of 1996, the Former Players' Association came into being linked to the Old Stars team which had been running for many years.

Moves were initiated by Martin Smith, son of the late England and Villa winger Leslie Smith who had started the original Old Stars team.

The Old Stars had raised thousands of pounds for local charities and good causes, but was running down badly with the lack of resources and fewer and fewer former players taking part.

As a result of Martin Smith's initiative, a more modern-minded, partially self-financing set-up was put into motion under the chairmanship of Neil Rioch and with Smith himself as secretary.

As a result, a whole battery of former players, including several from the Championship-European Cup years, returned to the claret and blue fold and the entire operation was given a kick-start.

The Former Players' Association, along with the Old Stars XI, organised social ventures, an executive trip to an away game, a re-union dinner to coincide with the Villa Park centenary and a banquet to celebrate the 40th Anniversary of the 1957 FA Cup victory in May.

When launched, the Executive Committee under Neil Rioch's Chairmanship was Andy Blair, Des Bremner, Alan Deakin, Colin Gibson, Tony Morley and David Goodyear.

Dennis Jackson continued as team Manager of the Old Stars. Patron of the dual organisation was Doug Ellis, while 1957 FA Cup-winning skipper Johnny Dixon was President and Charlie Aitken, holder of the Aston Villa appearances record, was the Honorary Chairman.

RESERVE TEAM RESULTS & SCORERS 1996-97

PONTIN'S CENTRAL LEAGUE

Aug	22	H	**West Bromwich Albion**	2-0	Walker 2
Aug	28	A	Sunderland	3-3	Davis (pen), Byfield 2
Sept	5	A	Sheffield United	1-2	Davis (pen)
Sept	18	A	Port Vale	3-1	Joachim 2, Carr
Sept	25	H	**Notts County**	1-2	Joachim
Oct	9	H	**Coventry City**	1-0	Johnson
Oct	21	A	Huddersfield Town	5-2	Joachim 3, Davis 2 (pens)
Nov	6	H	**Middlesbrough**	7-2	Hazell, Walker, Lescott, Joachim 2, Draper, Byfield
Nov	27	A	Blackpool	2-1	Byfield, Collins
Dec	3	A	Wolverhampton W.	4-1	Hendrie 3, Kirby
Jan	21	H	**Port Vale**	2-0	Kirby, Byfield
Jan	27	H	**Preston North End**	0-0	
Feb	12	A	Middlesbrough	4-0	Joachim 2, Davis 2
Feb	26	H	**Wolverhampton W.**	1-0	Law (og)
Mar	12	H	**Huddersfield Town**	3-2	Davis, Hendrie, Joachim
Mar	19	H	**Blackpool**	2-0	Farrelly 2
Mar	26	A	West Bromwich Albion	2-2	Davis, Joachim
Apr	2	H	**Sunderland**	2-2	Walker, Kirby
Apr	15	A	Coventry City	2-0	Joachim, Walker
Apr	17	A	Leicester City	2-3	Murray, Joachim
Apr	21	H	**Sheffield United**	4-1	Davis, Joachim 2, Walker
Apr	23	A	Notts County	4-0	Walker 2, Collins, Byfield
Apr	30	A	Preston North End	0-1	
May	6	H	**Leicester City**	5-0	Scimeca, Byfield 2, Farrelly, Hines (pen)

BIRMINGHAM COUNTY FA SENIOR CUP

Nov	18	A	Bolehall Swifts (Rd2)	2-0	Kirby, Birchall (pen)
Dec	10	A	Dudley Town (Rd3)	3-0	Lescott, Byfield, Jaszczun
Jan	15	A	W. B. Albion (Rd4)	1-1	Lee *(aet - Albion won 4-3 on penalties)*

Promotion the deserved prize for 'Beard's Babes' as youth shines

A season of 'only almost' winning silverware was the reward for the efforts of the Reserve and Youth teams.

For the whole of the season the mostly young Reserve team, now under the management of Malcolm Beard, battled for the Pontins League Division One title, but ultimately had to settle for runners-up place behind Preston North End.

The true yardstick of the section's success or otherwise, however, is that of young players making progress and in this regard there was much to enthuse over.

Welsh under-21 international centre-back David Hughes was the latest to come through the ranks of Tony McAndrew's youth squad and achieve first-team recognition via the Reserves.

The youth team often included several schoolboys who had to learn to cope mentally and physically against young professionals.

However, they reached the final of the Midland Youth Cup but, after recording a 1-1 draw at home to Stoke City, lost the away leg to settle for runners-up spot.

PONTINS LEAGUE DIVISION ONE TABLE

	P	W	D	L	F	A	Pts
Preston N. E.	24	16	6	2	42	14	54
Aston Villa	24	16	4	4	62	25	52
Notts County	24	12	5	7	38	35	41
Middlesbrough	24	10	8	6	42	36	38
Wolves	24	11	5	8	37	32	38
Leicester City	24	11	3	10	37	42	36
Sunderland	24	9	8	7	47	38	35
Huddersfield T.	24	8	5	11	32	39	29
Port Vale	24	7	6	11	30	37	27
Coventry City	24	6	8	10	22	25	26
W. B. Albion	24	6	6	12	21	36	24
Sheffield United	24	7	3	14	26	44	24
Blackpool	24	1	5	18	12	46	8

SOUTHERN JUNIOR FLOODLIT CUP

Sept 16	H	**Millwall**	2-4	Middleton 2

FA YOUTH CUP

Dec 4	A	Coventry City (Rd 2)	1-2	Vassell

MIDLAND YOUTH CUP

Oct 2	A	Derby County (Rd 2)	3-0	Burgess 2, Middleton
Nov 12	A	Port Vale (Rd 3)	1-1	Blackwood
Nov 26	H	**Port Vale** (Rd 3R)	3-1	Lee 2, Hickman
Mar 11	H	**Grimsby Town** (S/F 1/2)	1-0	Middleton (pen)
Mar 24	A	Grimsby Town (S/F 2/2)	2-1	Lee, Oswin (og) *Villa win 3-1 on aggregate*
Apr 28	H	**Stoke City** (F 1/2)	1-1	Blackwood
May 10	A	Stoke City (F 2/2)	0-2	*Villa lose 3-1 on aggregate*

MIDLAND MELVILLE YOUTH LEAGUE CUP

Oct 12	H	**Peterborough Utd** (Rd 2)	4-2	Middleton 2, Lee, Hadland
Nov 16	A	Coventry City (Rd 3)	0-1	

MIDLAND MELVILLE YOUTH LEAGUE

Aug	10	A	Birmingham City	1-1	Lescott
Aug	17	**H**	**Coventry City**	3-0	Sheridan, Burgess, Middleton
Aug	24	**H**	**Derby County**	1-0	Middleton
Aug	31	**H**	**Grimsby Town**	4-0	Hickman, Lee, Vassell, Middleton
Sept	13	**H**	**West Bromwich Albion**	3-0	Middleton, Lee, Vassell
Sept	21	**H**	**Northampton Town**	3-1	Hazell 2, Lee
Sept	28	A	Notts County	1-0	Middleton
Oct	5	**H**	**Walsall**	0-2	
Oct	16	**H**	**Lincoln City**	0-1	
Oct	19	A	Peterborough United	1-3	Appleby
Oct	26	**H**	**Port Vale**	4-3	Blackwood 2, Lescott, Blackburn
Nov	8	**H**	**Stoke City**	3-1	Lee, Vassell, Blackwood
Nov	30	**H**	**Mansfield Town**	4-1	Lee 3, Burgess
Dec	7	**H**	**Birmingham City**	0-5	
Jan	18	A	Derby County	1-0	Lee
Jan	25	A	Northampton Town	0-1	
Feb	1	**H**	**Notts County**	1-2	Sheridan
Feb	8	A	Nottingham Forest	1-1	Lescott
Feb	15	A	Port Vale	2-1	Own goal, Lee
Feb	22	A	Leicester City	0-2	
Mar	1	**H**	**Shrewsbury Town**	5-2	Lescott 2, Lee 2, Sheridan
Mar	7	A	Stoke City	3-1	Vassell 2, Lescott
Mar	15	A	West Bromwich Albion	2-0	Sheridan, Lee
Mar	19	A	Coventry City	2-1	Vassell, Middleton
Mar	22	**H**	**Peterborough United**	0-0	
Mar	29	**H**	**Wolverhampton W.**	3-1	Hadland, Middleton, Vassell
Apr	1	**H**	**Leicester City**	3-0	Lee 2, own goal
Apr	5	A	Wolverhampton W.	0-3	
Apr	12	A	Mansfield Town	1-2	Own goal
Apr	15	A	Shrewsbury Town	4-1	Blackwood 2, Lee, Middleton
Apr	19	**H**	**Nottingham Forest**	1-3	Sheridan
Apr	23	A	Grimsby Town	1-1	Lee
Apr	26	A	Walsall	1-0	Lee
May	3	A	Lincoln City	1-1	Blackwood

See page 133 for final Midland Melville Youth League Table.

RESERVE & YOUTH TEAM APPEARANCES

	CENTRAL LGE		SENIOR CUP		YOUTH LGE		YOUTH CUPS	
	Apps	Gls	Apps	Gls	Apps	Gls	Apps	Gls
Mark Appleby	-	-	-	-	13 (5)	1	3 (1)	-
Bradley Blackburn	-	-	-	-	11 (4)	1	4	-
Michael Blackwood	-	-	-	-	10 (11)	6	4 (4)	2
Mark Bosnich	1	-	-	-	-	-	-	-
Stuart Brock	3	-	2	-	-	-	-	-
Lee Burchell	1 (3)	-	2 (1)	1	-	-	-	-
Richard Burgess	-	-	- (1)	-	13 (2)	2	6	2
Darren Byfield	11 (9)	8	3	1	-	-	-	-
Jamie Cairns	-	-	-	-	- (1)	-	-	-
Gary Charles	1 (2)	-	-	-	-	-	-	-
Lee Collins	15 (2)	1	3	-	-	-	-	-
Neil Davis	14	9	-	-	-	-	-	-
Mark Draper	2	1	-	-	-	-	-	-
Phillip Elias	-	-	-	-	18	-	3	-
Steve Evans	-	-	-	-	1 (1)	-	-	-
Gareth Farrelly	20	3	1	-	-	-	-	-
Matthew George	-	-	-	-	14	-	7	-
Matthew Ghent	-	-	-	-	1	-	-	-
Guy Hadland	-	-	-	-	25 (4)	1	9 (2)	1
David Harding	-	-	-	-	2·	-	-	-
Reuben Hazell	6	1	1	-	27	2	11	-
Lee Hendrie	16	4	-	-	-	-	-	-
John Hickman	-	-	-	-	31	1	11	1
Leslie Hines	15 (3)	1	3	-	-	-	-	-
David Hughes	14 (1)	-	2	-	-	-	-	-
Tommy Jaszczun	11 (1)	-	2	1	-	-	-	-
Julian Joachim	16 (1)	17	-	-	-	-	-	-
Justin Keegan	-	-	-	-	1	-	-	-
Alan Kirby	6 (4)	3	3	1	-	-	-	-
Alan Lee	- (2)	-	- (2)	1	30 (3)	17	11	4
Aaron Lescott	4 (2)	1	1	1	27	6	10	-
Scott Matthewman	-	-	-	-	1	-	-	-
Alex Meredith	-	-	-	-	9 (6)	-	1	-
Darren Middleton	-	-	- (1)	-	23 (1)	8	8	6
Jonathan Miley	-	-	1 (1)	-	-	-	-	-
Brian Mulholland	-	-	-	-	2	-	-	-
Scott Murray	24	1	2	-	-	-	-	-
Michael Oakes	8	-	1	-	-	-	-	-
Ben Petty	21 (2)	-	3	-	-	-	-	-
Michael Price	-	-	-	-	2	-	1	-
Luke Prince	-	-	-	-	- (2)	-	-	-
Nathan Pulisciano	-	-	-	-	6 (5)	-	- (3)	-
Adam Rachel	12	-	-	-	-	-	-	-
Dominic Reece	-	-	-	-	24 (1)	-	11	-
Martin Ridley	-	-	-	-	22 (6)	-	8 (1)	-
Riccardo Scimeca	7	1	-	-	-	-	-	-
Darragh Sheridan	-	-	-	-	26 (3)	5	6 (3)	-
Richard Sindon	-	-	-	-	1	-	-	-
Ian Taylor	2	-	-	-	-	-	-	-
Stuart Thornley	-	-	-	-	4	-	- (2)	-
Phillip Tongue	-	-	-	-	10 (8)	-	- (1)	-
Darius Vassell	-	-	-	-	15 (14)	7	7 (4)	1
Richard Walker	15 (5)	9	3	-	-	-	-	-
David Warren	-	-	-	-	1	-	-	-
Trialists	-	-	-	-	4 (1)	-	-	-
Own Goals	-	-	-	-	-	3	-	1

Also played for the reserve team: Franz Carr 1 Lge, 1 goal; Tommy Johnson 3 Lge, 1 goal; Phil King 4 Lge, 1 sub Cup; Paul McGrath 2 Lge; Carl Tiler 9 Lge.

DEVELOPMENTS AT VILLA PARK

GROUND IMPROVEMENTS 'ON HOLD'

There was a deep sense of disappointment at Villa Park when plans for a multi-million pound development scheme in the Trinity Road main stand were 'deferred' by the city's Planning Department.

The surprise decision was announced in April, shortly before the work was due to commence, forcing the postponement of some 60 new jobs.

The major part of the scheme was a new roof with a trajectory and facia to match the other three sides and to standardise the overall appearance of the stadium.

Main stand supporters were to get an uninterrupted view of the pitch, due to the intended removal of the upright columns, arising from the installation of a huge supporting beam running the length of the stand.

The Planning Department deferred a decision pending sight of a model of the ground as it would be when a further development of the North Stand had been completed a year later.

Left with too little time to produce such an overall scheme in detail, the club had no alternative but to put the work back for a further twelve months.

The Trinity Road plan was also to include the installation of a new row of Executive Boxes to replace the original ones created, among the first in football, in 1970.

"This is as huge a blow to the club as it is to those supporters who would have benefitted from the improvements," said chairman Doug Ellis.

● In spite of the hold put on major developments, there are several projects which are going ahead in and around the ground this close-season.

The long awaited installation of new giant scoreboards, hereinafter known as 'Videowalls', is now taking place and they will hopefully be in place for the start of the season.

Also scheduled to be in operation for August is a new retail outlet within the old Holte Hotel, built with the intention of taking pressure off the Villa Village on match days.

The construction of the new Holte Suite is well under way and when completed will be the largest conference facility in the city. A part of the Suite will also be used as a supporters' club on match days.

Already serving, as we go to print, is the Corner Flag Restaurant, situated in the corner of the Trinity Road Stand and the North Stand, giving diners an uninterrupted view of the pitch.

THE PITCH

Plans to lay a new pitch at Villa Park for the second time in 12 months are going ahead in the close-season.

The new pitch will be along the lines of the one at the McAlpine Stadium, Huddersfield, which has been in place there for a season.

A machine is used to tie the roots of the grass together with nylon thread, which makes the roots stronger and gives them a longer life span. The method was first developed in Holland.

Villa director and secretary, Steve Stride, said, "Our groundsman, Tony Eden, travelled to have a look at the one used by Huddersfield and was impressed.

"They play rugby, reserve and first-team matches on it. In all, they have played 80 competitive games on it and it is still in great condition."

The work started immediately after the last game of the season, against Southampton, and is expected to be ready for use well in advance of the kick-off for the 1997-98 season; unlike last year when the relayed pitch had only a few weeks to bed in following the Euro 96 matches played at Villa Park.

COMPLETE PREMIERSHIP APPEARANCES & SCORERS

	LEAGUE		FA CUP		LGE CUP		UEFA CUP		TOTAL	
	Apps	Gls	Apps	Gls	Apps	Gls	Apps	Gls	Apps	Gls
Dalian ATKINSON *(Seasons played: 92/93, 93/94, 94/95)*	68 (5)	22	3	-	14	11	7	2	92 (5)	35
Earl BARRETT *(Seasons played: 92/93, 93/94, 94/95)*	105 (1)	1	9	-	15	1	7	-	136 (1)	2
Chris BODEN *(Seasons played: 94/95)*	- (1)	-	-	-	-	-	-	-	- (1)	-
Stefan BEINLICH *(Seasons played: 92/93, 93/94)*	7 (7)	1	-	-	-	-	-	-	7 (7)	1
Mark BLAKE *(Seasons played: 92/93)*	- (1)	-	-	-	-	-	-	-	- (1)	-
Mark BOSNICH *(Seasons played: 92/93, 93/94, 94/95, 95/96, 96/97)*	133	-	13	-	19 (1)	-	2	-	167 (1)	-
Matthias BREITKREUTZ *(Seasons played: 92/93, 93/94)*	3 (2)	-	-	-	- (1)	-	-	-	3 (3)	-
Paul BROWNE *(Seasons played: 95/96)*	2	-	-	-	-	-	-	-	2	-
Franz CARR *(Seasons played: 94/95, 95/96)*	1 (2)	-	1	1	-	-	-	-	2 (2)	1
Martin CARRUTHERS *(Seasons played: 92/93)*	- (1)	-	-	-	-	-	-	-	- (1)	-
Gary CHARLES *(Seasons played: 94/95, 95/96)*	48 (2)	1	5	-	8	-	-	-	61 (2)	1
Gordon COWANS *(Seasons played: 93/94)*	9 (2)	-	-	-	2	-	4	-	15 (2)	-
Neil COX *(Seasons played: 92/93, 93/94)*	22 (13)	3	4 (2)	1	5 (2)	-	1	-	32 (17)	4
Sasa CURCIC *(Seasons played: 96/97)*	17 (5)	-	2	1	1	-	-	-	20 (5)	1
Tony DALEY *(Seasons played: 92/93, 93/94)*	27 (13)	3	2	-	5 (1)	-	2	-	36 (14)	3
Neil DAVIS *(Seasons played: 95/96)*	- (2)	-	- (1)	-	-	-	-	-	- (3)	-
Mark DRAPER *(Seasons played: 95/96, 96/97)*	64 (1)	2	5	2	9 (1)	1	2	-	80 (2)	5
Ugo EHIOGU *(Seasons played: 92/93, 93/94, 94/95, 95/96, 96/97)*	127 (7)	7	10 (1)	1	14 (1)	1	6	1	157 (9)	10
Dave FARRELL *(Seasons played: 92/93, 93/94, 94/95)*	5 (1)	-	-	-	2	-	-	-	7 (1)	-
Gareth FARRELLY *(Seasons played: 95/96, 96/97)*	2 (6)	-	-	-	- (1)	-	-	-	2 (7)	-
John FASHANU *(Seasons played: 94/95)*	11 (2)	3	2	-	-	-	1	-	14 (2)	3
Graham FENTON *(Seasons played: 93/94, 94/95, 95/96)*	16 (16)	3	-	-	2 (5)	-	-	-	18 (21)	3
Steve FROGGATT *(Seasons played: 92/93, 93/94)*	24 (2)	2	3 (1)	-	1 (1)	-	-	-	28 (4)	2
Lee HENDRIE *(Seasons played: 95/96, 96/97)*	2 (5)	-	1 (2)	-	-	-	-	-	3 (7)	-
David HUGHES *(Seasons played: 96/97)*	4 (3)	-	-	-	-	-	-	-	4 (3)	-
Julian JOACHIM *(Seasons played: 95/96, 96/97)*	7 (19)	4	1	-	1	-	-	-	9 (19)	4
Ray HOUGHTON *(Seasons played: 92/93, 93/94, 94/95)*	83 (12)	6	7	2	11 (2)	2	4 (2)	1	105 (16)	11
Tommy JOHNSON *(Seasons played: 94/95, 95/96, 96/97)*	38 (19)	13	5 (2)	1	5	2	1 (1)	1	49 (22)	17

COMPLETE PREMIERSHIP APPEARANCES & SCORERS

	LEAGUE		FA CUP		LGE CUP		UEFA CUP		TOTAL	
	Apps	Gls	Apps	Gls	Apps	Gls	Apps	Gls	Apps	Gls
Phil KING *(Seasons played: 94/95)*	13 (3)	-	-	-	3	-	4	-	20 (3)	-
Dariusz KUBICKI *(Seasons played: 92/93, 93/94)*	1 (1)	-	-	-	1	-	-	-	2 (1)	-
Nii LAMPTEY* *(Seasons played: 94/95)*	1 (5)	-	-	-	2 (1)	3	-	-	3 (6)	3
Frank McAVENNIE † *(Seasons played: 92/93)*	3	-	-	-	-	-	-	-	3	-
Paul McGRATH *(Seasons played: 92/93, 93/94, 94/95, 95/96, 96/97)*	137 (5)	6	11 (1)	-	20 (1)	1	8 (1)	-	176 (8)	7
Savo MILOSEVIC *(Seasons played: 95/96, 96/97)*	65 (2)	21	8	1	7 (1)	1	2	-	82 (3)	23
Scott MURRAY *(Seasons played: 95/96, 96/97)*	4	-	-	-	-	-	-	-	4	-
Fernando NELSON *(Seasons played: 96/97)*	33 (1)	-	- (1)	-	2	-	2	-	37 (2)	-
Michael OAKES *(Seasons played: 94/95, 95/96, 96/97)*	18 (2)	-	-	-	2	-	2	-	22 (2)	-
Garry PARKER *(Seasons played: 92/93, 93/94, 94/95)*	66 (4)	12	5	-	12	-	- (2)	-	83 (6)	12
Cyrille REGIS *(Seasons played: 92/93)*	7 (6)	1	- (2)	-	1 (1)	-	-	-	8 (9)	1
Kevin RICHARDSON *(Seasons played: 92/93, 93/94, 94/95)*	100 (1)	7	7	-	13	3	8	-	128 (1)	10
Dean SAUNDERS *(Seasons played: 92/93, 93/94, 94/95)*	111 (1)	38	9	4	15	7	8	1	143 (1)	50
Riccardo SCIMECA *(Seasons played: 95/96, 96/97)*	18 (16)	-	5	-	2 (3)	-	-	-	25 (19)	-
Bryan SMALL *(Seasons played: 92/93, 93/94, 94/95)*	23 (5)	-	-	-	2	-	2	-	27 (5)	-
Gareth SOUTHGATE *(Seasons played: 95/96, 96/97)*	59	2	7	-	9	1	2	-	77	3
Nigel SPINK *(Seasons played: 92/93, 93/94, 94/95, 95/96)*	51 (4)	-	4	-	6	-	6	-	67 (4)	-
Steve STAUNTON *(Seasons played: 92/93, 93/94, 94/95, 95/96, 96/97)*	141 (3)	12	11 (1)	-	15 (2)	1	8	-	175 (6)	13
Ian TAYLOR *(Seasons played: 94/95, 95/96, 96/97)*	74 (6)	6	4 (1)	1	7 (1)	2	1	-	86 (8)	9
Shaun TEALE *(Seasons played: 92/93, 93/94, 94/95)*	104 (1)	2	8	-	13	2	4	-	129 (1)	4
Carl TILER *(Seasons played: 92/93, 93/94, 94/95, 95/96, 96/97)*	10 (2)	1	2	-	1	-	-	-	13 (2)	1
Andy TOWNSEND *(Seasons played: 92/93, 93/94, 94/95, 95/96, 96/97)*	130 (1)	8	12	-	20	2	10	1	172 (1)	11
Guy WHITTINGHAM *(Seasons played: 93/94, 94/95)*	17 (8)	5	-	-	4 (1)	1	2 (1)	-	23 (10)	6
Alan WRIGHT *(Seasons played: 94/95, 95/96, 96/97)*	84	3	8	-	10	-	2	-	104	3
Dwight YORKE *(Seasons played: 92/93, 93/94, 94/95, 95/96, 96/97)*	129 (19)	48	13 (2)	7	16 (2)	8	2	-	160 (23)	63
Own Goals	-	10	-	-	-	1	-	-	-	11

* On loan.   † On trial.

PREMIERSHIP ALL-TIME TABLE 1992-97

		P	W	D	L	F	A	Pts	1993	1994	1995	1996	1997
1	Manchester United	202	123	52	27	373	176	421	1st	1st	2nd	1st	1st
2	Blackburn Rovers	202	99	50	53	314	211	347	4th	2nd	1st	7th	13th
3	Liverpool	202	93	53	56	318	218	332	6th	8th	4th	3rd	4th
4	Arsenal	202	82	63	57	256	179	309	10th	4th	12th	5th	3rd
5	**Aston Villa**	202	82	57	63	253	215	303	2nd	10th	18th	4th	5th
6	Newcastle United	160	86	37	37	288	165	295	-	3rd	6th	2nd	2nd
7	Leeds United	202	73	64	65	249	234	283	17th	5th	5th	13th	11th
8	Tottenham Hotspur	202	72	57	73	274	272	273	8th	15th	7th	8th	10th
9	Wimbledon	202	72	56	74	264	289	272	12th	6th	9th	14th	8th
10	Sheffield Wednesday	202	68	67	67	278	274	271	7th	7th,	13th	15th	7th
11	Chelsea	202	68	66	68	254	261	270	11th	14th	11th,	11th	6th
12	Everton	202	65	55	82	247	270	250	13th	17th	15th	6th	15th
13	Coventry City	202	56	69	77	219	278	237	15th	11th	16th	16th	17th
14	Southampton	202	56	58	88	248	298	226	18th	18th	10th	17th	16th
15	QPR	164	59	39	66	224	232	216	5th	9th,	8th	19th R	-
16	Nottingham Forest	160	53	50	57	194	218	209	22nd R	-	3rd	9th	20th R
17	West Ham United	160	50	45	65	173	206	195	-	13th	14th	10th	14th
18	Manchester City	164	45	54	65	180	222	189	9th	16th	17th	18th R	-
19	Norwich City	126	43	39	44	163	180	168	3rd,	12th	20th R	-	-
20	Middlesbrough	118	32	33	53	140	185	126	21st R	-	-	12th	19th R
21	Ipswich Town	126	28	38	60	121	206	122	16th,	19th	22nd R	-	-
22	Sheffield United	84	22	28	34	96	113	94	14th	20th R	-	-	-
23	Crystal Palace	84	22	28	34	82	110	94	20th R	-	19th R	-	-
24	Oldham Athletic	84	22	23	39	105	142	89	19th	21st R	-	-	-
25	Leicester City	80	18	22	40	91	134	76	-	-	21st R	-	9th
26	Derby County	38	11	13	14	45	58	46	-	-	-	-	12th
27	Sunderland	38	10	10	18	35	53	40	-	-	-	-	18th R
28	Swindon Town	42	5	15	22	47	100	30	-	22nd R	-	-	-
29	Bolton Wanderers	38	8	5	25	39	71	29			-		20th R	-
	Totals	2146	1523	742	1523	5570	5570	5308					

Season	Div	Teams	Pos	P	W	D	L	F	A	W	D	L	F	A	Pts	Cup Honours
1888-89	1	12	2nd	22	10	0	1	44	16	2	5	4	17	27	29	*(FAC Winners in 1886-87)*
1889-90	1	12	8th	22	6	2	3	30	15	1	3	7	13	36	19	
1890-91	1	12	9th	22	5	4	2	29	18	2	0	9	16	40	18	
1891-92	1	14	4th	26	10	0	3	63	23	5	0	8	26	33	30	*FAC Runners-up*
1892-93	1	16	4th	30	12	1	2	50	24	4	2	9	23	38	35	
1893-94	**1**	**16**	**1st**	**30**	**12**	**2**	**1**	**49**	**13**	**7**	**4**	**4**	**35**	**29**	**44**	
1894-95	1	16	3rd	30	12	2	1	51	12	5	3	7	31	31	39	***FAC Winners***
1895-96	**1**	**16**	**1st**	**30**	**14**	**1**	**0**	**47**	**17**	**6**	**4**	**5**	**31**	**28**	**45**	
1896-97	**1**	**16**	**1st**	**30**	**10**	**3**	**2**	**36**	**16**	**11**	**2**	**2**	**37**	**22**	**47**	***FAC Winners***
1897-98	1	16	6th	30	12	1	2	47	21	2	4	9	14	30	33	
1898-99	**1**	**18**	**1st**	**34**	**15**	**2**	**0**	**58**	**13**	**4**	**5**	**8**	**18**	**27**	**45**	
1899-00	**1**	**18**	**1st**	**34**	**12**	**4**	**1**	**45**	**18**	**10**	**2**	**5**	**32**	**17**	**50**	
1900-01	1	18	15th	34	8	5	4	32	18	2	5	10	13	33	30	*FAC Semi-finalists*
1901-02	1	18	8th	34	9	5	3	27	13	4	3	10	15	27	34	
1902-03	1	18	2nd	34	11	3	3	43	18	8	0	9	18	22	41	*FAC Semi-finalists*
1903-04	1	18	5th	34	13	1	3	41	16	4	6	7	29	32	41	
1904-05	1	18	4th	34	11	2	4	32	15	8	2	7	31	28	42	***FAC Winners***
1905-06	1	20	8th	38	13	2	4	51	19	4	4	11	21	37	40	
1906-07	1	20	5th	38	13	4	2	51	19	6	2	11	27	33	44	
1907-08	1	20	2nd	38	9	6	4	47	24	8	3	8	30	35	43	
1908-09	1	20	7th	38	8	7	4	31	22	6	3	10	27	34	38	
1909-10	**1**	**20**	**1st**	**38**	**17**	**2**	**0**	**62**	**19**	**6**	**5**	**8**	**22**	**23**	**53**	
1910-11	1	20	2nd	38	15	3	1	50	18	7	4	8	19	23	51	
1911-12	1	20	6th	38	12	2	5	48	22	5	5	9	28	41	41	
1912-13	1	20	2nd	38	13	4	2	57	21	6	8	5	29	31	50	***FAC Winners***
1913-14	1	20	2nd	38	11	3	5	36	21	8	3	8	29	29	44	*FAC Semi-finalists*
1914-15	1	20	13th	38	10	5	4	39	32	3	6	10	23	40	37	
First World War																
1919-20	1	22	9th	42	11	3	7	49	36	7	3	11	26	37	42	***FAC Winners***
1920-21	1	22	10th	42	11	4	6	39	21	7	3	11	24	49	43	
1921-22	1	22	5th	42	16	3	2	50	19	6	0	15	24	36	47	
1922-23	1	22	6th	42	15	3	3	42	11	3	7	11	22	40	46	
1923-24	1	22	6th	42	10	10	1	33	11	8	3	10	19	26	49	*FAC Runners-up*
1924-25	1	22	15th	42	10	7	4	34	25	3	6	12	24	46	39	
1925-26	1	22	6th	42	12	7	2	56	25	4	5	12	30	51	44	
1926-27	1	22	10th	42	11	4	6	51	34	7	3	11	30	49	43	
1927-28	1	22	8th	42	13	3	5	52	30	4	6	11	26	43	43	
1928-29	1	22	3rd	42	16	2	3	62	30	7	2	12	36	51	50	*FAC Semi-finalists*
1929-30	1	22	4th	42	13	1	7	54	33	8	4	9	38	50	47	
1930-31	1	22	2nd	42	17	3	1	86	34	8	6	7	42	44	59	

VILLA'S ALL-TIME LEAGUE RECORD – SEASON BY SEASON

Season	Div	Teams	Pos	P	W	D	L	F	A	W	D	L	F	A	Pts	Cup Honours
1931-32	1	22	5th	42	15	1	5	64	28	4	7	10	40	44	46	
1932-33	1	22	2nd	42	16	2	3	60	29	7	6	8	32	38	54	
1933-34	1	22	13th	42	10	5	6	45	34	4	7	10	33	41	40	*FAC Semi-finalists*
1934-35	1	22	13th	42	11	6	4	50	36	3	7	11	24	52	41	
1935-36	*1*	*22*	*21st*	*42*	*7*	*6*	*8*	*47*	*56*	*6*	*3*	*12*	*34*	*54*	*35*	
1936-37	2	22	9th	42	10	6	5	47	30	6	6	9	35	40	44	
1937-38	**2**	**22**	**1st**	**42**	**17**	**2**	**2**	**50**	**12**	**8**	**5**	**8**	**23**	**23**	**57**	*FAC Semi-finalists*
1938-39	1	22	12th	42	11	3	7	44	25	5	6	10	27	35	41	
Second World War																
1946-47	1	22	8th	42	9	6	6	39	24	9	3	9	28	29	45	
1947-48	1	22	6th	42	13	5	3	42	22	6	4	11	23	35	47	
1948-49	1	22	10th	42	10	6	5	40	36	6	4	11	20	40	42	
1949-50	1	22	12th	42	10	7	4	31	19	5	5	11	30	42	42	
1950-51	1	22	15th	42	9	6	6	39	29	3	7	11	27	39	37	
1951-52	1	22	6th	42	13	3	5	49	28	6	6	9	30	42	47	
1952-53	1	22	11th	42	9	7	5	36	23	5	6	10	27	38	41	
1953-54	1	22	13th	42	12	5	4	50	28	4	4	13	20	40	41	
1954-55	1	22	6th	42	11	3	7	38	31	9	4	8	34	42	47	
1955-56	1	22	20th	42	9	6	6	32	29	2	7	12	20	40	35	
1956-57	1	22	10th	42	10	8	3	45	25	4	7	10	20	30	43	***FAC Winners***
1957-58	1	22	14th	42	12	4	5	46	26	4	3	14	27	60	39	
1958-59	*1*	*22*	*21st*	*42*	*8*	*5*	*8*	*31*	*33*	*3*	*3*	*15*	*27*	*54*	*30*	*FAC Semi-finalists*
1959-60	2	22	1st	42	17	3	1	62	19	8	6	7	27	24	59	*FAC Semi-finalists*
1960-61	1	22	9th	42	13	3	5	48	28	4	6	11	30	49	43	***LC Winners***
1961-62	1	22	7th	42	13	5	3	45	20	5	3	13	20	36	44	
1962-63	1	22	15th	42	12	2	7	38	23	3	6	12	24	45	38	*LC Runners-up*
1963-64	1	22	19th	42	8	6	7	35	29	3	6	12	27	42	34	
1964-65	1	22	16th	42	14	1	6	36	24	2	4	15	21	58	37	*LC Semi-finalists*
1965-66	1	22	16th	42	10	3	8	39	34	5	3	13	30	46	36	
1966-67	*1*	*22*	*21st*	*42*	*7*	*5*	*9*	*30*	*33*	*4*	*2*	*15*	*24*	*52*	*29*	
1967-68	2	22	16th	42	10	3	8	35	30	5	4	12	19	34	37	
1968-69	2	22	18th	42	10	8	3	22	11	2	6	13	15	37	38	
1969-70	*2*	*22*	*21st*	*42*	*7*	*8*	*6*	*23*	*21*	*1*	*5*	*15*	*13*	*41*	*29*	
1970-71	3	24	4th	46	13	7	3	27	13	6	8	9	27	33	53	*LC Runners-up*
1971-72	**3**	**24**	**1st**	**46**	**20**	**1**	**2**	**45**	**10**	**12**	**5**	**6**	**40**	**22**	**70**	
1972-73	2	22	3rd	42	12	5	4	27	17	6	9	6	24	30	50	
1973-74	2	22	14th	42	8	9	4	33	21	5	6	10	15	24	41	
1974-75	2	22	2nd	42	16	4	1	47	6	9	4	8	32	26	58	***LC Winners***
1975-76	1	22	16th	42	11	8	2	32	17	0	9	12	19	42	39	
1976-77	1	22	4th	42	17	3	1	55	17	5	4	12	21	33	51	***LC Winners***

VILLA'S ALL-TIME LEAGUE RECORD – SEASON BY SEASON

Season	Div	Teams	Pos	P	W	D	L	F	A	W	D	L	F	A	Pts	Cup Honours
1977-78	1	22	8th	42	11	4	6	33	18	7	6	8	24	24	46	
1978-79	1	22	8th	42	8	9	4	37	26	7	7	7	22	23	46	
1979-80	1	22	7th	42	11	5	5	29	22	5	9	7	22	28	46	
1980-81	**1**	**22**	**1st**	**42**	**16**	**3**	**2**	**40**	**13**	**10**	**5**	**6**	**32**	**27**	**60**	
1981-82	1	22	11th	42	9	6	6	28	24	6	6	9	27	29	57	*EC Winners*
1982-83	1	22	6th	42	17	2	2	47	15	4	3	14	15	35	68	*ESC Winners*
1983-84	1	22	10th	42	14	3	4	34	22	3	6	12	25	39	60	*LC Semi-finalists*
1984-85	1	22	10th	42	10	7	4	34	20	5	4	12	26	40	56	
1985-86	1	22	16th	42	7	6	8	27	28	3	8	10	24	39	44	*LC Semi-finalists*
1986-87	*1*	*22*	*22nd*	*42*	*7*	*7*	*7*	*25*	*25*	*1*	*5*	*15*	*20*	*54*	*36*	
1987-88	2	23	2nd	44	9	7	6	31	21	13	5	4	37	20	78	
1988-89	1	20	17th	38	7	6	6	25	22	2	7	10	20	34	40	
1989-90	1	20	2nd	38	13	3	3	36	20	8	4	7	21	18	70	*FMC Area Finalists*
1990-91	1	20	17th	38	7	9	3	29	25	2	5	12	17	33	41	
1991-92	1	22	7th	42	13	3	5	31	16	4	6	11	17	28	60	
1992-93	P	22	2nd	42	13	5	3	36	16	8	6	7	21	24	74	
1993-94	P	22	10th	42	8	5	8	23	18	7	7	7	23	32	57	*LC Winners*
1994-95	P	22	18th	42	6	9	6	27	24	5	6	10	24	32	48	
1995-96	P	20	4th	38	11	5	3	32	15	7	4	8	20	20	63	*LC Winners/FAC SF*
1996-97	P	20	5th	38	11	5	3	27	13	6	5	8	20	21	61	

VILLA'S COMPLETE LEAGUE RECORD

	P	W	D	L	F	A	Pts
Home	1931	1116	421	394	4039	2191	2815
Away	1931	523	461	947	2461	3480	1591
Total	3862	1639	882	1341	6500	5671	4406

2pts for a win up to season 1980-81, 3pts for a win from season 1981-82

Other honours:

World Club Championship runners-up 1982-83

FA Charity Shield joint winners 1981-82

FA Charity Shield runners-up 1910-11, 1957-58, 1972-73

FAC = FA Cup; LC = League Cup; FMC = Full Members' Cup; EC = European Champions' Cup; ESC = European Super Cup. Championship seasons in **bold** type, relegation seasons in *italics*.

VILLA'S ALL-TIME LEAGUE RECORD – CLUB BY CLUB

		Home					Away				
	P	W	D	L	F	A	W	D	L	F	A
Accrington	10	4	0	1	26	12	1	2	2	9	10
Arsenal	136	36	15	17	136	96	20	14	34	80	113
Barnsley	10	3	2	0	9	2	4	1	0	13	2
Birmingham City	96	23	13	12	82	60	16	12	20	68	74
Blackburn Rovers	130	35	17	13	138	83	18	12	35	89	137
Blackpool	62	16	9	6	65	39	10	7	14	44	51
Bolton Wanderers	128	35	15	14	138	81	16	13	35	66	126
Bournemouth	4	1	1	0	3	2	1	0	1	2	4
Bradford Park Avenue	10	4	0	1	12	4	1	2	2	8	16
Bradford City	28	9	2	3	32	12	4	4	6	17	23
Brentford	6	2	1	0	12	4	3	0	0	8	3
Brighton & Hove Albion	16	6	2	0	16	4	3	2	3	8	7
Bristol City	32	10	3	3	27	19	5	6	5	18	14
Bristol Rovers	8	3	1	0	8	3	2	1	1	4	4
Burnley	94	28	12	7	109	47	11	8	28	71	113
Bury	52	17	6	3	59	31	10	6	10	39	39
Cardiff City	44	14	3	5	39	20	8	2	12	23	30
Carlisle United	10	4	1	0	5	1	2	2	1	6	6
Charlton Athletic	38	10	6	3	41	18	5	6	8	22	33
Chelsea	100	27	12	11	104	70	16	10	24	62	75
Chesterfield	8	2	1	1	7	4	3	0	1	8	3
Coventry City	46	13	10	0	36	12	11	6	6	33	27
Crystal Palace	22	7	2	2	19	8	2	5	4	5	9
Darwen	4	2	0	0	16	0	1	1	0	6	2
Derby County	106	34	10	9	132	58	17	11	25	72	92
Doncaster Rovers	4	1	1	0	4	3	0	0	2	1	3
Everton	164	39	19	24	153	113	21	20	41	99	150
Fulham	34	8	5	4	30	22	2	5	10	20	34
Gillingham	2	1	0	0	2	1	0	1	0	0	0
Glossop	2	1	0	0	9	0	0	0	1	0	1
Grimsby Town	20	5	3	2	29	19	5	1	4	16	20
Halifax Town	4	1	1	0	2	1	1	0	1	2	2
Huddersfield Town	64	20	9	3	74	31	7	10	15	32	51
Hull City	16	4	3	1	21	8	2	2	4	7	12
Ipswich Town	40	11	6	3	40	17	5	4	11	20	30
Leeds United	66	16	10	7	57	40	6	11	16	31	56
Leicester City	70	17	6	12	74	55	6	9	20	48	88
Leyton Orient	10	4	1	0	8	3	1	2	2	3	6
Lincoln City	2	0	1	0	1	1	0	1	0	0	0
Liverpool	144	36	16	20	148	92	12	14	46	78	166
Luton Town	32	10	1	5	29	15	1	3	12	8	24
Manchester City	124	32	19	11	114	67	14	15	33	79	118

	P		Home					Away			
	P	W	D	L	F	A	W	D	L	F	A
Manchester United	128	32	16	16	134	93	10	15	39	61	132
Mansfield Town	4	0	0	2	0	2	0	1	1	1	3
Middlesbrough	106	30	10	13	121	59	18	14	21	70	81
Millwall	18	4	4	1	14	8	3	2	4	9	12
Newcastle United	118	31	14	14	117	65	12	9	38	78	133
Northampton Town	2	0	0	1	1	2	0	0	1	1	2
Norwich City	46	14	6	3	42	25	4	7	12	28	41
Nottingham Forest	106	33	10	10	108	53	16	16	21	74	97
Notts County	66	23	7	3	83	29	12	8	13	49	52
Oldham Athletic	30	9	3	3	34	8	7	6	2	29	17
Oxford United	14	4	2	1	9	3	1	3	3	8	11
Plymouth Argyle	14	5	1	1	19	9	2	2	3	12	12
Portsmouth	60	19	7	4	73	39	8	7	15	42	65
Port Vale	4	2	0	0	3	0	0	1	1	4	6
Preston North End	98	37	3	9	108	44	13	11	25	64	90
Queen's Park Rangers	38	8	4	7	32	26	3	3	13	14	29
Reading	4	2	0	0	4	2	2	0	0	7	3
Rochdale	4	2	0	0	3	0	0	1	1	1	2
Rotherham United	8	3	0	1	8	3	2	1	1	6	3
Scunthorpe United	2	1	0	0	5	0	1	0	0	2	1
Sheffield United	120	40	12	8	145	55	17	16	27	85	111
Sheffield Wednesday	122	43	8	10	153	63	15	8	38	84	131
Shrewsbury Town	6	3	0	0	6	0	1	1	1	4	4
Southampton	44	12	7	3	37	16	4	7	11	19	38
Stockport County	2	1	0	0	7	1	1	0	0	3	1
Stoke City	88	31	7	6	108	36	13	13	18	54	66
Sunderland	140	46	11	13	144	88	14	21	35	88	135
Swansea City	14	7	0	0	19	0	4	0	3	12	10
Swindon Town	10	3	1	1	10	5	2	2	1	6	4
Torquay United	4	1	0	1	5	2	0	1	1	2	3
Tottenham Hotspur	108	23	14	17	83	75	18	9	27	86	108
Tranmere Rovers	4	2	0	0	3	0	1	1	0	2	1
Walsall	4	0	2	0	0	0	0	1	1	1	4
Watford	12	3	2	1	11	6	0	2	4	9	16
West Bromwich Albion	124	39	8	15	118	74	19	15	28	86	99
West Ham United	68	18	6	10	69	45	6	10	18	44	77
Wimbledon	20	5	1	4	18	9	3	3	4	17	17
Wolverhampton Wan.	96	26	10	12	109	64	15	12	21	67	86
Wrexham	4	1	0	1	5	4	2	0	0	5	2
York City	4	2	0	0	5	0	1	1	0	2	1
TOTALS	3862	1116	421	394	4039	2191	523	461	947	2461	3480

VILLA'S RECORD IN EUROPEAN COMPETITIONS

1975-76 – UEFA CUP

Sep 17	R1/L1	A	Royal Antwerp (Belgium)	1-4	Graydon
Oct 1	R1/L2	**H**	**Royal Antwerp**	0-1	

Aggregate Score - Antwerp win 5-1

1977-78 – UEFA CUP

Sep 14	R1/L1	**H**	**Fenerbahce** (Turkey)	4-0	Deehan 2, Gray, Little
Oct 1	R1/L2	A	Fenerbahce	2-0	Deehan, Little

Aggregate Score - Villa win 6-0

Oct 19	R2/L1	**H**	**Gornik Zabrze** (Poland)	2-0	McNaught 2
Nov 2	R2/L2	A	Gornik Zabrze	1-1	Gray

Aggregate Score - Villa win 3-1

Nov 23	R3/L1	**H**	**Athletic Bilbao** (Spain)	2-0	Iribar og, Deehan
Dec 7	R3/L2	A	Athletic Bilbao	1-1	Mortimer

Aggregate Score - Villa win 3-1

Mar 1	R4/L1	**H**	**Barcelona** (Spain)	2-2	McNaught, Deehan
Mar 15	R4/L2	A	Barcelona	1-2	Little

Aggregate Score - Barcelona win 4-3

1981-82 – EUROPEAN CHAMPIONS' CUP

Sep 16	R1/L1	**H**	**Valur** (Iceland)	5-0	Morley, Donovan 2, Withe 2
Sep 30	R1/L2	A	Valur	2-0	Shaw 2

Aggregate Score - Villa win 7-0

Oct 21	R2/L1	A	Dynamo Berlin (E. Germany)	2-1	Morley 2
Nov 4	R2/L2	**H**	**Dynamo Berlin**	0-1	

Aggregate Score - 2-2, Villa win on away goals rule

Mar 3	QF/L1	A	Dynamo Kiev (USSR)	0-0	
Mar 17	QF/L2	**H**	**Dynamo Kiev**	2-0	Shaw, McNaught

Aggregate Score - Villa win 2-0

Apr 7	SF/L1	**H**	**Anderlecht** (Belgium)	1-0	Morley
Apr 21	SF/L2	A	Anderlecht	0-0	

Aggregate Score - Villa win 1-0

May 26	Final	N	**Bayern Munich** (W. Germany)	1-0	Withe

Played at the 'De Kuip' Stadium in Rotterdam, Holland

1982-83 – EUROPEAN CHAMPIONS' CUP

Sep 15	R1/L1	**H**	**Besiktas** (Turkey)	3-1	Withe, Morley, Mortimer
Sep 29	R1/L2	A	Besiktas	0-0	

Aggregate Score - Villa win 3-1

Oct 20	R2/L1	A	Dinamo Bucharest (Romania)	2-0	Shaw 2
Nov 3	R2/L2	**H**	**Dinamo Bucharest**	4-2	Shaw 3, Walters

Aggregate Score - Villa win 6-2

Mar 2	QF/L1	**H**	**Juventus** (Italy)	1-2	Cowans
Mar 16	QF/L2	A	Juventus	1-3	Withe

Aggregate Score - Juventus win 5-2

1982-83 – EUROPEAN SUPER CUP

Jan 19	L1	A	Barcelona (Spain)	0-1
Jan 26	L2	**H**	**Barcelona**	3-0 Shaw, Cowans (pen), McNaught

Aggregate Score - Villa win 3-1

1982-83 – WORLD CLUB CHAMPIONSHIP

Dec 12	–	N	Penarol (Uruguay)	0-2

Played in Tokyo, Japan

1983-84 – UEFA CUP

Sep 14	R1/L1	A	Vitoria Guimaraes (Portugal)	0-1
Sep 28	R1/L2	**H**	**Vitoria Guimaraes**	5-0 Withe 3, Gibson, Ormsby

Aggregate Score - Villa win 5-1

Oct 19	R2/L1	A	Spartak Moscow (USSR)	2-2 Gibson, Walters
Nov 2	R2/L2	**H**	**Spartak Moscow**	1-2 Withe

Aggregate Score - Spartak win 4-3

1990-91 – UEFA CUP

Sep 19	R1/L1	**H**	**Banik Ostrava** (Czechoslovakia)	3-1 Mountfield, Platt, Olney
Oct 2	R1/L2	A	Banik Ostrava	2-1 Mountfield, Stas og

Aggregate Score - Villa win 5-2

Oct 24	R2/L1	**H**	**Inter Milan** (Italy)	2-0 Neilson, Platt
Nov 7	R2/L2	A	Inter Milan	0-3

Aggregate Score - Inter win 3-2

1993-94 – UEFA CUP

Sep 15	R1/L1	A	Slovan Bratislava (Slovakia)	0-0
Sep 29	R1/L2	**H**	**Slovan Bratislava**	2-1 Atkinson, Townsend

Aggregate Score - Villa win 2-1

Oct 19	R2/L1	A	Deportivo La Coruna (Spain)	1-1 Saunders
Nov 3	R2/L2	**H**	**Deportivo La Coruna**	0-1

Aggregate Score - Deportivo win 2-1

1994-95 – UEFA CUP

Sep 15	R1/L1	A	Inter Milan (Italy)	0-1
Sep 29	R1/L2	**H**	**Inter Milan**	1-0 Houghton

Aggregate Score - 1-1, Villa go through after a penalty shoot-out

Oct 18	R2/L1	A	Trabzonspor (Turkey)	0-1
Nov 1	R2/L2	**H**	**Trabzonspor**	2-1 Atkinson, Ehiogu

Aggregate Score - 2-2, Trabzonspor win on away goals rule

1996-97 – UEFA CUP

Sep 10	R1/L1	**H**	**Helsingborgs IF** (Sweden)	1-1 Johnson
Sep 24	R1/L2	A	Helsingborgs IF	0-0

Aggregate Score - 1-1, Helsingborgs IF win on away goals rule

Aston Villa Bookshelf

RETURN OF THE LITTLE VILLAN

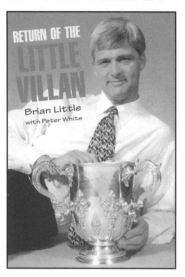

● Brian Little, one of Aston Villa's favourite footballing sons, made a dramatic return to take up the managerial reins at Villa Park in November 1994.

In this book, he gives a full and frank account of his first 20 months in charge, the turmoil surrounding his departure from Leicester City, insight into the transfer dealings and his personal A to Z guide to the Premiership.

● *Hardback*
● *£11.95*
● *180 pages*

IT'S NEVER TOO LATE TO GET INTO THE ASTON VILLA REVIEW

● The Aston Villa Review series, now in it's fifth year, is the club's official season -by-season record, and is the complete diary of Villa's five years in the Premiership.

All four previous issues are still obtainable for any-one wishing to complete the set.

● *Hardback*
● *£7.95/£8.95*
● *160 pages*

ASTON VILLA • DOUBLE WINNERS 1896/97

● One hundred years ago, Aston Villa celebrated the famous 'double' victory, winning the Football League and the FA Cup. Featuring match reports from the time, period illustrations and photos, this A4 booklet is a fascinating flashback and a must for any Villa fan.

● *Softback*   ● *£5.95*   ● *64 pages*

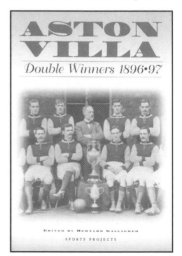

VILLA PARK 100 YEARS

● To celebrate the 100th Anniversary of Villa Park, a unique book has been published. VILLA PARK • 100 YEARS tells the fascinating story of one of the world's most famous football stadiums.

Packed with numerous stories and pictures, the book not only records the development of the stands and facilities, but also tells the stories of dozens of fans, players and members of the club staff who have played a part in the history of Aston Villa.

Devoted Villa fan and football ground expert, Simon Inglis, has compiled this magnificent publication which plots the development of the site, from neglected Victorian pleasure grounds through two World Wars up to the current day's 40,000 all-seater stadium.

● *Hardback* ● *£24.95* ● *240 pages*

STRIDE INSIDE THE VILLA

Club Secretary and Director, Steve Stride, gives a personal and often amusing account of 25 years working behind the scenes at Villa Park.

● *Hardback* ● *£8.95* ● *160 pages*

Title	Book Price	U.K. p&p	Europe	Elsewhere
Villa Park • 100 Years	£24.95	FREE	£5.00	£10.00
Return of the Little Villan	£11.95	£1.50	£3.00	£6.00
A.V. Double Winners 1896/97	£5.95	£1.00	£3.00	£5.00
Aston Villa Review 1993	£7.95	£1.00	£3.00	£5.00
Aston Villa Review 1994	£8.95	£1.00	£3.00	£5.00
Aston Villa Review 1995	£8.95	£1.00	£3.00	£5.00
Aston Villa Review 1996	£8.95	£1.00	£3.00	£5.00
Stride Inside The Villa	£8.95	£1.00	£3.00	£5.00

ORDERING BY POST

● Send your orders with a cheque or postal order for the correct amount to: **Sports Projects Ltd. 188 Lightwoods Hill, Smethwick, Warley, West Midlands B67 5EH**

Cheques made payable to Sports Projects Ltd.

0001 Neil Gallagher	0055 Michael Rose	0109 Sue Tilt
0002 Stewart James-Dyke	0056 Lynsey Dunbar	0110 Mick Tilt
0003 James W. Johnstone	0057 Elizabeth Dunbar	0111 Alan Percival
0004 Peter Lee Maddocks	0058 Warren H. McDivitt	0112 Damian Barrow
0005 Tony Spraggon	0059 Karen F. McDivitt	0113 Mark Barrow
0006 Susan Pudge	0060 Ellie S. McDivitt	0114 Glyn Howell
0007 Mark Lench	0061 Harry W. McDivitt	0115 Paul Palmer
0008 Michael Ridley	0062 David Eagle	0116 Peter Curry
0009 James Marcantonio	0063 Susan Eagle	0117 Yves Geens
0010 David Yeomans	0064 Oliver Eagle	0118 Pete Abrahams
0011 Glyn Richards	0065 Brian C. Seadon	0119 Nigel Iwanski
0012 Lorraine Richards	0066 Edward McNeill	0120 Ross Iwanski
0013 Caerwyn Richards	0067 Robert Gough	0121 Adrian Paul Rogers
0014 Celyn Richards	0068 Andy Perry	0122 Angela Perry
0015 Lars Nilsson	0069 Lisa - Holte End Nobby	0123 Adrian Perry
0016 Fraser Wilson	0070 Dr M. Wilson	0124 Keith Andrew Taylor
0017 Glyn Jones	0071 Master Karl Newton	0125 G. B. Jinks
0018 David Ian Jones	0072 Martin Kender	0126 N. I. Jinks
0019 Kathleen Jones	0073 Amanda and Karl	0127 B. R. Veal
0020 Mark Glyn Jones	0074 Nicholas Cox	0128 Gordon Cull
0021 Ralf Schulz	0075 Richard R. Carter	0129 Keith Stubbs
0022 Bill Greathead	0076 Simon Timerick	0130 Natalie Stubbs
0023 Denise Allibone	0077 Mr N. J. Harper	0131 Vicki Stubbs
0024 Thomas Johansson	0078 Alun L. L. Parish	0132 Keith Andrew Birch
0025 Kev Buttery	0079 Simon M. Wheeler	0133 Mark Evans
0026 Gido Kirfel	0080 Alexander Berwick	0134 Colin Perry
0027 Matthew James Gardner	0081 Daniel Berwick	0135 Derek Evans
0028 Tony C. Dacey	0082 R. Townsend	0136 Vera Ellen Ragsdale
0029 Malcolm Taylor	0083 Terry Wright	0137 Brig Flounders
0030 Ross Griffith	0084 Michael Halaj	0138 Scott Ginger
0031 Mark Stoneman	0085 Kevin Stratford	0139 Kevin A. Williams
0032 Mrs A. Mitchell	0086 Adam Paul Howlett	0140 Donna Green
0033 Helen L. Sutton	0087 Jonathan H. Wright	0141 J. Flynn
0034 Robin D. Wilkes	0088 John R. Ward	0142 K. Turner
0035 Roger H. Fullbrook	0089 Michael David Bromwich	0143 Scott Bradley
0036 Mary Petrakis-Birkby	0090 Keith Rickett	0144 James Wright
0037 Derek Day	0091 Darren Woodfield	0145 Louisa Winn
0038 Kerry Day	0092 Stephen Sturman	0146 Roger Winn
0039 Carly Day	0093 Alex Perkins	0147 Ken Noon
0040 Jean Day	0094 Mark Ford	0148 Paul Noon
0041 Antony Ibbotson	0095 Stephen Paul Naylor	0149 Peter Noon
0042 David Hodges	0096 Tina Garrigan	0150 Mr B. M. Dain
0043 Tracey Hatfield	0097 Marc Gill	0151 Mark Smith
0044 Roy Hatfield	0098 Peter Vos	0152 Carl Portman
0045 Caroline Crutchley	0099 Paul Vos	0153 Neil Harvey
0046 Kevin Fowler	0100 David F. Cox	0154 Martin Greenslade
0047 Amy Beard	0101 Bob Daniels	0155 Mark Hamblett
0048 Gareth C. Jones (Bones)	0102 Andrea Warren	0156 Michael Caiden
0049 Mick Wilkins	0103 David Woodley	0157 Anthony Woolley
0050 Darren Wilkins	0104 Sarah Kinsman	0158 Christopher Cottrell
0051 Philip Gray	0105 Stephanie Attenborough	0159 Andrew Cottrell
0052 Lee Day	0106 Martin G. K. Gibbs	0160 Antony Richard Joyner
0053 Mark David Goodwin	0107 Alison Jones	0161 Simon Peter Rawlins
0054 Stuart T. Swann	0108 Jamie Cash	0162 F. E. Oldham

0163 Mr David Byrne	0217 Jenny Bailey	0271 Trevor Statham
0164 Mrs Susan Byrne	0218 Antonio Durante	0272 Lisa Statham
0165 Peter Timms	0219 Nigel Renshaw	0273 Jake Wilkins
0166 Chris McCormack	0220 Norman Renshaw	0274 Ross Wilkins
0167 Veronica Stanyard	0221 Stephen (Rennie) Renshaw	0275 Patrick James Fenelon
0168 Beryl Stanyard	0222 Dan (Villa Man) Renshaw	0276 Matty 'Pughy' Pugh
0169 Paul J. Edwards	0223 Gareth Jackson	0277 Hinton
0170 Mick Brown	0224 Anthony L. McAllister	0278 Andrew Mitchell
0171 Yvonne A. Graves	0225 Neil Jones	0279 Martin Dillingham
0172 Mr S. C. Tovey	0226 Paul Aldhouse	0280 Carly Spearing
0173 Chris Harris	0227 Gordon Reynolds	0281 Bob Wardle
0174 Matthew Dale	0228 Steven Relf	0282 Karen Wardle
0175 Brett Moss	0229 Carl Davies	0283 Samantha Wardle
0176 Christine Rossiter	0230 Luke Davies	0284 Robert Jr. Wardle
0177 Bob Peach	0231 Colin Brown	0285 Alexander Wardle
0178 S. J. Lavery	0232 John Brealey	0286 Roy Sheard
0179 Gingerpud and Cadbury	0233 John A. Bullock	0287 Andy Collins
0180 Neil Byrne	0234 J. James Bullock	0288 Robert Leonard Taylor
0181 P. R. Haynes	0235 Robert A. Bullock	0289 Robert Andrew Taylor
0182 Gareth Jones	0236 Rev. Leo Osborn	0290 John (Villa) Power
0183 Trevor Jones	0237 Kenneth J. Marriott	0291 David Fletcher
0184 Raymond Warr	0238 Alan Jasper	0292 Richard Fletcher
0185 Reine Bladh	0239 Clive Platman	0293 Tom Fletcher
0186 Henrik Bladh	0240 Michele Platman	0294 Add, Andy, Bay and Phil
0187 Neal Sawyer	0241 Ian Tait	0295 Mr J. W. Johnstone
0188 Jonathan Sawyer	0242 Bridget Tait	0296 Adam Kynnersley
0189 Tony Brandal	0243 Peter Harrold	0297 Lisa Dickinson
0190 D. S. Willetts	0244 Gerald Chishick	0298 Jenny L. Walker
0191 Mark Napier	0245 Gregory Upton	0299 Christopher Mason
0192 Lee Baker	0246 Paul Ford	0300 Andrew Williams
0193 Rob Harvey	0247 Julie Harrison	0301 Gordon Williams
0194 Craig Ramsey	0248 Norman D. Crandles	0302 Gavin Morris
0195 Frank MacDonald	0249 Frank McNally	0303 Peter Miles
0196 Kevin Lowbridge	0250 Keith Potter	0304 Tracy Ashford
0197 David Hitchman	0251 The Fairfield Family	0305 Chris Ashford
0198 Peter Hitchman	0252 Patrick Fenelon	0306 Sara Tovey
0199 Clive Nicholls	0253 Gabrielle Fenelon	0307 Gary Lacey
0200 Bob Nicholls	0254 Sam Jarvis	0308 John Lacey
0201 Dean Strange	0255 Mr V. A. P. Kiely	0309 Paul Rostance
0202 Martin A. Bird	0256 John A. Gould (1934)	0310 Sebastian Power
0203 Duncan K. S. Laws	0257 Stephen Gould	0311 Vincent J. McKenna
0204 Dean Shepherd	0258 Mark Underwood	0312 Gavin Harris
0205 Karen Ellis	0259 Ian J. Walker	0313 Tracie Peagram
0206 Joseph Shepherd	0260 T. D. Measey	0314 Sarah Reynolds
0207 Mark Whitehouse	0261 Keith Gleadall	0315 Ray Matts
0208 Stewart Ray	0262 Paige Nevada Harris	0316 Aden Cole
0209 Ian Murphy	0263 David Hughes	0317 Diane Cole
0210 David John Peachey	0264 Amanda Elston	0318 Kevin Portley
0211 Matthew Smith	0265 Andrew Elston	0319 Stephanie Portley
0212 Daniel Smith	0266 Corey Barrett	0320 Jack Portley
0213 Maria Ganner	0267 Kallum Barrett	0321 Craig Vigurs
0214 Emma Ganner	0268 Ellisha Barrett	0322 Joe Browning
0215 Clare Ganner	0269 Lisa Barrett	0323 Andrew Friel
0216 Paul Bailey	0270 Dean Barrett	0324 Nicola Friel

0325 Mr David Bray BSc	0379 John Burns Snr	0433 David Foster
0326 The Doyle Family	0380 John Michael Anthony Burns	0434 Dave Skinner
0327 Paul Anderton	0381 Elaine Burns	0435 David Irwin
0328 Morten Esbjerg	0382 Tony Broadhurst	0436 Caroline Irwin
0329 Owen Suter	0383 John Knight	0437 Emily Irwin
0330 Edward Knott	0384 C. R. Aldous	0438 Julian Smith
0331 Jonathan Muir	0385 Graham N. Willetts	0439 Jason Wardle
0332 Graham Kinghorn	0386 David Clarkson	0440 Roger W. Linney
0333 Frank Antram	0387 Ian R. Wilson	0441 Adam O'Connor
0334 Ben Antram	0388 Adrian Hill	0442 D. J. Silver
0335 Jennie Taylor	0389 Lisa Hill	0443 The Moores
0336 Tony Morris	0390 Paul Tierney	0444 Michael Shrimplin
0337 Stephen Morris	0391 D. W. Close	0445 Alex Sandland
0338 Jo Rutherford	0392 J. D. Close	0446 Brett Rotheroe
0339 Wendy Jordan	0393 Debbie Swallow	0447 Harry Rotheroe
0340 Tony Corfield	0394 Richard Burton	0448 Duncan K. S. Laws
0341 Simon Kitchen	0395 Steve Hill	0449 Nick M. Salter
0342 Geoffrey Wright	0396 Claire Hill	0450 Paul Calvey
0343 John O'Brien	0397 Lauren Hill	0451 Craig Broadshaw
0344 Derek Wisdom	0398 Clare Beswick	0452 Michael J. Reidy
0345 Nick Wright	0399 J. McGeough	0453 Emma Lockey
0346 Gerald Leek	0400 Mr A. A. Bent	0454 Edmund Gajny
0347 Jason Paul Kennedy	0401 Rosie Rains	0455 Simon Phillips
0348 Ian Smith	0402 Tom Rains	0456 Sean Christopher Starrs
0349 Sue Glaves	0403 Paul Randle	0457 Matthew Dale
0350 Antony Rogers	0404 Mr R. C. Brown	0458 Matthew Lingard
0351 John Beale	0405 David Gilbert	0459 Charles Lingard
0352 Jennifer Beale	0406 Carolee Gifford	0460 Clifford Wiggett
0353 David Beale	0407 Geoff Elkington	0461 Stewart Marsh
0354 Keith Terry	0408 Darren Snelson	0462 Gareth Marsh
0355 Lisa Day	0409 Stuart Lancaster	0463 Stephen Healy
0356 Phil Innamorati	0410 Kath Leinster	0464 Josephine Clarke
0357 John Peter Reidy	0411 Mark Attwood	0465 Richard Henman
0358 Philip J. Etheridge	0412 Julia Attwood	0466 Christopher Henman
0359 Richard Prvulovich	0413 Alison (Helga) Smith	0467 Mary Henman
0360 Vincent R. Green	0414 Philip John Shakespeare	0468 Darryl M. Sankey
0361 G. Walden	0415 Valerie Shakespeare	0469 James Sankey
0362 Mark S. Waldron	0416 Thomas Shakespeare	0470 Edward Sankey
0363 Peter Brett	0417 Sara Tassa	0471 Henry Sankey
0364 Ken Phipp	0418 Glenn Douglas	0472 Rich Ford
0365 David Warman	0419 Daniel Baldwin	0473 Sue Ford
0366 Dave Alan Turner	0420 Ian Bousfield	0474 Dan Ford
0367 Adam France	0421 Lynsey Bousfield	0475 Julia Greenfield
0368 Andrew Richard Maddern	0422 John Bousfield	0476 Simon Kerr-Edwards
0369 Mark Thomas Randle	0423 Mr Jason Webb	0477 Esther Gilks
0370 Mark T. Lowndes	0424 Andy Johnson	0478 Richard Baker
0371 Noel Hickey	0425 James Cooke	0479 Steven Baker
0372 Paul McKenna	0426 Scott Maciver	0480 Jenny Baker
0373 Ian Hoskison	0427 Joe Ridout	0481 Richard Shutt
0374 Mr D. E. Cross	0428 Emily Ridout	0482 Andrew McAllister
0375 Graham Shearer	0429 Keith Ridout	0483 Philip R. Jones
0376 Andrea Burns	0430 John Cullen	0484 Jon Noden
0377 Robert Burns	0431 Frank Croft	0485 Mr Mark A. Sorrell
0378 Jack Burns	0432 Simon Croft	0486 Clive Foster

0487 David Foster	0541 Daren Reynolds	0595 Des Brennan
0488 Gary Foster	0542 Keith Stokes	0596 Graham Watkiss
0489 Janet Morgan	0543 Gareth Stokes	0597 Darren Hudson-Wood
0490 Gordon Parton	0544 Kirsty Stokes	0598 Matthew Buck
0491 Thomas Green	0545 Sarah Stokes	0599 Miss K. J. Taylor
0492 Benjamin Green	0546 Andy Downes	0600 Geoff Underhill
0493 Alan Green	0547 Adam Livesey	0601 Anne Smaje
0494 Helen Hollywell	0548 D. S. Willetts	0602 Laurence Smaje
0495 David Aust	0549 P. L. Bullock	0603 Andrew Webster
0496 Tony Taylor	0550 Ian Edward Beesley	0604 Bob Moore
0497 Jimmy Taylor	0551 Neil Alcock	0605 Hans Joachim Quade
0498 Darren Bedford	0552 Toni Alcock	0606 Deborah Corrall
0499 Alan Gee	0553 Roger Bailey	0607 Rob Rodway
0500 A. Congrave	0554 Liz Bailey	0608 Alan Mark Scrivens
0501 Carol Maguire	0555 Gemma Bailey	0609 John Henry Lane
0502 Jonathan Ahearne	0556 Becky Bailey	0610 Michael Bishop
0503 Christopher Homewood	0557 Trevor John Baker	0611 Mr S. A. Fowler
0504 Roy Stringer	0558 Daniel John Baker	0612 Mick Greaves
0505 Joy Stringer	0559 R. A. Clarkson	0613 Tom Greaves
0506 Simon Stringer	0560 Carol Smith	0614 Josh Greaves
0507 Bev Stringer	0561 Mr Dean Pedley	0615 John A. Willetts
0508 Nicholas Jones	0562 Dave Shipley	0616 Jon Jones
0509 Julian M. Turner	0563 Mr Alex Ashford	0617 Nigel Groves
0510 Rod Snelson	0564 Derek T. Hough	0618 Mark Clews
0511 Karen Green	0565 M. E. C. Wilson	0619 Sarah Woollard
0512 Richard Lawley	0566 Martin Hodson	0620 Richard Hands
0513 Adrian Chamberlain	0567 Mark Pearce	0621 Miss J. Cox
0514 Andrew John Francis	0568 Adrian Thorne	0622 Lloyd Hutchings
0515 Wesley Burrows	0569 Adam Rooke	0623 Stephen Donnelly
0516 Dean Burrows	0570 Craig 'Crusty' Putman	0624 Robert Moss
0517 Allen Souch	0571 Stuart Lancaster	0625 Terence Stone
0518 Philip Smith	0572 Nigel Lancaster	0626 R. E. Garratt
0519 Paul Virgo	0573 Debs Kendall	0627 M. Weller
0520 Mr David Poole	0574 John Kennedy	0628 Charles Stephens
0521 Ian Symes	0575 Jens Martin	0629 Colin Askey
0522 Karen Jeffery	0576 A. T. Martin	0630 Andrew Bignall
0523 Simon Lee	0577 George Barker	0631 Kevin Fern
0524 Paul Duffin	0578 Matthew Plant	0632 Jason Somerfield
0525 Oliver Sagols	0579 Matthew John Collinge	0633 David Watson
0526 Mr M. Murphy	0580 Andrew Collins	0634 Darren Bray
0527 Fran Bowdler	0581 Pamela Wood	0635 Ray Morris
0528 Alan Bowdler	0582 Aaron Hickman	0636 Emma-Jane 'Edge' Stallard
0529 David John Edward Clayton	0583 David Smith	0637 Rod Evans
0530 Michael Morgan	0584 Chris Newton	0638 Geoffrey P. Blaszkiw
0531 Philip Goldie	0585 Jonathan Handley	0639 Philip Busby
0532 Hilary Jennings	0586 Vincent J. McKenna	0640 Tony Hall
0533 Terry Hall	0587 Vernon Grove O.B.E.	0641 Liam Hall
0534 Dave 'AVFC' Knight	0588 Stephen Lammas	0642 Roger Levicki
0535 Mr Michael O'Brien	0589 Richard D. Webb	0643 Tim Levicki
0536 Robert York	0590 Michael Wurm Pedersen	0644 Andrew Levicki
0537 Sid Jeewa	0591 Nicholas Timothy	0645 Richard Wilson
0538 Philip Chandler	0592 John Timothy	0646 Jim McDonald
0539 Adrian Goddard	0593 J. K. Winters	0647 Paul Hawkins
0540 Caroline James	0594 Bill Willcox	0648 Rob Aston

0649 Mr & Mrs A. Smith	0703 Richard A. Hales	0757 Adrian Batsford
0650 Mr P. J. Smith	0704 Jack Welch	0758 Ian Smith
0651 Adam Hamlet	0705 Shaun Welch	0759 Gwenfyl Royles
0652 Mark A. J. Ward	0706 Neil Walton	0760 Nicola Royles
0653 Raymond J. Lewis	0707 Andrew James Harper	0761 Alison Royles
0654 Van De Sÿpe	0708 Dave Buet	0762 Scott P. I. Read
0655 Tony A. Bill	0709 Marg Buet	0763 Robert Cook
0656 Mr Mestre Didier	0710 Paul Buet	0764 Edward Mills
0657 Hayden Wakeling	0711 Neil Harris	0765 Chris Dennis
0658 Sheena Meredith	0712 Jason Russell Perry	0766 Mark Bradshaw
0659 Mr & Mrs De Rosa	0713 Andrew Mason	0767 Mark Wheeler
0660 Daniel Reeves	0714 Graham Brown	0768 Malcolm P. Price
0661 John Donohoe	0715 Barry Geddis	0769 Gordon Wilfred Price
0662 David Fortnam	0716 Wendy Geddis	0770 Ralph Willis
0663 Robin Peck	0717 R. Pearson	0771 David O. Cox
0664 Oliver Peck	0718 Lee Collison	0772 Keith Griffin
0665 Peter Day	0719 Corole Collison	0773 Shirley Blizard
0666 Joanne Preece	0720 Sophie Collison	0774 Geoff Blizard
0667 Richard Bennett	0721 C. J. Whitaker	0775 William J. Mottram
0668 Adrian Spray	0722 Mark Jenkins	0776 Mark Ferriday
0669 Sonia Greaves	0723 Andrew Smaje	0777 Daniel Lavander
0670 Chris Deakin	0724 Paul Hughes	0778 H. John Desaulles
0671 Daniel Burchell	0725 K. W. Powell	0779 James Powell
0672 Karen Cooper	0726 Adrian J. Mullis	0780 Mr James Lane
0673 Toni Cooper	0727 David C. Taylor	0781 John Simmonds
0674 Mick Long	0728 Ryan Cox	0782 Steve Hughes
0675 Wayne Richardson	0729 Mr Kelvin Cox	0783 P. J. Hadoulis
0676 Mr C. C. Wiseman	0730 Paul Gray-Davis	0784 John Adkins
0677 Brendan Shields	0731 Neil, Karen & Vikki	0785 Andy Armstrong
0678 Jeff Corfield	0732 David Hales	0786 Rachael Armstrong
0679 Mr Alan J. Dawson	0733 Luke Farrington	0787 Bradley Armstrong
0680 Ashley Dawson	0734 Andy Campkin	0788 Colin Smith
0681 Gerald Henry Lodwick	0735 Charles R. J. Clarke	0789 Lisa Cashmore
0682 Ian Dowell	0736 Rob Hale	0790 Andrew Webb
0683 Jim Stelfox	0737 Matthew Kenny	0791 James Daly
0684 Maurice Carter	0738 Andrew Kenny	0792 Colin Daly
0685 Mr J. A. Powell	0739 Nigel Ainge	0793 R. A. Jones
0686 Peter J. Ross	0740 Gordon Telfer	0794 Roger Nicklin
0687 Jack Stewart	0741 Robert Smith	0795 Steven Glen
0688 Freddie Stewart	0742 Robin Pleaden	0796 Charles R. Nelson
0689 Frank Hughes	0743 David Knight	0797 Cliff Paget
0690 Alan Adrian West	0744 Nathan Collins	0798 Joseph Michael Hopkins
0691 Sue Ramsay	0745 Mr Stuart Reading	0799 Alexander Thomas Berry
0692 John Meek	0746 Malcolm Morley	0800 Mark Fitzpatrick
0693 Pat Meek	0747 Daniel Howell	0801 Michelle Diggins
0694 Master Scott Cross	0748 Jenny A. Foster	0802 Kevin Joynes
0695 Nicholas Blewer	0749 Carl Morris	0803 Debbie Joynes
0696 Martin Attwood	0750 Sylvia Morris	0804 Christopher Hearn
0697 Liam Foley	0751 Darran Boulter	0805 Christopher P. Mansfield
0698 Katherine Waters	0752 Richard Allen	0806 Selina Travers
0699 Graham Walter Padmore	0753 Bernard Day	0807 Mary Travers
0700 Simon Padmore	0754 Mrs S. Scott	0808 Aidan Travers
0701 Martin Colin Roberts	0755 Benjamin Lee Icke	0809 Russ Brown
0702 Charlotte Louise Briggs	0756 Sid W. Walton	0810 R. L. Elwell

SUBSCRIBERS ROLL CALL

0811 Gary Wood
0812 Debbie Wood
0813 Stewart J. Draper
0814 Frank Allen
0815 Angela Webb
0816 Craig Webb
0817 Tony Webb
0818 Bruce Maciver
0819 Gavin Maciver
0820 Juliet Vaill
0821 Mr Alex Males
0822 Anita D. Harris
0823 Martin Lane
0824 Ian Robert Lane
0825 Philip Piper
0826 Kevin Piper
0827 Tracy Piper
0828 Jon O'Brien
0829 Anthony O'Brien
0830 Emma O'Brien
0831 David Swarts
0832 Suzy French
0833 Jim French
0834 Lee Pendrey
0835 Julie A. Empson
0836 D. H. Janes
0837 Mark Rogers
0838 Nick Becenna
0839 Matthew Gregory
0840 Robert F. Rea
0841 Dean Beresford
0842 Michelle Beresford
0843 Mark Keylock
0844 Peter Walker
0845 Lewis Poppitt
0846 Phil Cotter
0847 Tim Cotter
0848 Ken Wootton
0849 Pauline A. Holloway
0850 Jennifer Jones
0851 Christopher Jones
0852 Lynsey Holloway
0853 Laura Holloway
0854 R. J. Hall
0855 Paul Kenna
0856 Bobby Mendonca
0857 R. S. Hutchison
0858 P. Pilkington
0859 Jamie Taylor
0860 Mark Zeidan
0861 Daniel Richard Evans
0862 Mr Andrew G. Harris
0863 Miss Pamela J. Harris
0864 James Villans

0865 Mr Jason Ashley
0866 Dawn McCarrick
0867 Ashley Goodwin
0868 Luke John Clarke
0869 Peter Davies
0870 Paul Middleton
0871 Mr M. Lockley
0872 Thomas Blomberg
0873 Martha Osborne
0874 Chapman Family of Hartley
0875 Wintney
0876 T. Starbuck
0877 Barrie Bailey
0878 Henry Anthony
0879 Mark Thornley
0880 Kevin Gledhill
0881 Peter Gledhill
0882 Richard Gledhill
0883 Andrew Gledhill
0884 Barry Etheridge
0885 Steve Matthews
0886 Geoffrey James Turner
0887 James Michael Deeley
0888 Diane Swales
0889 Keith Puttick
0890 Tomkinson Family
0891 John Phillip Watkins
0892 Mr P. J. Stocker
0893 Jenny Balmforth
0894 Andrew Clayton
0895 Trevor Clayton
0896 Mr Kenneth F. Denham
0897 Butler Family
0898 Cathryn Morris
0899 Antony Morris
0900 Paul Perry
0901 John Downey
0902 Antony Rawson
0903 Ian Taylor
0904 Gary Sinnott
0905 Paul Cummins
0906 Sean W. Kelly
0907 Simon Booker
0908 Neal Strange
0909 Andrew R. Owen
0910 Marc Troth
0911 Steven Paul Butler
0912 Robert Cooper
0913 Lauren Clare Duff
0914 'Pele' Tomic
0915 Reza Bodiat
0916 Taariq Bodiat
0917 Yasser Bodiat
0918 Lindsey Roberts

0919 Simon Roberts
0920 Miss J. E. Elson
0921 Craig Marriot
0922 Paul Michael Trilloe
0923 John W. Daw
0924 Colin A. Holmes
0925 Nick Yates
0926 Nigel Sadler
0927 Graham Perry
0928 Asten Perry
0929 G. Foden
0930 Barry Livesey
0931 Dawn Taylor
0932 Robert Taylor
0933 Patricia Baker
0934 Bernard Baker
0935 Kay Lowe
0936 David Lowe
0937 Mark Lowe
0938 Kevin John Williams
0939 G. S. Clarke
0940 Carl Anthony Lewis
0941 Chris Russell
0942 Kiran Mahalingam
0943 Peter J. Baker
0944 Neil Edwards
0945 Don Vincent
0946 Angela Weir
0947 Walter Charles Kitley
0948 Liam Kiernan
0949 Michael Kiernan
0950 Charles Southby
0951 Terence Anthony Barker
0952 Sean Mullooly
0953 Amanda Ann Evans
0954 Matthew Robert Oakes
0955 Christopher Biggs
0956 Matthew Phipps
0957 Warren Enon
0958 David Enon
0959 Leonard Brian Reading
0960 Ian Shave
0961 Ross David Clarke
0962 Peter Goakes
0963 Paul Geraghty
0964 Ann Geraghty
0965 Robert Lerner
0966 Mr Anthony Harold
0967 Callum Fenlon
0968 Anthony Madigan
0969 Iain Fenwick
0970 Bully, Lisa, Leanne & Shannon
0971 Martin J. Watson
0972 Matthew Bond

0973 Patrick F. J. O'Reilly	1027 David Cleminson	1055 Natalie Langford
0974 Paul Groves	1028 Robert Cleminson	1056 John Millward
0975 Neil Gaskell	1029 Lloyd Marsden	1057 Ruth Millward
0976 Adam Thomas Barrett	1030 Sharon Thickett	1058 Jansen King
0977 M. A. Arscott	1031 Melvin James Thickett	1059 Julie King
0978 P. M. Arscott	1032 Matthew C. Thickett	1060 Heather King
0979 Paul Casley	1033 Michelle Thickett	1061 Jamie King
0980 Neal Casley	1034 Anthony Thickett	1062 John Hartley
0981 Barbara Casley	1035 Claire Wheeler	1063 Trevor Hartley
0982 Simon John Lane	1036 Richard Orton	1064 Catherine Hartley
0983 Iain Sheppard	1037 Daniel Adam Coleman	1065 David Hartley
0984 Vicky Sheppard	1038 Michael Alan Coldrick	1066 Andrew Hartley
0985 Mark Rowland (Skully)	1039 C. Eaton	1067 Steve Farr
0986 Andrew Mateer	1040 Les Stoddart	1068 Martin Farr
0987 Ted Geary	1041 S. A. Underhill	1069 James Allsop
0988 Jackie Rawlings	1042 Robert Head	1070 Claire Allsop
0989 Iain Rawlings	1043 Robert Kench	1071 Phil Lees
0990 Jack Pinnock	1044 Paul Webb	1072 Nadine Goldingay
0991 Leo Pinnock	1045 Andrew Bateman	1073 Terry Weir
0992 David England	1046 Tony Lennon	1074 Kate Atkins
0993 James Flood	1047 Martyn Bacchus	1075 Barry Atkins
0994 Simon Giles	1048 Danny and Suzy	1076 Robert Pittaway
0995 Josef Baker	1049 James H. W. T. Soden	1077 Molly Pittaway
0996 Andrew Hart	1050 Christopher C. Fleming	1078 Roger Pemberton
0997 Trevor Watts	1051 Frank Beach	1079 Neil Warner
0998 Matthew L. Watts	1052 Edie Beach	1080 Malcolm Vale
0999 Nicholas T. Watts	1053 Debbie Tidmarsh	1081 Betty Armstrong
1000 Paul Biddlestone	1054 Gareth Powell	1082 Neil Armstrong
1001 Robert Geaney		
1002 Nicholas English		
1003 Michael English		
1004 Jonathan Tebbutt		
1005 John Holmes		
1006 Richard C. Pike		
1007 Nigel Snowden		
1008 Derek Hollis		
1009 Mark Hall		
1010 Phillip Jemmison		
1011 Andrew Dawes		
1012 Richard Winter		
1013 Scott Davidson		
1014 Paul Fogarty		
1015 Ian Galbraith		
1016 Simon Galbraith		
1017 Harjinder Dosanjh		
1018 Kevin Whittick		
1019 William Eric Catherall		
1020 W. Kilmurray		
1021 Andrew Wibberley		
1022 Gary Arthurs		
1023 Derek Anthony Price		
1024 Jason 'Nobby' Crowley		
1025 William Lawrence		
1026 Joe Dixon		